T0336426

Additional Praise for *Soft Skills for the Professional Services Industry*

"As we increasingly enter a world of big data, where analytical skills and modeling ability are viewed as the only characteristics that matter, *Soft Skills for the Professional Services Industry* provides a timely and healthy reminder that without personal skills and emotional stability, modeling and numbers will not get you far."
—**Aswath Damodaran**, Professor of Finance, New York University

"Success in the professional services industry requires more than simply being a subject matter expert. I highly recommend *Soft Skills for the Professional Services Industry* as it is well written and an insightful guide to assist the reader in reaching their full potential."
—**Roger Grabowski**, FASA, Managing Director, Valuation Advisory Services, Kroll, LLC

"Andreas Creutzmann's analysis and guide to soft skills is a must-read for any professional wishing to improve and succeed in their work and indeed broader life!"
—**Nicholas Talbot**, IVSC Chief Executive

"Andreas Creutzmann's *Soft Skills for the Professional Services Industry* is a very useful and practical guide to assist consultants in achieving professional success through the development of well-rounded skills, beyond simply their area of expertise. Anyone providing professional services will benefit from Creutzmann's research-based advice and tips, particularly in these volatile, uncertain, complex, and ambiguous (**VUCA**) times!"
—**Mark L. Zyla**, CPA/ABV, CFA, ASA Managing Director, Zyla Valuation Advisors LLC

Soft Skills for the Professional Services Industry

Soft Skills for the Professional Services Industry

Principles, Tasks, and Tools for Success

ANDREAS CREUTZMANN

WILEY

For general information on our other products and services or for technical support, please contact our Customer Care Department within the United States at (800) 762-2974, outside the United States at (317) 572-3993 or fax (317) 572-4002.

Wiley also publishes its books in a variety of electronic formats. Some content that appears in print may not be available in electronic formats. For more information about Wiley products, visit our web site at www.wiley.com.

Library of Congress Cataloging-in-Publication Data is Available:

ISBN 9781119875536 (hardback)
ISBN 9781119875550 (ePDF)
ISBN 9781119875543 (ePub)

Cover Design: Wiley
Cover Image: © Donovan van Staden/Shutterstock

SKY10033110_032122

For Nicole

and

Alisa, Julian, Nicolas, and Shannon
for a happy and successful life

Contents

Foreword

FOR 30 YEARS I have been preaching to our membership the importance of mastering the soft skills (everything non-technical) required for building and managing a successful professional services practice. Unfortunately, it is this side of building a practice that is most difficult for a "master of numbers" to master. NACVA's members are highly intelligent technicians but given a choice to get training on, say, cost of capital or practice development, nine out of ten will choose cost of capital. Learning "soft skills" for many professionals is akin to learning a new language. The challenge from a teaching standpoint is not that soft skills is a difficult topic, it is just a challenging subject to layout in a way that is ingested in an organized, practical, and logical manner such that the student can easily absorb this new knowledge and soon-to-be-skills into their everyday activities. In other words, I have not seen anyone present or write on this topic in a way that had a long-lasting impact on the receivers of this information. Until now. Finally.

Andreas Creutzmann has written a masterful book that represents a significant contribution to the limited literature on the subject of soft skills for the professional services provider. This is easy reading that puts every aspect of building and managing a practice in perfect perspective. What I appreciated most, however, is that Andreas covers everything that constitutes soft skills, and by that I mean everything including the most often overlooked aspect of work-life balance, because it can't always be about business, right? If you have struggled to build your practice or feel like you're on a treadmill headed to nowhere, or you've been successful but feel like you could do more, then this book is a must read. In my humble opinion, this book just might be the missing link to a better and more fulfilling career.

Parnell Black, MBA, CPA, CVA, Chief Executive Officer
NACVA | National Association of Certified Valuators and Analysts
| www.NACVA.com GACVA | Global Association of Certified Valuators and Analysts | www.GlobalCVA.com
CTI | Consultants' Training Institute | www.theCTI.com

Preface

EXPERTISE IS A COMMONLY required prerequisite for professionals. The high requirements for passing the professional examinations document the formal qualification of a lawyer, Certified Public Accountant (CPA), or a Certified Valuation Analyst (CVA). On the way to becoming a lawyer, a CPA, or CVA (and) in their further professional lives, those with specialist knowledge dominate. Inherent in the profession is the willingness for lifelong learning. Qualification and competence are important prerequisites for a successful professional life. This is true not only for auditors and valuation professionals, but also for lawyers, doctors, and other professionals. At the very beginning of my studies, I asked myself a question that still accompanies me today: "Why are some people successful and others not?" I have always been interested in people who are successful through their own efforts instead of building on the success of previous generations through their heritage.

In my search for what distinguishes successful from less successful people, I began to read a variety of relevant books and to attend seminars. These books and seminars dealt with the topics of success, personality development, marketing and sales, rhetoric, psychology, and management as well as self-management, and personal productivity. To date, I have read several hundred books on these topics and attended an extensive number of seminars.

Most people think of the word success primarily in terms of professional and ultimately financial success. I consider this view of success too one-sided. A successful life is characterized by both a successful professional life and a successful private life. In a networked world in which everyone can be reached at almost any time from almost any place in the world via smartphone, the boundaries between professional and private life have become blurred. The two areas of life are intricately linked. People who do not have an intact private life will rarely be successful in their careers. If you only seek professional success, you shouldn't be surprised if your private life shows deficits. Through continuously reading books and attending seminars, it quickly became clear to me that the so-called soft skills of a person are crucial for personal success.

This book summarizes my theoretical and, above all, practical findings on the subject of soft skills from more than 30 years of personal experience. A strict separation between experience drawn from professional or from private life does not seem meaningful to me. The following soft skills apply for the most part to both professional and private life. I wrote this book as an auditor and certified valuation analyst for my professional colleagues. For this reason, the examples and practical advice refer to the profession of auditors and CVAs. In most cases, however, the transfer to other professions is remarkably simple. In this respect, the book is not singularly aimed at auditors, CVAs, and their employees. Even though auditors and valuation professionals are often individualists and tend to see themselves as something quite special precisely because of their high professional qualifications, the following soft skills are predominantly success factors that apply universally.

The individual chapters under the headings Principles of Successful Professionals, Tasks, and Tools can basically be read independently of one another. This means that the individual chapters are self-contained and, for the most part, do not build on each other. The Introduction, however, "Professionals in a Digital World," sets the framework and provides valuable information on how to use the book, which is why it should be read prior to all the other chapters.

"Does a successful life also lead to a happy life?" It might seem obvious that a successful life also leads to a happy life. If you read the individual chapters of the book and do not read the Conclusion at the beginning, this final chapter will also provide the answer.

The elephant on the cover impresses with its size and in many cultures also represents the symbol of wisdom, knowledge, and tranquility. This majestic animal is a popular symbol of power and intelligence. In Africa, the elephant is revered as a symbol of happiness and a long life. In China, the elephant embodies ingenuity, energy, and sovereignty. These are the three key words that best symbolize the wholesomeness of the elephant.

1. Wisdom
2. Steadfastness
3. Tradition

In many ways, humans and elephants are similar. The elephant teaches us to give these positive commonalities more space in our own lives. It points us to compassion, sensitivity, and patience, which must be either awakened or preserved in the current phase of our lives. With its help we can more easily absorb knowledge, understand wisdom, and remember the past. The elephant does not only represent wisdom, power, and strength, but also responsibility. Great power is known to bring great responsibility, which is why you can learn leadership from the elephant's qualities – while at the same time being a natural part of the community that respects us. The majestic elephant also stands for happiness, prosperity, and stability.

I hope you enjoy reading the book, and I look forward to your feedback.

Acknowledgments

FIRST, I WOULD LIKE to thank all the endorsers. Most especially, I want to thank Parnell Black, CEO of NACVA, who told me when EACVA was formed in 2005 that a Certified Valuation Analyst will only be successful if they can market themselves. NACVA has always supported its professionals with marketing. Parnell Black has inspired me to spread these thoughts in Europe as well.

Second, I would like to thank Anja. Anja is my partner's best friend. They have known each other since childhood. Anja's assistance with the English translation was a blessing for me. I knew that the publisher would make sure that the English translation would be grammatically perfect and that the book would not contain spelling mistakes and comma errors. However, it was much more important to me that the content be understandable to professionals in the United States and around the world. Anja is a German native speaker and has lived in the United States for 18 years. She made sure that the content and the translation are suitable for US professionals. Thank you, Anja.

I would also like to thank Elke. She has been my personal assistant for 15 years and has managed the format and scope of this translation, ensuring that this book meets the highest standards of accuracy and integrity. She usually does this with our appraisal reports. It is often incredible how meticulous she is in spotting and correcting errors. She is the rock in our office. Always dependable and conscientious. Thank you, Elke, for your support over the years. I appreciate it very much.

And most of all, my thanks go to my partner, Nicole. I have known Nicole since I was in school. I first fell in love with her after I graduated from high school. Nicole did not consider me as a partner at that time. We only fell in love after our failed marriages many decades later. Time for us was not yet meant for each other in the first half of our lives. In Germany, there is a saying that your partner is your "better half." I couldn't do anything with this phrase for a long time. It wasn't until I fell in love with Nicole that

I understood what was meant by it. Ideally, couples complement each other. The strengths of one partner and the strengths of the other partner make a couple really strong together. In this book, you will learn which four prerequisites must be fulfilled for a partnership to last. Perhaps for a lifetime.

Nicole's curiosity to just try things is inspiring to me. For example, when it comes to food, Nicole will try almost anything if there is an opportunity to eat something new. But Nicole is also interested in new things in many other areas of life. She has kept her childlike curiosity. A characteristic that many adults have lost in everyday life. But even more than things, Nicole is interested in people, and origin, education, and social status play no role in this. She is genuinely interested in others and gives them full attention during conversations. She is empathic, which is a quality that everyone should have.

If Nicole can help, she helps. So, it can happen that a supermarket shopping trip takes much longer than planned, because she helps an elderly and needy person find all their food.

She grasps life with all her senses. This especially includes her unique sense of smell and taste. She smells and tastes things and describes them in her unique way, which fascinates me every time. Qualities that I am sadly lacking. Unfortunately, I often don't smell or taste these subtle differences.

And finally, she has a creativity that is unique. When it came to the cover for this book, I asked her to help me. In less than an hour, she had this great idea with the elephant. And she found the right image for it right away, too. She also had the idea with the elephant because there are qualities that both Nicole and elephants have. They are intelligent and do not forget anything. It is known that elephants remember past things better than humans. This is true for both the elephant's sense of hearing and their sense of smell. For scientists, this is a clear sign that these animals are highly intelligent. However, elephants perceive the world much differently than we do, and their world also requires vastly different skills than ours. The soft skills that humans need to be happy and successful are presented in this book. That's why the elephant is the perfect symbol for the content of the book. Thank you, Nicole, for this great idea with the elephant.

But most of all, thank you for your unique way of loving me and thank you for every minute we spend together. You enrich my life every day with many small and important things. Thank you for helping me author this book. I love you and am grateful to be with you.

Introduction: Professionals in a Digital World

DIGITALIZATION AS WELL AS the pandemic are transforming our clients' businesses and the professional services industry. Disruption may mean that in the future, our clients' business models will no longer work in the future. But our own business models are also put to the test. In the future, how can we support our clients with our services? Are we paving the way and driving a successful future for our clients, or are we blocking important change processes with our consulting services? What are we doing in the professional services industry to successfully master digitalization? We need to find the right answers to these and many other questions.

Artificial intelligence, cryptocurrencies, social media, virtual and hybrid worlds, smartphones, Zoom, and MS Teams meetings have led to a complexity that is a particular challenge for every professional. To this we add the associated possibilities that we are able to call up information and communicate almost anywhere in the world while making decisions at every turn creates additional complexity. Professional private lives are often inextricably linked. Professional information can be transported almost anywhere in the world via smartphone. On the other hand, professionals receive information about their children's school grades, their life partner's problems, or other private matters at almost every location where they work. In work-life blending, the professional world merges with private life and the worlds become inseparable. In addition to a wealth of professional information, there are plenty of distractions in a professional's daily life.

Complexity has increased at all levels, and it has to be mastered. We live in a world of volatility, uncertainty, complexity, and ambiguity – a **VUCA** working world. Volatility refers to conditions that are unstable, unpredictable, and therefore hard to foresee. Nobody knows when a particular status will change and move into a different direction and what events will follow. Uncertainty refers to a state that is subject to unknown risks. We have less and less certainty about what will happen next. Known, earlier paradigms no longer apply, and it is unclear what actually still does. Predictions and forecasts are increasingly unreliable. Ambiguity means double or even multiple meanings of a fact.

Professionals have always had a particularly trusted and responsible role with their clients. To live up to this trust, the profession's service portfolio is under scrutiny in a changing world. Professional services providers are also in a state of upheaval due to digitalization. What impact does this have on the management of the firm and on self-management? **Does the ever-increasing complexity of everyday life in a VUCA world and the digital age require new principles, tasks, and tools from professionals in order to be successful?**

Professional services are occupations in the service industry that require specialized education and training in the arts or sciences. Some freelance services, such as those provided by architects, accountants, engineers, doctors, lawyers, and teachers, require a professional degree, or licensure and unique skills. I am a professional in the accounting and consulting industry with certifications as a German certified public accountant (Wirtschaftsprüfer) and Certified Valuation Analyst (CVA). I have professional experience in these industries. Therefore, most of the practical examples I provide throughout the book relate to the accounting and consulting industry. However, transfer to other industries is easily possible.

"Soft Skills for the Professional Services Industry" presents the principles, tasks, and tools of professionals that are necessary to master the increasing complexity of everyday life and the VUCA world. Effective self-management and the effective management of teams are more important today than ever before.

This book uses the profession of auditors as an example to demonstrate which soft skills are necessary to be successful. The principles, tasks, and tools also apply to a large extent to other professional groups, managers, and entrepreneurs. Successful professionals are characterized by excellent technical knowledge in their field of activity. In addition, they have a certain mindset and soft skills. Effective self-management as well as effective management of teams are indispensable for entrepreneurial success. Only those who can manage themselves effectively and efficiently have fulfilled an essential prerequisite for managing employees and teams successfully themselves.

NOTE

The principles, tasks, and tools outlined below are the basis for mastering complexity in a digitalized professional and private life and in a VUCA world.

TABLE I.1—PRINCIPLES, TASKS, AND TOOLS

Principles	Tasks	Tools
Principles that should be followed by performing tasks and using tools	Key-tasks related to self-management and the management of staff	Tools used to perform the task

Those who apply the Principles, Tasks, and Tools shown in Table I.1 will be more successful both professionally and personally.

Principles in this context should be adhered to when performing tasks and using tools. Adherence to the principles requires a certain degree of discipline. The principles can be learned more, or less easily. Since their application involves changes in behavior, it is essential that an individual understands that the principles are important for successful business transactions. If this insight is lacking, the tasks are usually performed unsatisfactorily. At the same time, they form the framework for the tasks and serve as an orientation for the use of the tools. The principles are not only valid for a CPA's or valuation expert's successful professional life, but also for lawyers and other expert groups as well as managers and entrepreneurs. Accordingly, they have a universal character. These principles are the most important and valuable soft skills of a successful personality. Those who adhere to them distinguish themselves significantly from others. They also apply to a significant extent to private life and therefore, serve as a basis for functioning relationships.

Tasks characterize a professional's work. Professional standards in particular often regulate certain duties. In the following, duties do not stand for the specialized duties of an auditor or lawyer, which are sufficiently well known. Therefore, it does not refer to a professional's given skill set. Where applicable, these are specified in detail in professional standards, laws, decrees, and so forth, to their specific field of expertise. They are special tasks predominately related to the auditor's own management and the management of employees. In this sense, they are the key tasks that are especially critical success factors. Those who perform these tasks poorly will not be as successful as professionals. At its core, the book deals with the professional tasks for successful self-management and management of employees. Transfer to personal life is possible for some tasks. For example, the "setting goals" task applies to both professional and personal life. Successful professionals can distinguish the essential from the non-essential. They know their key tasks and perform them in an above average manner.

Tools are the third element and are used to perform the tasks. Professionals are more likely to expect technical tools in this Part of the book when reading the term tool. Closely related to the term tools are apps. To prevent gaps in expectations at this point, Part Three, Tools is not essentially about technical aids. Technical aids can make it easier to perform the tasks described above. In the age of digitalization, there are a large number of apps that represent technical tools, and in the tools presented here, technical aids are mentioned only in passing. Rather, Part Three is about tools that have already been used in part by professionals long before the advent of digitalization. These are tools that successful professionals, managers, and entrepreneurs have also used in their daily work both skillfully and correctly. Since the tools I have presented are a selection of valuable soft skills, they were never a formal curriculum in training, in college, or in a professional exam. The tools presented here are the key to a successful professional life and happy private life.

However, mastering these tools requires a willingness to learn. Surely most people know that life consists of a lifelong learning process. Professionals in particular are accustomed to learning through regular continuing education. By contrast, soft skills are not trained and assessed in preparation for the professional exams as lawyers, tax consultants and auditors. Here, learning may be like learning a new language.

The tools will help you perform the tasks and adhere to the principles of successful professionals.

NOTE

Incidentally, professionals should ask themselves whether the following principles, tasks, and tools are useful. Before rejecting an idea, every professional should consider whether it could help in achieving professional and personal goals. Whenever an internal resistance to a statement arises, it could be a moment in your life that moves you forward. Analyze exactly why you are rejecting the thought. Anything that leads to a positive change in your life, that contributes to your personal development, is useful. And only the criterion of usefulness should be the yardstick for determining whether you reject the soft skills presented in this book or make them part of your life.

The following principles, tasks, and tools are partly based on management thinkers such as Peter F. Drucker and Fredmund Malik. Particularly in the case of the tools, but also in the case of individual principles and tasks, however, these have been supplemented, expanded, and adapted on the basis of my experience with the professional group.

This book is written in recognition of the fact that professionals in particular have excellent specialized training. This also applies to lawyers, doctors, and architects. These professions work in a very structured and analytical way. From training to the professional exam, or admission to the bar, it is always about expertise. The expertise and the hard facts are evaluated in the studies and in the exams. Personality does not play a decisive role. Those who are intelligent and diligent have a greater chance of passing the professional exams. However, anyone who has worked as an auditor or lawyer for several years knows that other factors are decisive for professional (and private) success. Soft skills regularly determine between success and failure.

The term "soft skills" has been used internationally in numerous languages for many years. It refers to the people skills that are generally necessary for professional and private success. We can learn or improve these skills through training. Anyone who enters the term "soft skills" in Google receives more than 784,000,000 references. On the one hand, this makes it clear that this term is of significant importance worldwide. On the other hand, the search results also show how important it is to have the "right" soft skills in order to be successful. This book is limited to the essential valuable soft skills that professionals should have if they want to be successful professionally and privately.

The term soft skills should be distinguished from the terms talent and aptitude, which are used synonymously below. In my understanding, talents and gifts are innate. Soft skills and the associated knowledge, however, can be learned. Accordingly, talents and gifts stand for innate potential and cannot be learned. Soft skills, on the other hand, are known behavior patterns or activities. A professional's technical and factual knowledge is acquired, and the high level of professional competence is documented by the examinations passed. However, a professional's outstanding performance only comes about when talent is combined with knowledge and soft skills in such a way that exceptional performance is achieved. This also requires appropriate professional experience, which young professionals can only acquire in the course of their professional lives. No matter how high the technical and factual knowledge of young professionals may be, the trust that clients place in a more experienced professional colleague because of their seniority is often related to their soft skills. Skills and insights they have acquired during their long professional lives. For this reason, it may well be that a client follows the recommendations of a seasoned professional colleague, even though the factual arguments of the young professional might be more convincing for those with expert knowledge.

On the one hand, the book points out those soft skills that are crucial and essential for professionals, and on the other hand, how these soft skills can be learned and trained. This is because knowing which soft skills are particularly relevant does not automatically mean that they can also be successfully applied in practice after reading the book once. Those professionals who practice a sport or have done so at some time know very well that only regular training brings the desired success. An athlete achieves proficiency only through training. That is why this book endeavors to encourage you to apply the knowledge you have acquired in your everyday life.

Closely related to soft skills is knowledge from psychology. This is certainly a subject area that professionals in particular do not usually deal with because technical and factual knowledge is omnipresent. The book likewise mentions the psychology of success in several places. Psychological knowledge is important if you want to be successful. But the psychological knowledge presented here has nothing to do with esotericism. It should help to understand why people are successful and why others fail. Those who learn and apply the soft skills presented in the chapters that follow will be successful in their professional and private lives.

This book is about success. Success is the achievement of personal goals, which can be professional as well as private goals. In both professional and personal life, soft skills are the key to success and personal happiness. In part, the soft skills associated with your private life are the basis for professional success. On the other hand, there are professional soft skills whose application will help you to be happy and successful in your private life. Professional and private soft skills sometimes merge. There is no razor-sharp distinction between a professional and private soft skill in that case. For this reason, there are chapters in this book that first describe a soft skill from the private perspective, for example, the task of "Setting goals." The transfer from private goals to professional or business goals is readily apparent. In this sense, the soft skills covered in this book are particularly valuable.

PART ONE

Principles of Successful Professionals

CHAPTER ONE

Self-Responsibility

THE PRINCIPLE OF SELF-RESPONSIBILITY is becoming increasingly important in a time when others are to blame. In both professional and personal life, there are situations where others are to blame for mistakes.

EXAMPLE

Auditors in particular are accustomed by profession to seeking and finding fault with others. After all, the central question in assessing an internal control system is, "What could go wrong and who controls what?" Even if there is no four-eyes principle, but only machine controls, there are people who are responsible for the programming. There is usually a "culprit" when something goes wrong with a client's internal control system (ICS). Chances are it's not the auditor and their staff. Since the company's accounting and ICS are the subject of the audit, it appears that it is always the "others" who are to blame for errors. The client's employees are then held responsible. Nevertheless, unless the auditor and his staff recognize that a control system is ineffective, they quickly get lost in excuses. Who likes to admit failures to a client?

In every company, one person, or a few people are in charge. It should go without saying for business owners that they are responsible for every project outcome. The larger the company, the more likely it is that unsuccessful projects will end up being just a matter of saving one's neck. The partner of a company blames his managers, or even customers (?) for the failure without realizing that perhaps they put together the wrong team, the tasks were not distributed properly, or the project control did not work.

Much worse, however, is often the complaining at all levels in the company and in private life and the proclamation of one's own helplessness.

> **NOTE**
>
> If you say, "I can't," you don't want to. Because, in reality, you can do everything. But everything has consequences. You can choose every day! And not to decide is also a choice. The point at which you stand today is based on earlier decisions and rejected alternatives. Everything that happens in the moment is the consequence of decisions in the past. And everything you do, you do voluntarily. However, everything has a price, and not everyone is willing to "pay" the price for a particular decision.

An employee who rebels against their superior must expect the possibility of not being considered in the next career round. A partner who wins all engagements by competing on low prices should not be surprised about negative contribution margins and possibly lower partner compensation. A person who does not spend time with their life partner and their children must not be surprised if these people distance themselves.

> **NOTE**
>
> "No time" means: Other things are more important to me. Everything in life is a question of priority: What you really want, you do! The exciting question, however, is: Why are you doing what you are doing right now?

This applies to both professional and personal life. The answers to these questions are important at every stage of life.

As an entry-level professional, most of the time we receive directions from others. As we advance in our career, we move from being the recipient of instructions to being the person who gives instructions. Those who are at the top of the company only give instructions and usually no longer receive instructions from colleagues. Many times, people do not go through these career phases with an awareness that would be necessary to successfully lead themselves and others. Too often, behavioral patterns and role models are unconsciously adopted by superiors, and the professional does not realize that at the top of their career they are often only a reflection of their former superiors.

Therefore, the psychological knowledge of the following regularities is particularly important.

 ## LAW OF CAUSE AND EFFECT

Everything has a reason, and every effect has its specific cause. Aristotle believed that we live in a world governed by laws and not by chance. He explained that there is a reason for everything, whether it is known to us, or not. There are one, or more causes for every effect. Every cause, or action has some effect. We do not always recognize the cause.

Based on this premise, success is no coincidence! Success has nothing to do with luck. Everything has a reason. However, this reason is not always apparent to everyone. "You reap what you sow" is a well-known saying from the Bible. Newton's third law, also known as the principle of interaction, the principle of counteraction, or the principle of reaction ("actio equals reactio"), states that for every action there is an equal and an opposite reaction.

Thoughts are causes and circumstances are effects. By changing the way you think, you change your life. All it takes is making a decision. You become what you think most of the time. What you feel and how you react is not determined by what happens, but by how you think about it. It is your inner world that is responsible for the conditions of your life. You yourself determine your feelings and behaviors by the way you view your environment and how you think about the things that happen to you.

> ## NOTE
>
> No event has any power over me except that which I give it in my thoughts!

For professionals, the law of cause and effect is relevant. If an ICS does not work, there is a risk that things will go wrong in the company and be incorrectly reflected in accounting. Lawyers know that missed deadlines lead to the rejection of requests at court. The law of cause and effect does not only apply to these easily understandable facts but to one's own management as well as to the management of others that finds its way into our private lives.

TIP

Pay attention to your thoughts! You become what you think most of the time. Thoughts are causes and effects are circumstances. If you control your thoughts, you can change your life. This applies to your professional life as well as your personal life. You cannot always influence the events in your life. In particular, strokes of fate, or things that you did not cause can have a significant negative impact on your life. You cannot change these things. The only thing you can influence is how you think about the things that happen to you. Your interpretation of events has a direct impact on how you feel. Consider the Serenity Prayer by U.S. theologian Reinhold Niebuhr:

"God, grant me the serenity to accept the things I cannot change, the courage to change the things I can, and the wisdom to distinguish one from the other."

Develop the habit of analyzing certain events to see if you or others were the cause. Be honest with yourself and take responsibility only where you were actually the cause of the event. This will be the case in many but not all instances. You are exactly where you are in your life now because of decisions you did or did not make in the past. Not deciding is also a decision. You are the cause of your life. Take responsibility for the choices you made in the past and make better choices in the future. Your thoughts are the key to a happy and successful future.

 LAW OF FAITH

What we believe deep in our hearts becomes reality. We believe not what we see, but what we already believe. We reject information that contradicts our already established opinions, regardless of whether our beliefs – or even prejudices – are based on fact or fantasy.

Henry Ford once said, "Whether you think you can, or think you can't – you are right."

Each of us has certain beliefs, or belief systems that are linked closely to our personal values. These belief systems make up several sets of beliefs. It's what we think about ourselves, reality, or the world. They determine our expectations. They indicate what we believe to be true and what we believe we can achieve. They are our inner beliefs.

Many of the thoughts we think are beliefs. Soliloquies are often based on beliefs, although we might not be aware of it. What we tend to think about ourselves and believe about life comes from our habitual thought patterns. However, we are not born with these beliefs and thought patterns. They are often formed in childhood and remain with us throughout our lives unless we replace them with others, be they positive, or negative. Negative beliefs often limit us, make us doubt ourselves, and prevent success. Positive beliefs, on the other hand, can give us energy and motivation. They can help in overcoming challenges and in achieving our goals. Beliefs are formed through upbringing as well as through our observations and experiences.

EXAMPLE

If a CPA deals exclusively with embezzlement audits, or is essentially involved with cybercrime, they will likely rarely see the good in people. If a lawyer deals exclusively with clients accused of crimes, their view of people, their thought patterns, and their beliefs are shaped by this. Professionals who are confronted predominantly with negative events will rarely be able to develop positive beliefs. This is obvious. It becomes particularly critical when this group of people then transfers their professional life to their private life.

The effect of beliefs was discovered by the French pharmacist Emile Coué at the beginning of the 20th century. He told his patients that they would surely get well very quickly with a particular medicine. His patients were also told to recite the following sentence 25 times a day, morning, noon, and night: "Every day, in every way, I am getting better and better."

From this, Coué developed the doctrine of autosuggestion. Nikolaus B. Enkelmann developed 14 basic laws of life development. In these basic laws, faith and positive thoughts are at the center of personality development. Enkelmann perfected the teaching of autosuggestion and expanded it to include mental training. The fourth basic law of life development is: "The subconscious mind – the construction site of life and the working space of the soul – has the tendency to realize every thought."

Every thought has the tendency to become a reality. Beliefs govern our daily lives because they reflect our beliefs, attitudes, and faith. We think countless thoughts every day. Of these, as a rule, only a few thoughts are positive and uplifting. Far more negative thoughts pass through our brains, often given additional weight via negative media coverage. In addition, we have a multitude of insignificant, neutral, and fleeting thoughts. When we memorize thoughts, it can have far-reaching consequences. First, a recurring thought becomes familiar to us until it becomes an inner conviction. Positive and negative actions can arise from this.

EXAMPLE

The following list shows examples of some negative beliefs:

- I never succeed
- I cannot do this
- I have always done it this way
- I always do everything wrong
- I am unimportant
- Others are always preferred
- I am too fat, too thin, too long, . . .
- I am not intelligent
- I am always late
- I am helpless
- I do not deserve attention
- My siblings are always preferred
- . . .

A Harvard University study found that each adolescent hears about 180,000 such negative suggestions by age 18. These suggestions can become beliefs through their frequent repetition. In this respect, what and how we say something is always important. This is true with our co-workers as well as with our family members and friends. If you want to do something good for those around you, always suggest positive beliefs to them.

TIP

A positive belief phrase is short, concise, and phrased in the present tense, and phrasing is always positive. It addresses the subconscious. Professionals have the opportunity to express a variety of positive beliefs to their employees on a daily basis. The following list shows examples of positive suggestions that become beliefs when constantly repeated:

- You will achieve this
- You can do it
- You will meet the deadline
- You can check the ICS
- You can pass the professional exam
- You are intelligent
- You are conscientious
- You are diligent
- You are willing to learn
- You are a helpful colleague
- . . .

In the mental training tool, the topic of beliefs is covered in more detail.

 ## LAW OF EXPECTATIONS

Whatever you expect with certainty becomes your self-fulfilling prophecy. You always have the function of a fortune teller in your life. Things become the way you think and speak about them. If you are convinced that good things will happen, they normally will. But if you expect negative things, there is a high probability that you will be right in this case as well.

Your expectations not only influence you, but also the people around you. Your attitude toward people and certain situations is essentially shaped by what you expect. In the 1960s, Robert Rosenthal and Leonore Jacobson discovered the Pygmalion effect as part of a research project. In this experiment, two school classes were randomly put together with other students. One teacher was told at the beginning of the school year that his class contained only highly talented students. The other teacher was told that there were only students in this class who were less gifted. At the end of the year, it was found that the class with the supposedly highly gifted students did significantly better than the class with the less gifted. Although there are now numerous studies that place restrictions on the age of the children in each class and the pedagogical skills of the teachers, the Pygmalion effect is recognized and established. According to this, the teacher's expectation of the students' abilities plays a crucial role in their learning success. Certainly, we all remember teachers who were either unaware of the Pygmalion Effect, or grossly disregarded it.

But what about our expectations of co-workers, or those close to us? Do we always expect the best from people, or certain situations? It doesn't take a psychology degree to realize that there are a multitude of self-fulfilling prophecies in each person's past. Oftentimes, sentences such as "I had a hunch," "I knew this would happen," or "If only I had listened to my gut/feeling" are uttered. The principle known as "self-fulfilling prophecy" is obviously known to many, but few people act accordingly.

TIP

By profession, an auditor has to adopt a critical attitude. This can lead to seeing only negative and bad things in everything. The focus is on the error. It is certainly not advisable for an auditor to automatically assume that all audits are effective, and that the correctness of the accounts is always guaranteed. The year-end audit looks for errors in systems, processes, and people. Those who habitually look only for the error tend to see an error in everything and everyone. If we transfer our professional life to our private life, we should not be surprised when people turn away. For auditors in particular, it is advisable to adopt a fundamentally critical attitude only towards internal control systems and with regard to the correctness of accounting. For other life situations as well as dealing with employees and other people, it is advisable to always expect the best. Expect only the best from yourself as well. Give your employees positive feedback when there is a reason to do so. Tell your employees that you believe in them and that you are proud of them. The same goes for your life partner and children. Tell them as often as possible that you believe in them, that you love them, and that you are proud of them.

 LAW OF ATTRACTION

You are a living magnet. This means that in your life you will inevitably attract those people, situations, and circumstances that fit your predominant thoughts.

You attract everything in your life through your mindset and personality. You can change your life by changing your mindset. You have most likely heard the saying, "Birds of a feather flock together."

The law of attraction also shows up in a completely different form. Have you ever thought intensely about a person and a few minutes later this person called, or you ran into them? Or has it ever happened to you that your counterpart yawns and you automatically have to yawn too? Or someone smiles at you, and you smile back without thinking? The research of mirror neurons explains such behavior. Mirror neurons are a resonance system in the brain that makes other people's feelings and moods resonate in the receiver. What is unique about these neurons is that they already send out signals when someone merely observes an action. The nerve cells react in exactly the same way as if you had performed what you saw yourself. The best comparison comes from playing music: When we pluck a guitar string, we also make the other strings of the instrument vibrate; we create a resonance. To feel compassion, joy, but also pain, is only possible in this way.

Thoughts are forces. We attract into our life what we think about most of the time. If we want to become successful, it is best to surround ourselves with successful people.

TIP

In the future, observe your surroundings carefully. This applies to both your professional and personal life. When people are in resonance, their posture and way of speaking are similar. Neurolinguistic Programming (NLP) refers to this resonance behavior as pacing. What is meant by this is that the body language of two people mirrors each other.

In football, it has long been standard practice for players to consciously adopt a positive and confident body language after a touchdown. This is because negative body language has an immediate effect on the subconscious and then makes it more difficult to score points for their own team.

For professionals, this means in daily practice that they should consciously have a positive expression and body language.

 LAW OF CORRESPONDENCE

Your outer world is a reflection of your inner world and corresponds to your prevailing thought patterns. Since our outer world is in every way a reflection of our inner world, we often encounter only that which corresponds to our innermost beliefs.

> **NOTE**
>
> The perception of your outer world is only a reflection of your inner world.

If we want to change, we have to start inside our thinking. Our relationships always reflect the personality we are inside. Our attitudes, our health, and our material conditions are reflections of how we think in these areas. "Nothing changes unless I change," Nikolaus B. Enkelmann, a famous German personality trainer, says in his seminars. There is only one thing in the world that you can really control: That is your own thinking. By taking control of your thinking, you get control of all other aspects of your life. By thinking about and talking about only the things you want, and by refusing to talk, or think about things you don't want, you become the architect of your own destiny.

> **TIP**
>
> By changing the quality of your thinking, you change the quality of your life. When you think, you ask yourself questions in an inner dialogue, which you answer yourself. The starting point are the questions you ask yourself every day. The quality of your questions and the quality of the answers determine your quality of life. They are the cause of whether or not you lead a successful life. They are also the starting point for the happiness in life.
>
> Everyone can choose and change their behavior every day. Not to choose, as I have mentioned before, is also a choice and everything that happens at the moment is the result of choices you once made in the past. Whoever has gained this realization can choose anew every day. Whoever chooses what they do, always does what they have chosen. That is why conscious choice is so important, because everything you do, you do voluntarily. If you are looking for a helping hand, you will always find it at the end of your arms. Self-responsible action is what particularly distinguishes successful professionals.

There are **two central life decisions** of every human being. In my opinion, they are the most important decisions you will make in your life:

The choice of profession.
The choice of a life partner.

Both decisions will have a lasting impact on your life and are not easily reversible. When it comes to choosing a profession, the vast majority of readers of this book have already made up their minds. You may be a CPA, or a lawyer, or you may be on your way to becoming a professional. This decision was probably well-considered in light of the difficulty of the professional exams. After passing the professional exam, some auditors move to an industrial, or service company, to a bank, or an insurance company. Then the professional exam was a means to an end and the profession not a vocation or calling. Regarding the second important life decision, the choice of a life partner, I will present a valuable tool in Chapter 17.

Almost every decision is associated with more or less significant risks. The principle of self-responsibility should help you become aware that with almost every decision, decisions in favor of alternatives would also have been possible. So, if you have decided in favor of something, you have thereby also immanently rejected the alternatives.

I advocate elevating the principle of self-responsibility to a maxim of life. This applies to both professional and private life. I am not suggesting that you should slip into a victim role. Assume responsibility only for what you are in fact responsible for. It is often mistakenly assumed that you are at a certain point in your life only because you made "right" or "wrong" decisions before. Warren Buffett once said, **"You have to do very few things right in life as long as you don't do too many wrong."**

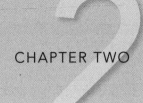

CHAPTER TWO

Result Orientation

W HAT IS GENERALLY ACCEPTED in sports is not always taken into account in everyday professional life. In football, baseball, soccer, tennis, or golf, the only thing that counts are the results. If you play beautifully and lose, the reference to the "beautiful game" is usually not very meaningful. If you deliver an exceptional presentation and don't get the job, or don't convince your superiors, you have lost. This is why the principle of result orientation is so important. Successful people always focus their thoughts and actions on results. They already have the end in mind at the beginning.

There are many parallels between top athletes and consultants, which is why top sports can serve as a model of success for professionals. Especially when it comes to understanding the principle of result orientation and integrating it into a professional's everyday work.

You might object at this point that the results will not always meet your client's expectations and ask yourself what the use of the principle of result orientation actually is? In this case, it is especially important because you're already in the mindset of how you can "sell" an "undesirable" result in a positive way. If you start thinking about how the client might react to the result of your work only shortly before the presentation, you have lost valuable time during the preparation.

TIP

Effective professionals focus all project planning on the result at the beginning of a project. The result may be a presentation, an audit report, an expert opinion, an appeal, or a written statement. Only the deliverable sticks with the client. You may have done everything right, the motivation of the team may have been excellent, but if the client is not enthusiastic about you at the end of the project, all effort was in vain. That is why it is especially important for professionals that not only the material form of reporting is perfect, but that formal aspects reflect the quality of the service as well. Just as eating an eye-pleasing and perfectly cooked meal in a restaurant, it is important that the external appearance of a professional's reports do not contain any errors. If you have any spelling mistakes or incorrect punctuation in your texts, if you format tables incorrectly, or set up graphics poorly, you should not be surprised if clients draw conclusions about the quality of the service. Therefore, it is advisable not only to work in a technically outstanding manner, but also to present a perfect formal appearance.

Outstanding successes of top athletes at the Olympic Games, playoffs in the NFL, NBA, or NHL are duly celebrated by the public. There is extensive media coverage. Journalists often scrutinize and analyze the success factors behind these extraordinary athletic achievements. For the daily application of the principle of result orientation, it is advisable in a first step to point out similarities between top athletes and professionals. In a second step, essential traits and characteristics of successful top athletes are presented. Finally, in a third step, essential success factors of top athletes are shown, which are also valid for successful professionals.

SIMILARITIES BETWEEN TOP ATHLETES AND PROFESSIONALS

At world championships, Olympics, or other sporting events, athletes go through a process that typically comprises three phases. Figure 2.1 illustrates the process and lists key activities:

The transferability to the processes of professionals is immediately apparent. Audit and consulting projects as well as trials have to be prepared, assignments are conducted and, finally, new consulting assignments should follow the completion of projects.

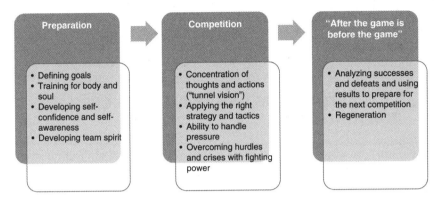

FIGURE 2.1 Processes in elite sports and key activities

The ability to analyze successes and defeats accurately and to draw the right conclusions for the future is another common key component among successful top athletes and successful professionals.

Those who seek explanations rather than excuses have also already taken the first step toward a fresh start. For German goalkeeper legend Oliver Kahn, a defeat is a single image of success. It creates an opportunity to think everything through again, to review and possibly realign everything once more. For Kahn, the setback provides important clues as to where one needs to make improvements, or what one might do completely differently. In this way, the setback creates the prerequisite for being able to really take off. The principle of personal responsibility should apply to both top athletes and professionals.

> ## NOTE
>
> Defeats are part of the "game" for both athletes and professionals. Almost all of those who are at the top and celebrate success have suffered some defeats along the way and have drawn their conclusions from this; otherwise, they would not have reached their current positions. It shows sovereignty to admit one's own mistakes instead of blaming failures on a chain of unfortunate circumstances.

In sports as in business, there are rules of the game to be observed. Fair play wins. Most world-class athletes have observed this important principle in competitions. Those who observe the rules of the game and behave fairly in their dealings with their competitors win twice. Fairness pays off. Fair play and top performance do not have to be opposites. Respect and honesty are a better basis for success.

CHARACTER TRAITS AND TRAITS OF SUCCESSFUL TOP ATHLETES

There are certainly a variety of traits and characteristics that distinguish top athletes. The following can be observed in world-class athletes in a wide variety of sports.

- Passion and enthusiasm
- Perseverance and discipline
- The ability to "fight"
- Self-confidence and self-assurance
- Winning mentality and concentration

The biographies of successful athletes show that **passion and enthusiasm** are an important source of energy for them. Top performances are no coincidence. In the beginning, there is usually passion and enthusiasm for a certain goal. Oliver Kahn says that it is the love for something, the intensity with which we dedicate ourselves to it, and the degree to which we identify with what we are doing that makes us successful. Beyond that, passion and enthusiasm are infectious. We can only inspire others if we are enthusiastic ourselves.

Passion and enthusiasm are an essential driving force to deliver the necessary **perseverance and discipline** to achieve certain goals. A person who wants to win a gold medal or become a world champion needs perseverance and discipline. They must be able to overcome obstacles and train with discipline towards the goal.

Closely related to the ability to muster endurance and discipline is the willingness of a top athlete to fight. With fighting strength, hurdles and crisis are overcome. In soccer, sports commentators often credit victories primarily on the team's fighting ability. Combative athletes' characteristics are patience and a high tolerance for frustration. When we fight, we act. Action makes us confident, which increases the chances of success. Often, these athletes fight for every single point.

Self-confidence and self-assurance are important characteristics of successful top athletes. If you don't believe in yourself, you have lost already.

Successful top athletes believe in themselves, even when their backs are against the wall. Self-confidence and self-assurance go hand in hand with past sporting success. Having already successfully mastered difficult situations in training, or other competitions is the basis for the necessary self-confidence in critical competitive situations.

The most successful athletes have a **winner's mentality** and have the ability to focus completely on the moment in certain situations. They have the ability for what is called "tunnel vision." This is about completely surrendering to the situation and acting intuitively out of the situation. This is the state of "flow." Flow is the highest level of concentration in one's own performance. It is a trance-like, meditative state, the result of correctly dealing with one's own emotional and thought world. Oliver Kahn describes this state in the final match of the 2001 Champions League when taking a penalty kick as follows: "I was no longer aware of anything except the ball and the shooter. It was as if I were in an empty, silent room. I didn't hear anything from the 80,000 spectators in the stadium. I left everything to my intuition. I was completely in the flow." Professionals who possess the same traits and characteristics as athletes are more successful than others who do not. These are characteristics that you can also learn or train for.

 ## SUCCESS FACTORS OF ACCOMPLISHED TOP ATHLETES AND PROFESSIONALS

Top athletes use six central factors to be successful. Figure 2.2 shows an overview of these six factors and the principles and techniques behind them:

In the following, these important success factors of top athletes are explained in more detail, and it is shown how professionals can use them profitably for themselves.

 ## GOAL CLARITY AND WILLPOWER

Clarity of purpose and willpower are the first success factors of particularly successful top athletes and professionals. Ever since he was a child, Tiger Woods dreamed of becoming the best golf player in the world. Boris Becker also knew when he was still a child that he wanted to win Wimbledon one day. With an unshakable will, both worked towards achieving their goals. Both top athletes and professionals should clearly know what goals they want to achieve.

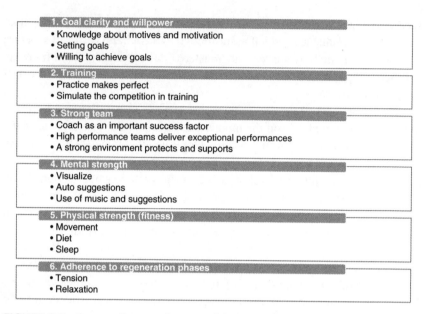

FIGURE 2.2 Success factors of successful top athletes and professionals

The clearer the goal, the easier it is for the subconscious mind to help achieve those goals.

As a child, or teenager, athletes are usually unaware of the motives and motivation behind their actions. Often it is fun, passion, and enthusiasm for a certain sport as well as the talent necessary for success that can lead children to top performances at an early age. It is only in adulthood that some athletes become aware of their motives and motivation as part of a process of self-discovery. In any case, sustainably successful professionals should be aware of their motives and the motivation behind their consulting activities. Those who do not know why they work as professionals or do so solely for monetary reasons should not be surprised if sooner, or later "burn-out" syndrome appears.

 TRAINING

The saying "practice makes perfect" comes from sports and is equally valid for successful professionals. Anyone who conducts a certain consulting activity (e.g., business valuations) once a year should not expect results better than those of an amateur athlete who plays golf or tennis once a year. Successful world-class athletes specialize in a particular sport and train for it until they reach the world championship. No top athlete would think of wanting to win Wimbledon, or the US Open in tennis and become a Formula 1 world champion at the same time. In essence, this applies equally to all athletes in all classes. With this in mind, all generalists in the consulting professions should ask themselves whether they want to know a little about each of many areas, or an above-average amount in one specialty. Who would want to have heart surgery performed by a general practitioner? Probably nobody. Anyone would prefer a cardiologist, who specializes in heart surgery, for such a procedure. Any generalist who can credibly convey to their customer that they have the necessary specialized professional knowledge in all of these fields is an excellent salesperson, but not really a good consultant.

TIP

What could the training plans for professionals look like in order to provide above-average successful consulting services? The already specialized consultant knows that they have gained experience with each completed assignment and have, as it were, passed through practice a situation similar to that of an athlete in a competition. An essential part of the training of any specialist is, therefore, their practice. For the professional who is not yet a specialist, it is important to acquire the necessary specialized knowledge through appropriate further training and education. But even the specialist must continue to train, i.e., educate themselves through self-study and seminars. Only constant repetition of theory and practice leads to mastery among consultants. Only permanent training and participation in competitions lead to world-class performance in athletes. It applies equally to athletes and professionals that they should simulate competition already during training.

STRONG TEAM

When you ask top athletes about the reasons for their success, they often point to their team. In both individual and team sports, the success of an athlete is closely linked to the performance of the entire team. Ultimately, however, in my opinion, the team does not only include coaches, doctors, physiologists, and psychologists, but also the family and private environment. An intact family environment is an essential basis for athletic success. The private environment supports and protects in crisis situations.

In today's consulting environment, high-performance teams also deliver exceptional performance. In almost every major consulting assignment, teams of consultants provide the services. It is necessary to select the right "mix" of consultants for the project. The professional working as a "lone wolf" quickly reaches his limits. He cannot fall back on ideas that creative teams develop but is always on his own. Likewise, he cannot use the group dynamics and the feedback from other project members during the consulting project to the benefit of his customers. Finally, he runs the risk of lacking important resources that high-performance teams have.

 ## MENTAL STRENGTH

Mental training is a valuable tool not only for top athletes, but also for professionals, which is why we will discuss this tool in detail in Part Three. The goal of mental training is for you to become mentally strong. For top athletes, it is the crucial tool to focus on results. Meanwhile, many successful athletes, or teams have hired mental coaches. Time and again, athletes and coaches are quoted as saying that games, or competitions are won, or lost in the mind. We constantly send thoughts from our subconscious to our conscious. These are not always constructive thoughts. Negative beliefs and thought patterns have a decisive influence on success. Only those who really believe in success will succeed. In this context, everything we have absorbed from conception through birth to the present day has an unconscious effect on our actions. This includes, for example, our upbringing, our biographical experiences (successes as well as failures), and our convictions and belief patterns. This is why the ability to control one's thoughts and to put oneself in a state of deep conviction and confidence is so important. This is where mental training comes in, which we discuss in detail later under Tools.

Visualization techniques are most commonly used in elite sports. The idea is that optimal movement sequences, or game situations are anticipated in the mind as often as possible so that they can be called up in competition situations and the desired results brought about. Success is to be programmed deep into the athlete's subconscious. The goal is to intensely visualize the desired victory, or success over and over again. Our brain cannot distinguish between the imagined and what is actually experienced, because both are activated by the same brain areas. This topic is also deepened during the mental training.

> **NOTE**
>
> The conservative professional, who has traditionally trained their analytical thinking skills in their education, will ask themselves whether they can and should use such techniques in their consulting work. It is worth noting that the ability to focus all attention on one point at the decisive moment, to block out everything that interferes and thus to focus all forces willfully, is substantially important for professionals. The ability to concentrate is a critical and decisive factor in being able to call on one's full potential at important moments.

The longer and more intensely you can concentrate, the more constant and higher your performance will be. Lack of concentration always occurs when your thoughts digress from what is really important. Only absolute concentration will enable professionals to withstand the pressure in critical situations. In this context, physical fitness has a significant impact on the ability to concentrate.

 ## PHYSICAL STRENGTH (FITNESS)

It is obvious that the top athletes have to be physically strong in order to be successful. However, Tiger Woods, the world's best golfer, has shown in his most successful times the significant importance of the mental strength described above. Although doctors advised him against starting at the US Open in the summer of 2008, he played five days with a fatigue fracture and torn cruciate ligament in what is probably the toughest golf tournament in the world. Tiger Woods said before the tournament, "I'm going to play, and I'm going to win."

Although the injury worsened during the tournament, Tiger Woods did not give up. Golf Journal magazine praised the achievement as follows: "The possibility of giving up on a tournament is obviously beyond his imagination."

It is certainly not the norm for an athlete who is not in good health to perform exceptionally well. Fitness is assumed in athletes. But are all professionals physically fit? Many are so professionally active that they think they have no time for activities that lead to physical strength and fitness. But given that the time in a week is the same for all professionals with 7 days of 24 hours each, it is obviously a matter of priority. There are three starting points to significantly strengthen the physical fitness and consequently the concentration ability of consultants:

- Exercise
- Healthy diet
- Sufficient sleep

Those who exercise regularly, learn to switch off and often have the best ideas during or afterwards. These should be aerobic sports (running, cycling, etc.) performed at a reasonable heart rate. Regular exercise and the physical fitness that comes with it prevent illness and create reserves of strength and energy for everyday work.

Other lifestyle factors can also contribute positively to physical fitness. This includes a healthy diet and sufficient sleep. Performance absolutely needs breaks and rest. Fitness, sleep, and proper nutrition are the foundations of the ability to concentrate.

 ## REGENERATION PHASES

Neither top athletes nor top consultants can perform their activities without any breaks. They need to recharge their inner batteries, both physical and mental, from time to time. This requires regular regeneration every working day as well as a vacation period after exhausting months of intensive work. Only those who perform their job with 100% commitment of body and mind are at the top of their game. This total exertion must be followed by an equal relaxation in order to achieve regeneration and thus re-emergence (Latin "regeneration"). The following applies: Those who are in good physical condition recover more quickly. In elite sports, the rhythm of activity and active rest form the core of all training methods worldwide. Periodic instead of linear loads enable success here.

Energy is recovered at the same rate it is expended. The right work-life balance, which I present later in Part Three, Tools, can help significantly in achieving this. The difference between successful consultants and less successful consultants is their effectiveness and efficiency. Top consultants create a balanced ratio between input and output, which is proven by the quality of their results. Extremely long working hours of consultants are no proof of above-average performance and can often indicate exhaustion.

CONCLUSION ON THE PRINCIPLE OF RESULTS ORIENTATION

The principle of results orientation is recognized in sports and is the dominant principle. Winning comes first. Preparation, competition during the game, and regeneration after the game to prepare for the next game are always oriented to the result. Action is focused on the results. In this respect, top-level sport serves as a model of success for successful professionals. The similarities between successful top athletes and professionals have been highlighted. The traits and characteristics as well as central success factors apply equally to successful athletes and top consultants.

In the meantime, personnel managers are increasingly looking at applications to see whether the applicant was or is active in sports. Particularly successful athletes with the same qualification profile are given preference over other applicants. HR departments now know that certain characteristics are already present in athletes and do not have to be developed first. Many top managers were at one time also exceptionally good athletes. Zittelmann's dissertation on the "Psychology of the Super-Rich" found that there was no correlation between performance at school and university and the degree of their financial success. With a few exceptions, however, all of the interviewees were either far above-average amateur athletes, or even competitive athletes. "As such, they learned to deal with victories and defeats and to prevail against competitors, they acquired a tolerance for frustration, developed self-confidence in their own ability. Team athletes learned teamwork skills. But most interviewees were not team athletes, they were individual athletes."

Malik and Drucker agree with the principle of results orientation as a crucial factor in successful and effective managers. In his expanded new edition, "Leading, Performing, Living," Malik says, "A consistent pattern in the thinking and the actions of competent managers is their focus on results. They are predominantly – occasionally exclusively – interested in results. Everything else is secondary, or of no interest to them." "Management," he says, "is the profession of making results happen. The touchstone is achieving goals and accomplishing tasks."

TIP

Professionals should base their actions on the principle of results orientation. The lessons learned from top-level sports can serve as a model for success. At the beginning of each activity, audit plans and project plans should be reviewed to determine whether they comply with the principle of results orientation. The results of professionals are largely handed over to the client in the form of a written report. In addition, there is often an oral presentation of the results. Even if the results produced by a professional are not in the client's interest, it is important to sell these results in a professional manner. The client will remember the way of reporting. High-quality work is to be expected from a qualified professional. Beyond that, the external form will be remembered as well. If a professional has formal errors in his reporting, conclusions are often drawn about the quality of the deliverables.

As an example: An annual audit loses significant value from a client's perspective if the audit report has a large number of formal errors. An auditor and their team may have observed all quality assurance instruments in the course of the annual audit and arrive at the correct material results, but if there are formal errors in the audit report, or in the auditor's opinion, this counteracts the entire work of the audit team.

CHAPTER THREE

Focus

FOCUS IS THE CENTRAL key to professional and private success. It is important to concentrate on a few essentials. Focus is the key to results and ultimately to success. You can be busy with many things at the same time, but you cannot be successful in many areas at the same time. Reduce everything in your professional and private life to the essentials. In other words, ignore all the things you could be doing and instead do only what you should be doing. The principle of focus means that you recognize that not all things are equally important. You need to identify the things that are most important, the things that are top priority.

> **NOTE**
>
> Applying the principle of focus makes the difference between success and failure. The key to a professional's success is that they know their key tasks. Professionals should work only on those.

This is why the principle of focus is so important. Your lack of focus will bog you down in details. Those who cannot distinguish essentials from non-essentials will not be able to manage themselves, or others well. The results will be far from a top-notch performance. A professional who does not know exactly what the essential things on the to-do list are, is not a professional, but an amateur.

TIP

Hidden champions, secret winners, or unknown world market leaders are relatively unknown companies that are market leaders in their industry. They are characterized by the fact that they operate in a specialized niche. Professionals have a broad field of activity in their professional tasks. From the audit of financial statements to the preparation of annual financial statements, tax consulting, business consulting, IT consulting, and so forth, there are a wide range of services that the professional can offer its clients. However, smaller professional services providers, in particular, quickly reach their limits here, as qualified consulting in the individual areas of activity is associated with the corresponding know-how. In addition, there is a trend towards ever larger professional services providers, although this does not necessarily mean that the size of a professional's practice is a surefire indicator of the professional's specialized knowledge.

That is why specialization – especially for medium-sized companies – is the most important differentiation strategy against competitors. Many larger companies have specialists. But too many professionals in medium-sized practices still believe that it is better to accumulate the broadest possible knowledge. The all-rounder, who seems to know the answer to every question, may be able to sell themselves well to their clients. The specialist knows that all too often there is a lack of substance.

For the same reason, specialization, and sound expert knowledge in a narrowly defined field of activity do not mean that all generalists among professionals will no longer be needed in the future. However, the generalists among the professionals need highly specialized experts among their colleagues, or at least a particularly good network in order to be able to provide qualified consulting services. Here, too, the principle of focus is helpful. The smaller a professional's practice is, the more specialized it should be. As their size increases, medium-sized professional services providers should occupy additional consulting fields with proven experts as part of strategic corporate planning.

How can the principle of focus in self-management and external management be systematically and effectively learned? This question is especially important for all professionals who have been bogged down so far. One tool that helps to apply the principle of focus in everyday life is the Pareto rule. It goes back to Vilfredo Pareto (1848–1923), an Italian engineer, economist, and sociologist, who recognized the Pareto distribution in the course of his research. Pareto studied the distribution of land ownership in Italy and found that about 20% of the population owned roughly 80% of the land. In addition, he studied the distribution of people's income and wealth. Again, he was able to identify a recurring mathematical relationship. The Pareto Principle is derived from this. It basically states that with a resource input of about 20%, about 80% output can be generated. The Pareto rule is also called the 80/20 rule.

The Pareto rule is an effective tool for focusing on the few essential things in both professional and personal life. In management, the Pareto rule states that about 20% of the activities deliver 80% of the results. Those who believe in this principle know that 20% of the essential activities contribute to 80% of the project's success. Figure 3.1 shows the Pareto Principle.

EXAMPLE

As part of the analysis of customer and supplier relationships, the sales figures attributable to individual customers and suppliers are examined periodically in more detail. If the cumulative sales of the 20 largest customers and suppliers are analyzed in this context, professionals often find that these account for a cumulative 80% of sales and purchasing revenues. Even though the distribution can sometimes be 70/30, or 90/10, these deviations from the 80/20 rule are relatively minor and confirm the basic principle. It is usually the major customers and suppliers that account for a sizable proportion of sales. Provided that auditors do not perform mathematical sampling procedures in their result-oriented audit procedures, but make a conscious selection, they benefit from using this knowledge in their audit procedures.

Accordingly, if 80% of the results are typical as a result of 20% of the time commitment, then one must necessarily also accept that 80%, i.e., the vast majority of the time, will yield only 20% of the results. This does not mean, however, that the other 80% is generally dispensable. In every profession there are activities that have to be done but are often not particularly productive. This includes answering e-mails, for example. To do without this and to concentrate only on the other 20% is not practicable. However, the organization and use of time for such tasks can be optimized at least to such an extent that the share of work input for them falls below 80%.

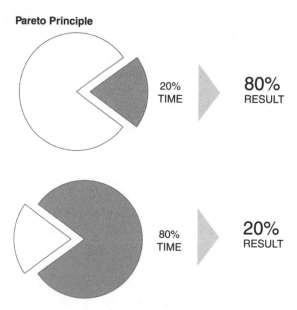

FIGURE 3.1 Pareto Principle

Summarizing, the 80/20 rule is about focusing on the essential things to improve your productivity, for example. In essence, it's about how everyone chooses the right activities in their different areas of life so that a successful life gradually emerges. In this respect, the principle of focus illustrates the principle of results orientation presented earlier, because it shows a professional that they must concentrate on a few, essential things if they want to be successful.

Digitalization leads to increasing complexity in everyday professional and private life. As complexity increases, however, there is a growing risk of getting too absorbed in the process. The distraction in everyday professional life is immense.

EXAMPLE

It is common requirement for professionals to have periods of concentrated reading. This might relate to briefs, audit reports, expert opinions, technical papers, and the like. In many cases, there will be a landline phone, smartphone, tablet, or PC/notebook on the desk, or in close proximity to the desk. The risk of distraction from calls, incoming mail, text messages, or colleagues coming into the office is substantial. Anyone who gets distracted by such disruptions knows that the learning curve afterwards is huge. This is accompanied by an enormous loss of productivity.

There's a Russian proverb that says, "If you chase two rabbits at the same time, they'll both slip through your fingers." Multitasking is an opportunity to do multiple things at the same time incorrectly. The ability and intention to do more than one task at a time is deeply ingrained in our subconscious because it was most likely a survival necessity in the earliest history of humankind. While many people can do two or more things at the same time, they cannot effectively focus on two things at once. Distractions are natural. Don't let them take your focus. Multitasking takes its toll. If you try to do too much at once, you'll end up doing nothing right. Figure out what things are most important right now and give them your undivided attention. Multitasking won't get more done. Thinking you can accomplish more by multitasking is wrong.

Not everything is equally important. Many professionals use to-do lists for their planning. You will find a variety of professional and private activities. However, not all activities are equally important to your success. Successful people can distinguish between the essential and the unessential items on a to-do list. Often, however, the activities on a to-do list are unrelated to productivity and success, so we end up being neither productive nor successful. Thus, to-do lists become pure survival lists that get you through the day and through life. However, they do not turn every single day into a milestone for the next milestone in your life, so that it gradually turns into a successful life.

TIP

For this reason, to-do lists should become so-called success lists. Unlike a to-do list, which often has a multitude of activities, success lists are short. Successful people know their priorities that lead to the right decisions and ultimately, to success. To-do lists contain both activities that should be done and activities that could be done. The challenge for each individual is to do exclusively the things that you should do to achieve your professional and personal goals.

While the Pareto Principle states that about 20% of the activities deliver about 80% of the results, the "Extreme Pareto Principle" focuses on finding the ONE Thing that leads to success. Gary Keller and Jay Papasan have summarized the surprisingly simple truth about extraordinary success in a book called *The ONE Thing*. According to this, whoever takes the first step of the

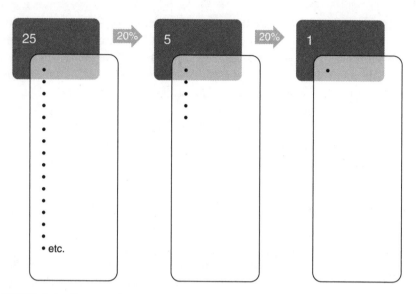

FIGURE 3.2 Extreme Pareto Principle

Pareto Principle and applies it again to the remaining 20% of activities leads to extraordinary success until they finally land on the ONE Thing that leads to success. Figure 3.2 shows the approach.

Here, the Pareto Principle remains the starting point for identifying the ONE Thing that leads to success. While the Pareto Principle states that about 20% of the activities deliver about 80% of the results, the "Extreme Pareto Principle" focuses on finding the ONE Thing that leads to success. Accordingly, whoever applies the Pareto Principle from the first step to the remaining 20% of the activities again and again, until finally only the ONE Thing that provides the decisive contribution to success is left, will create an opportunity to achieve extraordinary success. The central idea of the book is the constant reduction to the ONE Thing. The concept of "the ONE Thing" is essentially based on a focusing question and three success habits.

 THE FOCUSING QUESTION

The quality of your life is determined by the quality of the questions you ask yourself and the quality of the answers you give to those questions. If you ask the wrong questions, you will get the wrong answers. Great questions are the best way to great answers. If you want to be exceptionally successful, you need to ask yourself just one question in all areas of your life and answer it correctly. The key focusing question that leads to extraordinary success is:

"What's the ONE Thing I can do such that by doing it everything else will be easier or unnecessary?"

Extraordinary success depends on the choices we make, and the activities required to achieve them. The answer to this question is not always easy. The question implies several points to consider in finding the right answer.

The question is aimed at the ONE Thing. Not at two, or three things, but at the ONE Thing.

It is about what I can do. Not about what I should do, or wish I could do, but what I can do specifically.

The goal is for the ONE Thing to create a domino effect so that everything else becomes easier, or unnecessary.

The term "everything else" describes the biggest possible domino effect. Ideally, the domino effect that makes everything else superfluous.

The question of the ONE Thing implies both a "big-picture map" and a "small-focus compass."

The question of the ONE Thing aims at having a bigger picture in mind. THE Big Picture. On the other hand, you can stay focused on a daily basis by asking, "What is the ONE Thing I can do right now that will make everything else easier, or unnecessary." Asking "right now" will lead you to always focus on the most important activity in the present. The following three points form the basis for focused thinking regarding the ONE Thing:

- Not everything is equally important. There is always one thing that is more important than anything else.
- Successes are sequential, not simultaneous as the semantics of the word success suggests: Something must take place or be preceded in order to be successful. You start by doing the right thing, and that leads to your subsequent decisions being right as well."
- Ask great questions, find great answers, and act on them.

THE SUCCESS HABIT

"Success is simple. Do what's right, the right way, at the right time," says Arnold H. Glasow, an American businessman and publisher. Asking for the ONE Thing I can do so that in doing that thing, everything else becomes easier

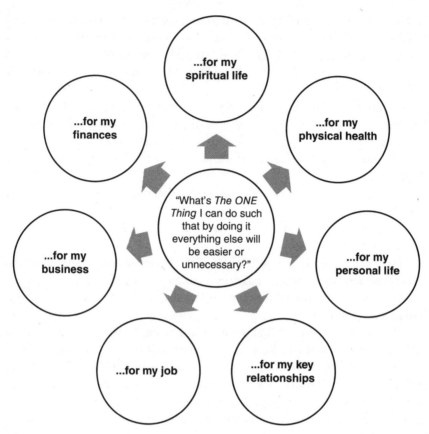

FIGURE 3.3   Focus question for the individual areas of life according to Keller and Papasan

or unnecessary is the underlying guideline that applies to all areas of life. (See Figure 3.3.)

Proceed from the question of the ONE Thing and then answer in the various areas of life on this in a clockwise direction starting at 12:00. Your spiritual life and physical health are the basis for a happy personal life. Without good relationships with the important people in your life, you will have difficulty achieving professional and business success, which in turn is the basis for your financial well-being. Make finding the ONE Thing a daily habit. Understand the concept and apply it. After 66 days, it will have become a routine in your life and will lead you to extraordinary success. We will cover mental training in Chapter 14. That's where you'll learn how to use the subconscious mind to program habits for success.

THE PATH TO GREAT ANSWERS

"People do not decide their futures, they decide their habits and their habits decide their futures," says F.M. Alexander, an Australian author and speaker. Great questions are like great goals. They are big and specific. Exceptional success requires great questions and great answers (see Figure 3.4).

Great and extraordinary questions lead to great and extraordinary answers. The quality of your life is determined by the quality of the questions you ask yourself every day. If you take a closer look at the process of thinking, you will find that thinking is nothing more than constantly asking questions and giving answers. When you think about something, you ask yourself a question on that specific point and give yourself an answer to it in your thoughts. So, if you ask yourself the "right" questions and give yourself the "right" answers, you will be more successful. Especially successful people ask qualitatively especially good questions and find especially good answers to these questions.

TIP

In all the areas of life described above, check what questions you have asked yourself and what answers you have arrived at. For your practice, this means starting with a situation analysis to examine which entrepreneurial questions you have asked yourself in the past up to the present, and what answers you have found. The questions should include your service offering as well as your relationships with your clients and your staff. Write down the questions and answers and let them sink in. Be honest about the answers.

The starting point for your questions and answers are your goals. These should be ambitious and specific. Think about what is possible. Setting a doable goal is like writing another task on your to-do list that you can just check off.

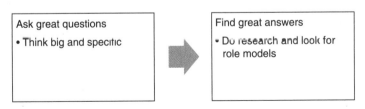

FIGURE 3.4 The path to great answers

A demanding goal is more challenging because you have to work harder to achieve it. Think of people and companies that have completely reinvented themselves. They are good examples of extraordinary success. An example of a great and specific question in a business setting might be, "What can I do today to double sales in a particular area of activity within six months?"

CHAPTER FOUR

Leverage Strengths

ABOVE AVERAGE PROFESSIONALS HAVE special talents. At the beginning, I define talent and aptitude as innate potential and distinguish them from the things we can learn. We can learn specialist knowledge in the same way as we can learn soft skills. Our talents, on the other hand, are innate. That's why it's so important that we know exactly what our own talents are. We will return to the basic knowledge presented here when we look more closely at employee development in Part Two. After all, if we don't know our own talents, how can we identify the talents of our employees? Self-awareness is a prerequisite for successful personnel development.

The principle of "using strengths" is about using our own strengths in a targeted way for our job in order to achieve good, or better yet, very or exceptionally good results. The principle of "using strengths" aims at using already existing strengths and talents. Unfortunately, many managers are weakness oriented. They point out employees' weaknesses and continuously pointed out. It should be obvious that motivation falls by the wayside. Why are so many people weakness-oriented?

They have taken their schooling into their professional lives. Our school systems are mostly aimed at identifying the mistakes of students. Ergo, the biggest goal of a student is to avoid mistakes. The same is often true in child-rearing.

Parents punish their children when they "misbehave." Thus, children avoid "mistakes." The principle of "reward and punishment" also works with animals. Dogs are rewarded for certain behavior with a treat. This Pavlovian conditioning may lead to the desired behavior under certain circumstances, but it fails to recognize that behind some supposed misbehavior of a human being there is a hidden strength in a completely different area. Instead of promoting this strength, however, it is neglected and not developed.

Incidentally, error avoidance is often a reason many people do not take action or are not action oriented. If you don't act, you don't make mistakes. It is as simple as that. Let's analyze the geniuses of the last epochs: What do Goethe, Mozart, Picasso, and other successful people in world history have in common? They all focused on their strengths. They became experts in one field. They made the most of their strengths. Success does not lie in versatility, but in concentrating on strengths. But how do you recognize your strengths? Our school systems are designed to grade students on their verbal intelligence and logical-mathematical intelligence. However, Howard Gardner found that there are a total of eight different basic intelligences. For many professions, the combination of different intelligences is necessary to perform them with above-average success. According to Alexander Christiani and Frank Scheelen, talent is the combination of ten basic intelligences and possibly other personality traits that enable people to excel in a particular field of activity. In their book "Stärken stärken – Talente entdecken, entwickeln und einsetzen" (Strengths – Discovering, Developing and Using Talents), they deal extensively on the topic of using strengths. Referring to Howard Gardner's eight basic intelligences, Christiani and Scheelen summarize a total of ten intelligences in a table. In doing so, they give examples of the central characteristics, typical occupational groups, and prominent representatives. Table 4.1 is based on Christiani and Scheelen and gives an overview of ten different basic intelligences of people.

Even though Gardner acknowledged the spiritual intelligence, or existential intelligence, he only added the natural history skills to his original seven intelligences later on. The associative-creative intelligence does not originate from Gardner.

Professionals indisputably have their talents in the linguistic intelligences and the mathematical-logical intelligences.

In the past, it was important for professionals and their employees to have both linguistic and mathematical-logical intelligence. In the age of digitalization and disruption, I believe this is only a necessary condition, but in itself not

TABLE 4.1 Basic Intelligences According to Howard Gardner

Intelligence	Characteristics	Professional groups	Outstanding representatives
Linguistic intelligence	Sensitivity to written and spoken language Ability to use language for its intended purpose Ability to learn languages	Lawyers, auditors, tax consultants Writers Poets Journalists	William Shakespeare Mark Twain Ernest Hemingway Stephen King
Logical-mathematical intelligence	Ability to analyze problems logically Perform mathematical operations Scientific investigation of problems	Scientist Mathematician Programmers Business economists	Euclid Aristotle Albert Einstein
Associative-creative intelligence	Connecting thoughts in an arbitrary way (not logical and not causal) Giving meaning (associating facts with values) Discovering, creating Label-free observation	Inventors, discoverers Design and development engineers	Walt Disney Daniel Boone Thomas Alva Edison
Spatial intelligence	Theoretical and practical sense for large and small spaces	Sailors Pilots Architects Sculptors Graphic artist	Leonardo da Vinci Michelangelo Vincent van Gogh Picasso Salvador Dali
Musical intelligence	Talent for making music, composing, and sense of musical principles	Musician Singers Composers	Wolfgang Amadeus Mozart George Gershwin Leonard Bernstein Prince

(continued)

TABLE 4.1 (Continued)

Intelligence	Characteristics	Professional groups	Outstanding representatives
Physical kinesthetic intelligence	Ability to precisely use individual body parts, or the entire body for movement sequences	Dancer Athletes Actors Surgeons Artisans Mechanics	Michael Jackson Michael Jordan Charlie Chaplin Christian Barnard
Naturopathic intelligence	Ability to recognize and classify the environment	Natural scientists Biologists Marketing experts Trend researchers	Charles Darwin Isaac Newton Albert Einstein
Intrapersonal intelligence	Ability to understand oneself, to develop a realistic picture of oneself – with one's desires, fears, and abilities – and to use this knowledge in everyday life	All those who are at the limits of their own performance Top athletes Lone warriors (military)	Thomas of Aquin Jesus Buddha Arnold Schwarzenegger Usain Bolt
Interpersonal intelligence	Ability to understand the intentions, desires, and motives of other people and to be able to cooperate with them successfully	All those who perform management tasks Managers Teachers Politicians	Mahatma Gandhi Mother Teresa Martin Luther King John F. Kennedy
Spiritual intelligence	Ability to recognize and understand things that are beyond the cognitive limits of our world	Priests Shamans Healers Wisdom teachers	Jesus Buddha Popes

EXAMPLE

Based on my professional experience as a German certified public accountant (Wirtschaftsprüfer) specializing in business valuations, I have found that in many employees, linguistic intelligence and mathematical-logical intelligence are not equally strong. Often, employees who are particularly strong in financial modeling are less strong in writing valuation reports. An employee with a particularly high mathematical-logical intelligence finds it easy to create complex valuation models. For them, even the most complex Excel models are easy to develop. The same employee, however, finds the textual presentation of the valuation results in an expert opinion much more difficult. Formulating texts does not come easily to this type of employee. Employees who can do both equally well are exceedingly rare indeed.

a sufficient one if we want our professional practices to continue to flourish in the future. Associative-creative intelligence plays a key role in successfully mastering the complexity of a changing environment. Until now, associative-creative intelligence has been rather frowned upon in an auditor's working environment that is highly structured on the basis of checklists. An employee of an auditing practice could not make a career if they were a creative lateral thinker. As a rule, well adapted employees who act in line with their firm are successful. In a daily work routine dominated by checklists and structured workflows, associative thinking is not a top priority. Most professionals are also not assumed to be creative people. They don't like to leave familiar thought patterns and have a challenging time with change. However, in an environment that is changing ever faster, resilience is an important quality. Often, resilient people are associative-creative people.

According to Christiani and Scheelen, associative-creative intelligence comprises three elements:

- The ability to associate freely and make new connections without reference to causality, order, or meaning.
- The ability to associate and connect and to produce novel compositions in diverse ways and by different means.
- The ability to block out concepts, labels, and conclusions in order to enter the world of direct perception.

Our educational system has not yet recognized that associative-creative intelligence is likely the most important intelligence for mastering the challenges of the future and of digitalization. This would be an important starting point for comprehensive educational reform in our school system. What is not demanded and promoted in schools must be replaced by companies. Think tanks and other institutions aim their focus precisely on empowering employees to be associative and creative.

TIP

As a first step, professionals must identify the employees who have a pronounced associative-creative intelligence. Presumably, this type of employee will rarely be found in a professional's practice, as this intelligence is not primarily necessary to overcome academic hurdles and pass professional exams. Experience has shown that the partners of a professional services provider do not sufficiently encourage young professionals or their full potential in associative-creative intelligence. In such cases, external advice is often the only option. This advice could come either from professional colleagues who have associative-creative intelligence, or from consultants outside the profession. It is important to pay attention to a possible lack of innate acceptance among new and established colleagues. After all, professionals are rather reluctant to take "advice" from others given that they are used to giving advice themselves.

In an age of digitalization, where information is becoming less of a bottleneck, the ability to innovatively link data into meaningful content is increasingly becoming a critical success factor. Data analytics, artificial intelligence, and machine learning are becoming key factors in future economic success. Added to this is the ability to think outside of existing rules. This is particularly difficult for professionals, as they are used to thinking and acting on the basis of (legal) rules.

The principle of leveraging strengths has major consequences for us and our employees. This applies to training, employee selection, job creation, staffing, performance appraisal, and potential analysis. The starting point is a comprehensive analysis of talents, or our various intelligences. There are now a number of different test procedures that make it possible to identify our own strengths and those of our employees. It makes sense to use test procedures that can identify the aforementioned forms of intelligence.

NOTE

In many professional service firms, there is still an outdated behavior in dealing with employees. Namely, the principle applies that in projects in which no criticism is expressed to an employee, the behavior of a supervisor is understood as praise. It appears that those who treat their employees exclusively with negative criticism are always looking for the deficit in people's actions. This is the opposite of focusing on strengths. Incidentally, this behavior shows as a deficit in managers. If they observe people against the background of their strengths, the manager will quickly discover that almost everyone has at least one, often several, strengths. The most important task of a manager in dealing with employees is therefore to place them where they show their strengths. The more that professionals can succeed in matching strengths and tasks in employees, the more optimized results can be achieved and will serve as a motivational accelerator to the individual.

Does the principle of strength utilization mean that professionals should ignore their own weaknesses, or those of their employees? The answer is clearly no! You must know both your own weaknesses and those of your employees in order to be sure that you, or your employees do not predominantly perform activities in which it would be disastrous if this weakness were to dominate their workplace. The goal must always be to ensure that people are deployed where they can contribute their strengths. Weaknesses should be managed in such a way that they do not become an impediment.

EXAMPLE

If, for example, a professional has a very pronounced logical-mathematical intelligence and is less gifted in languages, it could become difficult for them to conduct business with internationally active companies. In this case, foreign language skills must be developed in such a way that they do not become a critical success factor. The lack of talent in the area of linguistic intelligence remains, but it does not have to become a bottleneck of a particular activity.

Malik speaks decidedly against people changing their personalities in his new edition "Managing Performing Living". His reasoning is convincing: By their thirties, when many people are in leadership positions, their personality structures are solidified in such a way that changes very rarely take place anymore.

In psychology, the term personality is not defined uniformly. It is often defined as the sum of all behavioral characteristics of a person. Science distinguishes between largely unchangeable (traits) and changeable personality characteristics (also known as states). The traits of a person have a stable quality. Among these are genetic predispositions, largely unchangeable basic structures, such as a person's anxiety. States are environmentally determined and changeable traits that are influenced by socialization, culture, and situational conditions. These are transient states, such as being afraid.

Thomas Staller and Cornelia Kirschke write in "The ID 37 Personality Analysis: Importance and Effect of Life Motives for Efficient Self-Direction" that we remain true to ourselves even when we change. They claim that people only change within their personality. People who believe that they have changed fundamentally in their personality and claim that they are a completely different person today than they were in the past are usually mistaken. Christian E. Elger writes in his book "Neuroleadership" on the stability and changeability of personality that genetic traits influence a person's character by 30-60%. The rest is socially acquired and can therefore be changed again.

That is why the environment in which one stays in predominantly both professionally and privately is especially important. This applies to every phase of life. Due to the social environment in childhood and adolescence, many personality traits are already highly developed by the age of about 20, so that a change is only possible with a correspondingly great will of one's own. This does not mean that people beyond the age of 20 can no longer change their behavior. Behavioral changes relate to personality traits that can be changed. Personality traits are closely related to certain behavior patterns of a person. Behavior patterns, in turn, are strongly influenced by a person's motives, which we will deal with more in depth in Chapter 6, Action Orientation.

Behavioral changes will only take place when a person decides for themselves that they want to change something in their life. In essence, this is about one's own personality development. To use the words of Nikolaus B. Enkelmann again, "Nothing changes unless I change." Consequently, these behavioral changes will only occur if you yourself want them to. Certainly, this change can come from an external impulse. Events, or people can influence you. Anyone who once wanted to lose weight, or stop smoking knows that they will only succeed at all if the person really wants it. Extrinsic motivation alone will never lead to success. Only intrinsic motivation will.

Malik says that changing people is not the task of management: "The task of management is to take people as they are, to find out their strengths and, by designing their tasks accordingly, give them the opportunity to work where they can perform and achieve results with their strengths."

Accordingly, Malik does not see it primarily as the task of companies that they should further develop their employees in terms of their personalities, but rather that employees should be deployed in alignment with their strengths. I share this principle in essence. However, the growth principle is already inherent in nature. Think of trees which, if they are healthy, grow year after year. This growth affects both the branches and roots in the earth, which are not visible. Similarly, people should develop in personality year after year. A conditio sine qua non for this is, however, that the professional wants this personality growth equally for themselves. Incidentally, this book aims precisely at the aspect of personal development. In it, the soft skills that are valuable for professionals are presented in combination with their own individual management and the management of employees. If these were unchangeable personality traits, there would be little point in presenting these soft skills. They are all soft skills that are more, or less easy to learn or train for. In the end, success is also a question of character, or personality.

The master plan for a strength-centered life is to first know your own strengths in detail. You can either have these determined via various test procedures, or also discover them relatively easily via self-analysis. Analyze what comes easily to you. Often, these are the things that you are particularly good at and that belong to your strengths. However, it is often the case that what comes easily to you does not stand out to you, precisely because it comes easily to you.

The principle of results orientation and the use of strengths are closely related. If you want to achieve exceptionally satisfactory results, you have to make the best possible use of your strengths. In doing so, you must also accept weaknesses. Weaknesses cannot be eliminated on a regular basis, but they must be managed, or compensated for. Wanting to develop one's personality from year to year should be part of every person's lifelong learning process. The starting point is always an intrinsic motivation and never an extrinsic motivation.

CHAPTER FIVE

Think Positively

THE AUDITORS AMONG YOU might say that it is part of your professional ethics to maintain at least a critical basic attitude throughout your work as an auditor. This includes questioning information, paying particular attention to signs that could indicate a misrepresentation, and critically assessing audit evidence.

Before we deal with the principle of positive thinking and its application in practice, it makes sense to consider why people think positively or negatively. It makes obvious sense to ask whether positive or negative thinking is innate. Does thinking positively or negatively depend on hereditary factors? And if so, what possibilities does a person who has a genetic tendency to think negatively have to change their behavior? Can a negative-thinking person even become a positive-thinking person, or are they trapped in their genetic makeup?

Researchers at the University of California have been studying people's personalities comprehensively and found that a person's personality depends on both hereditary factors and environmental influences. Five psychological factors were identified for measuring individual differences in personality:

- *Extraversion Versus Introversion:* characteristics include talkativeness, assertiveness, and a high level of activity;
- *Neuroticism Versus Emotional Stability:* traits are negative thinking, more anxious, depressed;

- *Agreeableness Versus Antagonism, Hostility:* traits are cooperative, compassionate;
- *Conscientiousness Versus Unreliability:* traits are diligent, self-disciplined;
- *Openness to Experience Versus Closed-mindedness:* traits are intellectual inquisitiveness and creativity.

In their study, the researchers analyzed genetic variations among the five personality traits. According to the researchers, the traits are largely genetically distinct from psychiatric disorders. They found, among other things, that there was a high genetic correlation between extraversion and attention deficit hyperactivity disorder (ADHD) and openness and schizophrenia. Neuroticism was genetically linked to internalized psychopathologies, such as depression and anxiety disorders. Based on a further analysis, the researchers were also able to make statements regarding the genetic inheritance of the five personality factors. According to this the following percentages are genetically inherited.

- Extraversion by 18%
- Neuroticism by 11%
- Openness to experience by 10%
- Conscientiousness by 9%
- Agreeableness by 8%

Research illustrates that we are just beginning to understand the genetics of personality and its relationship to mental illness and that further studies must follow.

This means that negative thinking would theoretically only be 11% genetically inherited and largely dependent on environmental influences. As already shown in previous chapters, positive thinking is more socially influenced than negative thinking, which has its cause in hereditary factors.

Check if you grew up in a family, or social environment that had Positive Thinking in its mindset. If so, there is a relatively high probability that you are also more likely to be a positive thinking person. Conversely, this means that even if you grew up in a negative thinking environment, today you have the possibility to become a positive thinking person even if you have a hereditary tendency to think negatively. Therefore, everyone should examine for themselves whether they surrounded themselves with people who think positively, or rather negatively in their childhood, youth, and in their professional and private life. In an environment full of negative thinking people, it is significantly more difficult to think positively.

EXAMPLE

I can confirm this finding based on my own experiences in my youth. My father has been politically active since he was 20 years old. For many years he was active as a volunteer. Later, he also worked as a professional politician. He was elected to the state executive committee of his party in 1983 and has been its state treasurer ever since. Before that, his party had not been reelected to the state parliament and no longer had a stable base in the state. The party was devastated. It had to be built up again, and my father was more often in the state capital and rarely with his family. Whenever he returned home from meetings of the state party at that time, he would say as he entered our house, "Things are looking up!" This (auto)suggestion became a common saying in our family after a few weeks, and he then didn't have to say anything at all when he entered the house because one of the family, or all of us would say in chorus, "Things are looking up!" Today I understand this better today than I did as a teenager:

That was Positive Thinking at its purest, and unconsciously it must have had a substantial impact on me at the time, because I realized as a teenager that even when you're down, you're always going to get back up, and it was positive autosuggestion that, according to the law of faith, had the tendency to become reality.

Incidentally, the party was elected to the state parliament again in 1987. It entered the state government, and the suggestion became reality.

In this context, emotions have a central influence on our lives. The hedonistic principle of avoiding pain and seeking pleasure and joy often applies. The subconscious mind controls our behavior in many cases. If you have often heard in your childhood that you cannot do something, are not talented enough, or had to accept many defeats, you should not be surprised if negative beliefs burrowed themselves deep into your subconscious and produced the "wrong" result at important moments in life. A positive self-image as well as the "right" beliefs are therefore an essential prerequisite for Positive Thinking.

You can train yourself to think positively. This requires knowledge and regular training. To use the words of Robert H. Schuller (1926–2015), one of the world's most famous pastors: Become a Possibility Thinker. In his book "If It's Going to Be, It's Up to Me: The Eight Proven Principles of Possibility Thinking," he shows how you can become a possibility thinker step by step. If you follow his eight principles, you will become a Possibility Thinker and thus practice Positive Thinking:

- Possibilities must be weighed
- Priorities must be swayed
- Plans must be laid
- Commitments must be made
- The price must be paid
- The timing may be delayed
- The course must be stayed
- The trumps will be played

The meaning of this saying is paraphrased but it shows quite clearly a central tenet of Schuller's principle in his book:

$$Possibility + Responsibility = Success$$

The eight principles of Possibility Thinking are a guide to Positive Thinking. What prevents people from thinking positively? Often it is the already mentioned beliefs that are deeply anchored in the subconscious and were formed in childhood. We dealt with beliefs in Chapter 1 in the principle of self-responsibility. In the Positive Thinking Principle, it makes sense that we understand how to reprogram these beliefs. In Chapter 14, Mental Training we look at mental training. However, this first requires some basic knowledge from psychology, which we will discuss below. One important insight is that many beliefs unconsciously prevent us from thinking positively. The following picture shows the connection between the conscious mind, the subconscious mind, and the superconscious mind. (See Figure 5.1.)

With an iceberg, typically only one third is visible, whereas two thirds of the iceberg are under water. It is the same with our consciousness as well as our subconsciousness and the primal knowledge.

By consciousness we understand everything that fills our attention at the moment. This includes the presence and the perception of thoughts, sensory impressions, feelings, memories, ideas, planning, and evaluations.

In contrast, the subconscious is the area that is not directly accessible to consciousness. Only through dreams, trance, or hypnosis can contents of the subconscious rise to the consciousness and become visible. The subconscious stores all the experiences a person has had from the moment of conception. It

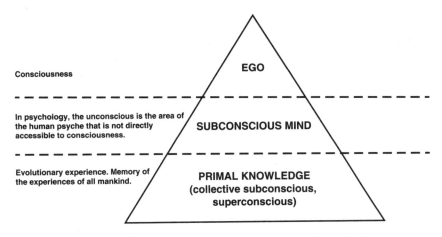

FIGURE 5.1 Consciousness – subconsciousness – primal knowledge

does not begin with birth. The subconscious is comparable to an unrecorded hard drive. From the moment of conception, all feelings and experiences are recorded in the subconscious. Even an unborn child senses in the womb whether it is loved, or not. It recognizes the mother's voice and can distinguish it from other voices after birth. Information that is consciously ignored also flows into the subconscious. Therefore, everything that we have unconsciously "taken in" can be retrieved there. Thus, all good and bad experiences, joys, and sorrows are stored in the subconscious of a person. The fact that the subconscious has a strong influence on our thoughts and actions is generally accepted and is expressed colloquially in phrases such as "I did that unconsciously." Accordingly, a person's subconscious includes all individual experiences of that person and the elements stored in their subconscious.

The subconscious is an executive organ. It does not evaluate. It does not care who gives it an order. It only carries out every command properly. Therefore, it is decisive for a person in their life, which spiritual and mental "food" they take and from whom this "food" comes. Since the subconscious mind takes in all positive and negative information equally, it is especially important for Positive Thinking that you take in as much positive information as possible on a daily basis.

Primal knowledge, also called collective subconscious, or superconscious, has emerged from the history of humankind and is stored because of its evolutionary importance. That is why it is also called evolutionary experience. The

TIP

Some people deliberately shut themselves off from all negative information by not listening to news programs on the radio or watching television. Nor do these people seek out newspapers, or (social) media that spread negative information. However, those who know the philosophy of yin and yang know that life is bipolar. The opposites, such as light and dark, healthy and sick, war and peace, success and failure, etc., are part of life. In this respect, a total shut-off of all negative information seems to me to be ignorance of the reality of life. The idea, however, of consciously controlling the dosage of negative information that you allow to pour in on you on a daily, or weekly basis is something I not only find worth considering but have been practicing for many years. Consciously decide what negative information you take in daily and when you take it in. You should never take in negative information before going to bed. If possible, always take positive thoughts with you to sleep. Can't think of anything positive to say on certain days? Then be grateful before you go to sleep. There is always something for which you can be grateful. Look for it.

collective subconscious does not develop individually but is inherited. Accordingly, it is all the experiences, all the knowledge of all humankind from all times. In animals we often call this instinct.

Humans often explain decisions made from the gut as intuition. These are often decisions that they cannot justify. Their mind does not give them a logical explanation.

EXAMPLE

Professionals, who as previously mentioned have a strong analytical mind and use their intellect in their daily work, often find it difficult to rely on their intuition. However, anyone who has already spent a few years in the profession will have realized in retrospect that they would have been better off relying on their intuition in connection with certain clients, or when hiring employees. But professionals in particular are often so convinced of their intellectual superiority that in the process, they have long since destroyed faith in their primal knowledge.

This is where it is important to be able to mentally program yourself to tap into your collective subconscious. When we tap into our collective

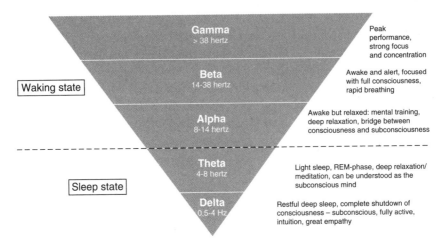

FIGURE 5.2 Brain waves and states of consciousness

subconscious, we unleash our creativity. Our intuition develops, and we often have excellent ideas. However, if we don't use the access to our primal knowledge, then no matter how hard we try, we won't have the one brilliant idea.

The crucial question thus is, how can we use this knowledge to practice the principle of Positive Thinking on a daily basis? If you look at Figure 5.2, you will notice that the lines between the areas are merely dashed. This shows that the boundaries between the various levels of consciousness are permeable. In a state of relaxation, we can cross these boundaries. The more relaxed we are, the easier we can work with all our levels of consciousness.

Very few of my professional colleagues complain about not having enough work, and because of the heavy workload, only a few professionals are often in a relaxed state. Often, they even bring their work with them on vacation, so there is a lack of much-needed relaxation here as well. With the help of an electroencephalogram (EEG), it is possible to measure the rhythm of brain waves. In this way, scientists and doctors can recognize the state a person is currently in. Basically, four different brain frequencies are distinguished, whereby the fifth brain wave is almost unexplored. The following figure shows the different brain waves.

In the delta and theta states, we are asleep. The body regenerates best in dreamless and deep sleep in the delta state. The delta state is measured up to 4 hertz. The body is most relaxed here. Delta brain waves correspond to the unconscious and are present during deep sleep when all other brain waves are undetectable. Delta accompanies the restful part of deep sleep. People who have high amplitude Delta waves are often intuitive and have learned through trial and error to trust their sixth sense. Delta is often associated with great empathy. At 4 to 8 hertz, we are in a light sleep phase and not as deeply relaxed. We are asleep or meditating. This state is called theta. Theta brainwaves are active in dream sleep and in deep meditation and relaxation. They can be understood as the subconscious, the part of your consciousness that is a level between the conscious and the subconscious. Theta contains a lot of memories, perceptions, and feelings. Even though these experiences are not accessible to the conscious mind, they can still influence, or even determine your attitudes, expectations, and behavior. Our intuition and creativity can flourish very well in this state of brain activity.

At a wavelength of 8 to 14 hertz, we are in the alpha state. In this phase, we are mentally awake but completely relaxed. Alpha waves occur during daydreaming, fantasizing, and visualizing. The alpha state is the bridge between the conscious and subconscious mind. When alpha is absent, the connection to the subconscious is broken. Our thoughts are calm, we breathe deeply and evenly, and feel at ease. In this state we can solve problems well. We see from different perspectives and can develop holistic and comprehensive solutions. In the alpha state, our intuition is active, and we can be associative and creative. In this state, positive thinking is much easier. The gateway to the subconscious and the collective unconscious is open.

However, when our brain frequency exceeds values of 14, we are in the so-called beta state. The beta state is synonymous with hectic rush, stress, aggression, and even fighting. Your heart is pounding, your temples are pulsating, your breath is rapid, and you can't think clearly. Your thinking seems out of control and your beta brain waves are in turmoil. We are awake and alert, fully conscious; often tense inside and out, internally tense and bitter. A one-sided view is a particular characteristic of beta. If you are in a Beta state, you will not find the most optimal solutions. Positive thinking will be difficult here. Beta state is often accompanied by health complaints, such as muscle tension, headaches, migraines, and stomach cramps.

The gamma state is still largely unexplored. Brain waves in the gamma state are measured from 38 to 100 hertz. They are associated with peak performance, strong focus and concentration, high information flow, and integration of new knowledge, as well as mystical and transcendental experiences. Peak mental performance is achieved.

In the seventies, scientists were convinced that only the alpha state held the key to a higher state of consciousness. In the nineties, theta and delta range came more into focus. Some claimed that theta and delta were much more important than beta and alpha. Anna Wise says in her book "Awakened Mind

Training," that no one brainwave type is better than another, but all work together in a variety of ways to create the full range of our mental, emotional, and spiritual states of consciousness.

It is a widely held view that the left hemisphere is the logical, or thinking part of the brain, while the right hemisphere is responsible for creativity and artistic activities, and that we mostly engage only one of the two sides.

In fact, our brain is an integrated whole in which both sides are constantly active. Mental training and brainwave training can improve the use of the brain.

The more often a person is in a beta state, the more nervous and consequently tense they are. This shows in their behavior and actions and reactions. Their voice is usually high-pitched, and breathing is fast. The brain is typically no longer supplied with enough oxygen and therefore cannot work optimally. The gate to the subconscious is closed and solutions can only be worked out with great difficulty. Positive thinking is almost impossible in this state.

Positive thinking means constructive thinking. A positive thinking person thinks about the solutions and not exclusively about the problem. In every project there are smaller and bigger problems. Often in teams only the problems are discussed and not enough energy is put into problem solving. Valuable time is lost here. Those who have learned to think only in solution categories consistently will manage projects more successfully – regardless of whether they work on them alone, or in a team.

TIP

There is a simple method to learn solution-oriented and positive thinking. It is called mindstorming. Formulate your problem or task as a question. Then write down at least 20 answers to this question. Do not leave your workstation until you have found 20 answers. If you use this method consistently, in a brief time, you will learn solution-oriented thinking. The best time of day to use this method is in the morning shortly after getting up because this way, the subconscious mind has the opportunity to search for solutions overnight. The question should therefore ideally be formulated the night before.

As professionals, we are predominantly using our left-brain hemisphere for thinking analytically. When practicing the method of mindstorming for the first time, we will notice that we might have trouble falling asleep that first evening because we want to find solutions immediately.

However, this clearly indicates that you should then first work on how you can relax at the "push of a button." You will learn how to do this during mental training. If you can fall asleep well despite this task, you will find that some solutions will come very quickly the next morning. Even though the number 20 seems unattainable at the beginning, I would like to encourage you, nevertheless, not to leave your workplace before you have 20 solutions. You will most likely only succeed if you are willing to write down the most abstruse solutions. This requires courage. Many of the solutions you will discard and never put into practice. However, this will teach you to use your right brain hemisphere. Your creativity will increase from exercise to exercise. Your ability to associate becomes better and better. If you practice the method of mindstorming regularly, you will not only become a person who is always looking for solutions to problems, but you will become a possibility thinker and a positive thinker with a fascination for others.

Most people only see the problem and think in terms of problems. Especially if they are professionals. This is because they are paid to identify problems. But it is more important to focus on solving our clients' problems. A professional who has understood this and practices the method of mindstorming sees the world with different eyes. Problems are a gift for them. Because they know that people's primary task is to solve problems and, if possible, not to cause them. Companies pay professionals to solve problems. Clients pay specialists to solve problems. Therefore, professionals should always be equipped with the mindset of a problem solver. In practice, however, it is often the other way around: Professionals point out problems to their clients. They point out risks and problems related to internal control systems, embezzlement, and cyber security. They point out tax risks and educate about business risks. Often, they overemphasize the problems and risks instead of focusing on problem solving.

There, are, by the way, quite a few people who prefer to use the term challenges instead of problems. For them, the term "problem" seems to be too negative. Every problem is also a challenge. This appears to be obvious. The challenge in solving a problem is to find a solution that is appropriate and suitable for the purpose. Therefore, not using the word "problem" and talking about challenges does not change the fact that it's the solutions we are focusing on. I prefer a clear language to embellishment. The same applies when an optimist says that the glass is half full, whereas the pessimist claims that the glass is half empty. As an auditor, I always say that for me the glass is 50% full.

In my understanding, positive thinking also includes a high degree of realism. Jack Welch, the former CEO of General Electric, demanded a sense

NOTE

Many years ago, I made it a habit in my companies that employees always had to develop solution proposals themselves if they wanted to discuss problems with me. This method has proven to always lead to effective meetings. The problem is first described in detail and the first alternative solutions come from the employee themselves. Anyone who organizes their professional practice differently will often find the pattern that has been tried and tested from childhood when problems arise in their company as well. Wasn't it often the case in childhood that when a child had a problem, they came to their parents, who were then supposed to solve the problem for the child? It could be homework, or other things. If parents raised children in such a way that the children always had their problems solved by the parents, people in companies should not be surprised if this behavior pattern remains in later professional life. The parents are then replaced by the supervisor. So positive thinking always starts with you first. And positive thinking means solution-oriented thinking.

of reality from his employees. He wanted to be the market leader, or at least the runner-up in a market. This meant, first of all, accepting the existing reality as it is. Realism is an important skill for a professional. It is even more important when you work as a manager. In companies and often in private relationships, things are glossed over. However, a sense of reality means seeing things as they actually are. Not worse, but not better either. Now you will probably object and say that everything is subjective and that the perspective of each observer must also be considered here.

EXAMPLE

If internal control systems are not effective, an auditor should expect accounting irregularities. Their task is to point out these irregularities and insist that they be eliminated. A sense of reality and positive thinking are therefore not contradictory. The same applies to the financial situation in a corporate crisis. Often, company managers in crisis situations tend to view things much more positively than they are. When auditors eventually point out that insolvency is imminent, or that the company is already insolvent, managers often refuse to see things realistically and instead of accepting it, they deny reality.

It is, however, necessary to assess objectively whether there is a realistic chance of achieving a goal. For example, someone who although he's already 30 is starting to think about becoming a professional football player, golfer, or tennis player probably has little sense of reality. Even though there may be talent, the right time to start a sports career as a professional is long past.

In my lectures, in connection with the reference to a sense of reality, I like to show a photo of a small boy facing an adult sumo wrestler in the ring. The boy weighs an estimated 40 kg. The adult sumo wrestler weighs about 200 kg. It does not correspond to any sense of reality to believe that the little boy has even the slightest chance against the adult sumo wrestler in a fight with normal means. Perhaps he could eliminate the sumo wrestler with the help of a slingshot trick as in the legend of David and Goliath.

Another method that is closely related to practicing Positive Thinking is **"Zero Based Thinking."** I learned of this method through Brian Tracy. The starting point of this method is that you make it a habit to revisit important decisions that you have made in the past. Ask yourself the following question: **Is there anything that you would from your current point of view, not do again?** Try to answer this question with your current knowledge and put yourself back to the time of the decision. You can apply this method to all areas of life. If you have to answer this question in the negative, then the next question should be: How do you get out of the situation as quickly as possible? The decision you made at that time cannot be reversed. However, in many cases, you can develop positive approaches to change in the current situation by using the Zero-Based Thinking method.

EXAMPLE

For example, if you hired an employee that you would not hire again based on your current level of knowledge, then you should part ways with them. If you have accepted a mandate that you would not accept again based on your current level of knowledge, then you should terminate them.

The Zero-Based Thinking method does not only help you with the method of Positive Thinking, but it also makes a significant contribution to change in certain situations.

Jean-Baptiste Massillon, a French preacher and theologian, said, "Gratitude is the memory of the heart." It's surprising how often people are not grateful for what they have, but rather grumble about many other comparatively unimportant things in life. Yet it is often the people who experienced true blows of fate, such as the death of their life partner, or their own children, who face their fellow human beings with confidence and positive thoughts. There is another method of learning gratitude and thus making a big step towards positive thinking. Ask yourself the following questions as a ritual in the morning and in the evening:

To set the mood in the morning for a positive day:

■ What am I grateful for?
■ What am I especially looking forward to today?
■ What is the ONE Thing I want to do today?
■ What makes me happy in my life right now?
■ Which people are important to me?
■ What am I proud of in my life right now?

To attune in the evening before sleep:

■ What am I grateful for?
■ What have I learned today?
■ What successes did I have today?
■ How can I use the day as an investment into my future?
■ What was the ONE Thing I worked on?

The principle of Positive Thinking can be anchored in the subconscious mind through the right techniques. For this purpose, as mentioned under the tools in mental training, I will discuss in later chapters how this works.

CHAPTER SIX

Action Orientation

ONLY THOSE WHO ACT will be successful. Successful people are action oriented. For this reason, successful entrepreneurs do the right things at the right time. Certainly, this principle is easier said than done, especially in larger companies. There are clear hierarchies and anyone who oversteps them should be prepared to face negative consequences. Action is not really desired equally everywhere.

The principle of action orientation is highly significant in start-up companies. Their current motto is often like the Nike slogan: "just do it." And more and more established companies are letting entire departments "just do it" to find answers to questions related to digitalization and disruption.

Successful people in particular tend to be distinctly action oriented. They align their actions with their goals. Those who want to be commissioned should be in frequent contact with their clients. Those who want to climb the career ladder in a company are well advised to act in the interests of their superiors and keep in regular contact with them. In order to pass a professional exam, you have to work to prepare for it. That means making sacrifices.

But what is it that drives a person to act? In this context, the avoidance of pain and the creation of joy are closely related. According to this, people aim at bringing about those events that lead to positive emotional states by either striving for something (appetence) or avoiding it (aversion).

Whoever deals with the principle of action orientation cannot avoid dealing with the concepts of motives and the motivation of a person. The terms "motive" and "motivation" both derive from the Latin verb "movere" (to move, to drive). Motives and motivation are closely related. However, they must be distinguished from one another.

Motives are directional, situation-independent stimuli for action. They are deeply rooted in the personality. In part, they are genetically determined and vary in intensity from person to person. In this context, motives are motivations for behavior in the sense of a guiding, activating, direction-giving force. When we say that we give a motive a high priority, it is both a qualitative and a quantitative statement. The qualitative statement is that the motive names the reason we act. We give priority to one motive over another. We ask ourselves what is really important to us and for what do we strive? The expression of a motive, on the other hand, also makes a quantitative statement. How often, or intensively should the motive be satisfied? For one person, for example, going to the nearby butcher, or baker is physical activity enough for the day, whereas another person strives for physical exhaustion, and there is nothing better than hard training sessions. Thus, there is a very low and a very high level of motive expression within a motive scale. A person whose motive expression is in the middle range can show both tendencies in their behavior. In this case, it is much more difficult to make a statement about their motive characteristics. Motives must always be considered in a certain context. How a person lives with their motives and what motivates them also depends on their environment.

The process of motive stimulation is called motivating. It is triggered by incentives. The result of motivating is a person's motivation. It triggers an action in a person towards a positively expected goal. Psychology distinguishes between intrinsic and extrinsic motivation. In intrinsic motivation, an activity is performed for its own sake. A person acts on their own initiative. No external incentive is needed to perform an activity joyfully and persistently. In contrast, extrinsic motivation involves an external stimulus, such as an incentive. The incentive for doing something lies primarily in the consequences of the action. Extrinsically motivated behavior depends on external impulses and expires when these impulses cease to exist. It is scientifically proven that extrinsic incentives do not only lose their effect quickly, but they also need to be continually increased in order to retain their effect.

Steven Reiss (1947–2016) is considered one of the best-known motivational researchers in the world. He identified 16 central life motives on the basis of scientific research by questioning more than 25,000 people up to the year

1998. According to the study, 16 basic needs of people can be assigned to certain life motives. The Reiss Motivation Profile (RMP) clearly shows which values and personality traits a person has. The terms values and motives are not congruent. However, they are closely related and mutually dependent. Values are not innate. They are shaped by the environment. Motives, on the other hand, provide important clues to a person's conception of values. Staller and Kirschke, following Frank H. Sauer (https://www.wertesysteme.de/nuetzlicheinfos/frank-h-sauer-uber-werte/) define values as a person's evaluative thoughts and attitudes about important things in life with regard to oneself, friends, or society and how people treat each other (for example, trust, honesty, politeness). Values are a part of one's identity and personality. This is because they also provide information about what is important or unimportant to a person. Unlike motives, values are not innate, but are formed during a person's life as a result of the social environment and the imprinting associated with it. Families, schools, professional life, and the respective immediate environment of a person have an influence on their values. A person's fundamental values will not change significantly after the age of 20.

Knowledge of life motives as well as values and the associated personality traits of a person provide information about factors that make a person decide when and when not to act. This is why life motives are important for one's own management as well as for the management of employees and in dealing with people close to us. Especially if we want to apply the principle of action orientation. If a particular life motive is strongly pronounced, or a certain value has a particularly high priority with a person, they will show a high motivation and willingness to act.

However, people often do not live in harmony with their own values and motives. Eventually, this might lead to burn-out syndrome and illnesses. Only those who act in harmony with their values, or motives will experience happiness in their professional and private lives in perspective. In my opinion, the dropouts in their 40s or 50s clearly show that their profession was not a calling, but a means to an end. Someone who loves their profession does not drop out. In the case of professionals, I am not aware of any colleagues in my specialty who have left their chosen profession. Nevertheless, there will always be some. I also know colleagues who work for large companies and have contracts that stipulate that they have to stop at a certain age. But many colleagues are often reluctant to quit.

The 16 life motives according to Steven Reiss function as a driving force in the principle of action orientation. Everyone has all of the 16 basic needs. However, Reiss gives them different priorities and claims that he can predict a person's behavior in certain life situations by knowing what priority a person gives to the 16 basic needs and how they combine them. Staller and Kirschke see it the same way and, based on Steven Reiss' life motives, have developed their ID37 Personality Analysis, which – also based on similar 16 life motives – analyzes a person's personality.

Table 6.1 shows the 16 life motives according to Steven Reiss in alphabetical order and describes a low and high level of expression in each case. On one hand, the intensity of the expression indicates how a person is perceived by other people and which characteristics are important to them in connection with their expression. The boundaries can be fluid. There are also more or less strong dimensions within a proficiency. The characteristics are merely exemplary and serve as orientation.

Motives are motivations of individual behavior. They explain why a person acts and are therefore important for the principle of action orientation. Knowledge of one's own central motives in life and their manifestations are an important prerequisite for understanding one's own personality. A person who does not know themselves well will not develop good knowledge of human nature in others either. The characteristics shown in the columns of weak and strong expression serve only as a guide. Because within a weak as well as within a strong expression there are different strong bandwidths of the respective expression. The high number of characteristics shown for the different expressions helps to assess oneself more thoroughly, but also to identify more quickly which life motives other people have.

People act to satisfy their life motives. The different life motives of a person show which priorities someone has in their life and to what extent they desire to satisfy them. Intrinsic motivation arises when someone pursues their personal goals, and they are in harmony with their life motives. The complex interaction of the 16 life motives describes the uniqueness of each person.

There are a number of different test procedures for determining one's own life motives as well as one's own Reiss Profile. These procedures are also available online, although I do not want to make a recommendation for a particular test at this point. Anyone who has passed the age of thirty should be able to recognize for themselves what their dominant life motives are. In particular, the classification of life motives – what is personally important and what is less important – should be done regularly. Someone who, after reading Table 6.1, cannot make their own judgment about their life motives, should indeed then take one of the many tests. This is especially true for young readers.

TABLE 6.1 The 16 life motives according to Steven Reiss

Weak expression	Life motive	Strong expression
• self-confident and positive self-image • optimistic • deals constructively with criticism • is not dependent on the approval of others	ACCEPTANCE	• lack of self-confidence • insecurity • feelings of inferiority • social acceptance • does not want to be criticized
• introverted • shows no interest in people, often loner • lives withdrawn, often lonely • distant, serious, and withdrawn • often has few friends	SOCIAL CONTACT	• extroverted • sociable • affable • charming • amiable • extrovert • informal • lively • often has many friends
• disloyal • immoral • calculating • opportunistic • word-breaking	HONOR	• loyal • trustworthy • reliable • honest • principled • steadfast • truthful
• little interest in sex • abstinent • chaste • platonic	ROMANCE	• active sex life • sex and passion are given a high value • sensual/erotic • with extremely strong expression sex-obsessed
• little appetite • rarely thinks about food • moderate eater • possibly thin	EATING	• food gives great pleasure • likes different food • perhaps overweight • insatiable • voracious
• duties associated with children are burdensome • no desire to have children • does not spend much time on raising children • parents often absent • possibly childless	FAMILY	• family-oriented • wants to have children and spend an important part of time raising them • family is essential for happiness • family life and parental role is important

(continued)

TABLE 6.1 (*Continued*)

Weak expression	Life motive	Strong expression

• injustice is part of life
• uncompromising
• pragmatic
• realistic
• tends to look the other way
	IDEALISM	• fairness and social justice
		  are important
		• volunteerism and humanitarian
		  thoughts are important
		• altruistic
		• compassionate
		• do-gooder
		• possibly martyr

• inactive person
• flabby and listless
• prefers sedentary lifestyle
• lethargic
• fitness and muscular strength
  are unimportant
• not physical
	PHYSICAL ACTIVITY	• active person
		• sport is an important
		  part of life
		• fitness, vitality, strength, and
		  stamina have a high value
		• physical

• no will to assert themselves
• lets things go without trying
  to influence them
• has no demanding perfor-
  mance goals
• intrinsic reluctance to control
  or influence others
• not assertive
• not directive
• without ambition
	POWER	• leadership roles
		• seeks challenges
		• wants to achieve goals
		• advisor
		• ambitious
		• determined
		• focused
		• strong-willed
		• controlling

• likes to keep mental activity
  to a minimum
• rarely reads books
• does not enjoy intellectual
  conversations
• prefers to speak through
  actions rather than words
• thoughtless
• action-oriented
• not intellectual
• practically inclined
	CURIOSITY	• intellectual
		• inquisitive
		• thoughtful
		• enjoys intellectual pursuits
		  such as thinking, reading,
		  writing, and talking ach other
		• theoretical knowledge,
		  ideas, and truth are of great
		  importance
		• needs constant mental
		  stimulation
		• often has a wide variety
		  of interests

TABLE 6.1 (*Continued*)

Weak expression	Life motive	Strong expression
• flexibility is important • does not like structures • does not like to stick to rules and schedules • focuses on the "big picture" and not on details • fickle • disorganized • tardy • untidy • spontaneous • hates plans	ORDER	• organization and punctuality are important • perfectionist • attention to details, rules, and schedules • likes rituals • not spontaneous • meticulous • systematic • orderly • well prepared • thorough
• avoids confrontation, fights, and violence • cooperative • polite • kind • non-aggressive • peace oriented	VENGEANCE	• competitive • pugnacious • belligerent • aggressive • vile
• risk-taking • fearless • unafraid • calm • relaxed • adventurous	TRANQUILITY	• personal safety is important • many fears, worries • cautious • timid • cowardly
• spendthrift • extravagant • dissolute • takes less care of things in his possession	SAVING	• collector • has the need to accumulate things • does not like to throw things away • thrifty • stingy
• is not easily impressed by wealth and fame • does not care much what others think about them • identifies with the middle and lower class • down-to-earth • egalitarian attitude • not formal • informal	STATUS	• wealth and material things are important • belonging to a social class and social associations are important • social prestige and titles are important • respectful • proud

(*continued*)

TABLE 6.1 (*Continued*)

Weak expression	Life motive	Strong expression
• relies on others to satisfy their needs • appreciates psychological support, especially when making decisions • likes to rely on his intuition • humble • interdependent • shows a preference for overly emotional experiences	**INDEPENDENCE**	• personal freedom is important • independence has a high value • does not like to be subordinated • logic, science, and rationality are important, intuition less so • autonomous • discomfort with overly emotional experiences

NOTE

Many years ago, when I dealt with the life motives according to Steven Reiss, I put them all in order from 1 to 16. This approach is not absolutely necessary. I had deliberately decided to put them in order for myself. Another division would have been to classify them into three different groups. For example, you could classify the life motives as strong, average, and weak in terms of their importance to your life. However, I believe it is important that you clearly know the life motives that are central or dominant in your life.

It is worthwhile to deal with one's own personality. In addition, all professionals who manage employees should be able to get a picture of another person's personality. Following Staller and Kirschke, I summarize the main reasons why it is beneficial to deal with one's own personality:

- Self-awareness and self-control
- Learning to understand motivation and behavior
- Learning to classify and regulate emotions
- Understanding others
- Recognizing, avoiding, and solving conflict situations
- Shaping relationships
- Reflective self-perception and perception of others
- Motivating oneself and not demotivating others

The principle of action orientation is related to the principle of result orientation. Only those who act will achieve results. If we act wrongly, we will achieve the wrong results. On the other hand, if we don't act at all, we could miss many opportunities. The 16 life motives show why people act, or do not act.

In the case of the life motive "curiosity," the column shows the characteristic "action-oriented" if it is weak. Accordingly, people for whom the life motive curiosity does not play a key role would be more action-oriented than for those of us with a strong expression of the life motive curiosity. In my opinion, this is often true. People with a strong expression of the life motive curiosity are indeed mostly intellectual, inquisitive, and thoughtful. However, these are precisely the qualities that keep people from taking action. Those who constantly weigh arguments against each other and focus on the problems instead of the solutions should not be surprised if they end up not acting at all.

EXAMPLE

In 2005, I founded the European Association of Certified Valuators and Analysts (EACVA). The aim was to provide people who professionally perform business valuations with the Certified Valuation Analyst (CVA), an internationally recognized independent designation. At the time of the foundation, it was not foreseeable whether there would be a market for this in Europe. However, as with so many start-ups, my hope was that those professionally involved in business valuations might also have an interest in acquiring qualification credentials for business valuators. In the meantime, more than 1,200 people have attended our CVA-trainings, and with around 900 members, EACVA has become firmly established, and is Europe's biggest association of valuation professionals. This is an example of the application of the principle of action orientation. Because if I hadn't "just done it," there still might not be an independent qualification certificate for company assessors today.

Unfortunately, many ideas fizzle out when people fail to act. The principle of action orientation is important if you want to achieve goals. An entrepreneur takes action, as the very name implies. Every action also implies failure. In my practice, I notice repeatedly that analytically driven professions often find arguments that prevent action. In a corporate culture that consists of doubters, it should not be surprising if no action is taken. It is much more important that the risks associated with failure are calculable and manageable. By contrast, anyone who does the right things at the right time will much more likely succeed and move toward their goals.

Someone who is in motion tends to stay in motion. Most people are familiar with the feeling when everything is going really well. Mihaly Csikszentmihalyi calls this phenomenon the "flow state." In the final phases of large projects, all forces are mobilized. Everyone acts toward the goal in good project management. People who do something every day that moves them toward their goals are ahead of others and are usually more satisfied with themselves than those who do not act in line with their goals, or who don't act at all.

PART TWO

Tasks

T HE PRINCIPLES PRESENTED EARLIER should be adhered to when performing your tasks and using the tools. They provide the framework for the tasks as outlined in the chapters that follow. It has already been mentioned that the following tasks are not the professional's activities related to the provision of various services. Rather, they are key tasks related to the management of a professional services provider's practice as well as self-management. Key tasks are critical success factors that are essential and decisive for the professional's success. Those who perform these tasks poorly will not be successful in conducting business. Even if a professional is one of the most qualified consultants jobwise – if they do not perform the following key tasks exceptionally or at least well, they will not achieve great success and, in the worst case, will fail.

The following key tasks apply equally to professionals working in a solo practice without other employees and to those who work in a partnership with others. The latter are familiar with the important management principles of delegation. The ability to delegate properly is not a skill all professionals have in common automatically. In particular, proven experts often take the position that they themselves are their best employee. This group of people finds it difficult to delegate both professional and other activities to employees or business partners because, in their view, they can do everything best themselves. If you assign management tasks to such professionals in a partnership, they will not only be overburdened, but will also perform these tasks poorly. Effective management, therefore, includes knowing your own strengths as well as those of your associates, partners, colleagues, and employees.

Professionals who work in management need competencies in the tasks listed below. For the most part, these can be trained for and learned. Malik sees management as a profession itself and clearly demarcates the management of factual tasks. For example, he would classify marketing as a factual task of a manager and not as a management task. In the case of professionals, I do not think a classification into factual and management tasks is appropriate and instead recommend a classification into key tasks. If professionals want to be successful and effective, this is more purposeful than a division between factual and management tasks.

In Malik's understanding, management can be learned and, in his view, it must be learned. Successful professionals have certain things in common. On the one hand, they base their actions on the previously outlined principles. On the other hand, they perform certain key tasks with special care. In doing so, they use certain tools, which will be presented in Part Three.

CHAPTER SEVEN

Marketing

THE MOST IMPORTANT TASK of a successful professional is marketing. This is even more true if they work in a solo practice because in this case, they are not only responsible for providing the services, but also for acquiring new potential clients as well as retaining existing clients. In a partnership or in larger entities, there is usually a division of labor, which means that there are only a few professionals – sometimes only one – who are able to acquire and retain new clients. The employees of such companies are aware of the significant importance of these individuals for the success of the company. Any professional, no matter how qualified, can only validate their qualifications if clients express their trust in the business and demand the services offered.

The high importance of marketing and sales for the success of a company might be a bothersome necessity for many professionals. Those who enjoyed an academic education prior to their professional examinations may still remember fellow students who focused on marketing during their studies instead of issues related to accounting, auditing, and tax law. This group of people differed significantly from the group of prospective professionals. At times, there was definitely a negative attitude towards students who had chosen marketing instead of accounting, auditing, and taxation as their focus. I experienced this firsthand. My majors were marketing, human resources, and psychology. This probably makes me an outlier among auditors. However, the main advantage

I have over my accounting colleagues is that I studied marketing and learned how to sell from scratch in financial consulting. This made me aware of how important marketing is for the success of a company.

It is increasingly known that marketing is an integral part of larger accounting and international law firms. This is why international accounting firms in particular have in-house business development departments. Business development can be understood to mean the expansion of existing client relationships, including the acquisition of new clients. The aim is to professionalize marketing, and as a rule, professionals do not head these departments. In the specific concentration of accounting and financial consulting, the business development department employees are also non-professionals. Outside of their professional activities, marketing is the most important task of a professional, which is thus often delegated to employees without the required advanced education and special qualifications of the professional.

EXAMPLE

For almost three decades, I have been a member of the association DIE FAMILIENUNTERNEHMER and – up to the age of 40 – of DIE JUNGEN UNTERNEHMER. The association represents the interests of family businesses vis-à-vis politicians and the public. I have been the chairman of the Rhine-Neckar metropolitan region since 2018 and have participated in many events in the region over the years. I can still remember very well a champagne reception for an event many years ago when I was making small talk with two renowned lawyers from the region, and a smartly dressed woman of about 30 years of age joined us. After a few minutes of small talk, one of the lawyers, who at 60 years of age could have been the young woman's father, asked her what she did for a living. The woman replied that she worked in business development for an international accounting firm. As a certified public accountant, my ears pricked up immediately, since my colleagues usually work either in auditing or tax consulting or in consulting (business management consulting or IT consulting, etc.). When I asked, it quickly became clear that the young woman went to such events, among other things, in order to win new potential clients or network partners for her auditing firm. She was therefore neither a professional employee nor did she have the professional qualifications of an auditor or tax consultant. The young woman remained in my memory and that of the members present because of her positive external appearance. However, I could not see any real chance of winning a potential new client for her auditing company or a network partner that evening.

It seems to be normal for auditors to often only accept professional colleagues who also have the auditor's qualifications. However, if an auditor only accepts another auditor in terms of professional authority and competence, why should potential clients have confidence in marketing experts who have no professional qualifications? To make matters worse, in my example above, the young lady was demonstrably a marketing expert who, due to her youthful age, could not have had much professional experience after her studies. In any case, she had no experience in the project management of the services of an auditing company. The international auditing company (Big Four company) could indisputably solve any problem of a member of DIE FAMILIENUNTERNEHMER in all service areas of an auditing company. The young lady was also aware of her firm's prominent level of problem-solving expertise and its wide range of services. Only she could not credibly sell a service. She was lacking the professional competence to do so. I still remember that evening, even though it took place many years ago. The acquisition of potential new clients is not transferable to business development staff! Certainly, business development staff can assist partners with marketing. The following information provides various starting points for this. The actual acquisition or networking activity cannot be delegated.

In the Anglo-American world there are a multitude of books about the marketing of lawyers, accountants, and valuators. The literature in German-speaking countries is comparatively small. The bibliography contains valuable sources in connection with the marketing of professionals or professional services providers, as the companies of accountants and lawyers are called in the US.

Up to now, with a few exceptions, the literature on the marketing is predominantly by authors who are not professionals themselves. After more than 30 years of professional experience and the establishment of several auditing and tax consulting companies, I have been able to gain substantial experience in connection with the marketing of our profession. In this context, I consider it highly expedient in marketing to make a distinction on several levels. Figure 7.1 shows the different perspectives.

The figure distinguishes between marketing at the level of the company and at the level of the professional on the one hand, and in terms of strategy and activities on the other. In the case of a solo practice, both coincide. I consider this distinction essential when drawing up marketing plans.

The marketing plan should include a marketing strategy and marketing activities. In a solo practice, there will often be only one marketing plan. Depending on the size of the individual practice's business, an according

> **NOTE**
>
> The preparation of a marketing plan concerns every professional who wants to become or remain a partner or shareholder of a service provider in their field. For a solo practitioner anyway. Accountants and tax advisors who believe that they have nothing to do with marketing are unsuitable as partners or shareholders and should in no case become entrepreneurial. This statement will have a polarizing effect on one or the other professional colleague and generate fierce opposition. However, please note the important addition that I am referring here to partners or associates of professional services providers. In many companies, especially larger ones, professionals – with the status of partner or associate – often act like salaried managers. In my understanding, however, a partner or shareholder should act like an entrepreneur, even though they often cannot do so within their company due to the established rules. A professional, however, can always think and act like an entrepreneur on the level of their own person. However, anyone who also does not want to create marketing plans at the level of their own person is not an entrepreneur and should not have the status of a partner or shareholder within a company. By the way, this does not mean that a professional should counteract the marketing strategy and marketing activities at the level of the company with his own marketing plan. It is obvious and needs no further explanation that this is not highly effective and cannot be in the best interest of the company. My point is that marketing concerns every partner and shareholder in the company and is not the exclusive domain of a marketing department or business development department. Marketing at the level of the professional concerns every partner and shareholder and cannot be delegated. Marketing at the level of the firm can, of course, be delegated to individuals or, in the case of larger firms, be conducted by separate marketing departments or business development departments. However, marketing plans from the marketing departments of larger companies will only have a chance of success if a majority of the partners and shareholders consider them promising and support them. Ideally, all partners and shareholders should agree. The more that partners and shareholders have doubts about the success of the marketing plan, the more likely it is to fail.

distinction is also quite useful. This is especially the case if there are multiple professionals employed in the solo practice.

For larger firms, the marketing plan includes both the firm level and the partner and associate level. The principle of focus means concentrating on a few things. This, of course, also applies to marketing. For this reason, only the

Marketing Levels

Business Level	STRATEGY ACTIVITIES	Professional Level
Auditing / tax consulting company		Auditor Tax consultant

FIGURE 7.1   Marketing at the level of the company and at the level of the professional

central aspects of the marketing of a professional or professional services provider are presented below. Since entrepreneurial success depends on focusing on the few essentials, marketing is about asking the right questions and providing the right answers.

 ## MARKETING STRATEGY

A successful marketing strategy is based on the right positioning. Figure 7.2 shows the areas in which strategic decisions need to be made.

The brand strategy, the service strategy, and the price strategy are at the heart of the marketing strategy. This applies both at the level of the professional and at the level of the company. The cycle is intended to express that the respective strategies influence each other mutually. The marketing strategy will only be successful if the brand, service, and price strategies are aligned. A strategic decision in one area influences the other two and vice versa.

Most books for professionals desperately try to apply the marketing mix familiar from their studies to our industry. Then the product, pricing, promotion, and sales place are adapted by authors who are not specialists in the

FIGURE 7.2 Marketing strategy

---

field. The following information obviously contains elements that could also be assigned within the marketing mix. However, based on my practical experience, I consider the division into marketing strategy and marketing activities to be much more expedient.

BRAND STRATEGY

If you cannot sell yourself and your company convincingly, you will not be successful in the long run. It is important to consider the sequence: First, the professional sells himself and only in the second step they sell their company. Those who believe that they can hide behind the brand of a large international auditing, law, or consulting firm show their lack of self-confidence as a manager. This will not really convince the clients, as the label of these "big" companies is interchangeable. The people behind the label, on the other hand, are unique and not interchangeable.

At its core, brand strategy is about your own positioning as a professional and about the positioning of the company. (See Figure 7.3.)

This initially requires a change in thinking. The vast majority of people think about the corporate brand when it comes to brand strategy. However,

own brand as a professional		corporate brand

FIGURE 7.3 Own brand and corporate brand

since the success of professionals depends much more on the bond between the professional and the client than on the bond between the company and the clients, it makes sense to deal with the branding of the professional in the first step and only with the branding of the company in the second step. Accordingly, branding takes place at the level of the professional level and at the level of the company.

EXAMPLE

For more than 15 years I have been working at various universities as a lecturer in the field of business valuation. In the years 2006 to 2010, I held a part-time professorship in this capacity. As a member of the board of directors and managing director of two auditing companies and as the chairman of the board of directors of a professional association for business valuators, my professorship gave my teaching activities an exposed position. In close temporal connection to the appointment as professor, one of my auditing companies changed its company name and logo three times within one year. What seemed to be a disaster for me at the time, I was able to sell as an advantage on the market. I realized that, in addition to the corporate brand of my accounting firm, it made sense to see myself as a professional with my own brand. Consequently, in 2006, I started to launch my personal website – detached from the websites of my companies. At **www.creutzmann.eu** you can get comprehensive information about me.

Branding on the level of one's own person is unknown to most professionals even though it goes hand in hand with the renewed self-confidence and self-image of a professional. Certainly, the managers of large international auditing companies might object that such an approach is neither in line with pre-existing service contracts, nor, from their point of view, in the best interests of the company. The larger the company, the more importance is attached to the fact that only the corporate brand is being sold and that the professional not appear as a separate brand next to it. However, if the principle that our business is a so-called "people's business" still applies, then the relationship between the professional and the client plays a decisive role. Professionals should ensure that their clients receive personal and individual service in the interests of the company. In this context, values such as experience, competence, trust, and quality are the basis for a successful client relationship. These values apply equally to the business as a whole as well as to the professional themselves. It therefore makes a great deal of sense for a professional to present themself on the one hand and visibly embody the corporate philosophy to the outside world on the other.

Many professional services providers do not want their partners and associates to present themselves this visibly to the outside world. This is even more true when it comes to international accounting firms. The more partners and shareholders succeed in retaining clients, the more dependent the firm is on these professionals. In my opinion, the risk of a strong partner or shareholder leaving a firm and then taking the clients with them to the new firm is just as high if the professional does not have an active brand strategy of his own. In addition, the respective partners and shareholders can be obligated to always carry the company brand in connection with their own brand presence in public. For me, this has been a matter of fact for years since it is always in my interest to communicate the corporate brands in direct connection with my own brand.

The forward-thinking professional may object that in the age of digitalization, technology is becoming more and more important and people are becoming less important. The question arises: Why invest time in building your own brand as a professional? Modern technologies will quickly change processes. That is undoubtedly true. And those who don't use the modern technologies for their business success are likely to lose clients. However, the profession of valuators and accountants thrives particularly in a special relationship of trust with its clients. This relationship of trust develops over time and through personal discussions. The focus is therefore on the individual! In my opinion, this will not change in the future. No matter what changes are yet to come with digitalization.

 ## SERVICE STRATEGY

Based on the marketing mix, the service strategy is comparable to the product policy. The starting point of the service strategy should be a situation analysis. Here, too, it is useful to distinguish between what services a professional can credibly provide themselves on the basis of their qualification profile and what services the company can credibly provide with its human resources.

The following questions help to determine the position of the professional and the company:

- What exactly are the services provided by:
  a. me and
  b. by my company?
- With which services
  a. do I achieve and
  b. with which does the company generate the most revenue?
- Are the main revenue generators also the main revenue sources?
- Which clients bring
  a. me and
  b. the company the most profit?
- What qualifications do
  a. I and
  b. my employees provide?
- Are there any special skills in our company?
- What exactly distinguishes
  a. me and
  b. my employees from other competitors?
- With which knowledge and services can
  a. I and
  b. my employees bring the most benefit to our customers?
- Why do our customers hire us and how do we win new customers?

If you can answer these questions clearly and unambiguously, you have done the groundwork for an analysis of strengths, weaknesses, opportunities, threats – a SWOT analysis. In the first step, write down your own **s**trengths, **w**eaknesses, **o**pportunities, and **t**hreats resulting from your current professional situation. In the second step, record these for your company as well. This strategic groundwork is necessary in order to develop a strategy that fits your personal situation and circumstances on the one hand and a corporate strategy on the other. The situation analysis should show you where you can find the best starting point to your service strategies according to your strengths and the enterprise with its strengths.

In essence, the service strategy is about your own positioning as a professional and about the positioning of the company. The decisive factor is not how you and your team perceive yourself, but how you are perceived or want to be perceived by your customers.

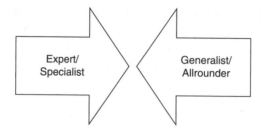

FIGURE 7.4 Professional as expert or generalist

There are two basic positioning strategies for professionals in services (see Figure 7.4):

The result of one's own situation analysis should be the starting point for strategic decisions. Being perceived as an expert requires lead time and does not happen overnight. The necessary marketing activities for this will be presented later in this chapter. First of all, the professional must make a fundamental decision whether they want to assume expert status. Once this fundamental decision has been made, two steps are required:

1. Determination of the Field of Activity as an Expert
2. Building up competence in the specific field of activity through professional practice, external training, and a great deal of self-study.

A professional will only be credibly perceived as an expert if they have an appropriate qualification as an expert. First of all, the professional acquires this qualification for themselves internally. Through the right marketing activities, these then become visible externally in the market to potential clients. In his book "Outliers: The Story of Success," Malcolm Gladwell, referring to studies by Anders Ericsson as well as Ralf Krampe and Clemens Tesch-Römer, claims that it takes an average of 10,000 hours to become an expert in a field. The key message is that through diligence and practice, everyone will be among the best in their field after 10,000 hours. Although Ericsson later qualifies his research results and, in addition to diligence and practice, also establishes talent to a considerable extent as a prerequisite for exceptional performance in a particular field, in my opinion the basic statement is still valid. What every athlete takes for granted is too often negated by professionals. No matter in which sport someone is active, only through regular training and practice is above-average performance possible. No athlete, whether amateur or professional, will deny this. The fact that talent is required for exceptional performance also needs no special explanation.

NOTE

My professional career started in 1992 with one of the Big Four auditing companies. As early as 1993, I assisted an experienced professional colleague with a business valuation. Initially, I was only sporadically active in the field of business valuations. However, as I was fascinated by the field of activity as a valuation professional, I started reading books related to business valuations. After passing the exam to become a certified public accountant in 1999, I started to focus on the field of business valuations. My interest was so great that I began to read almost everything related to business valuations. Looking back, I confirm that it takes an average of about 10,000 hours to have the necessary expertise as an expert in a particular field.

Most professional colleagues will object that they do not have the time to invest 10,000 hours in a particular field in order to acquire expert status. This judgment should not be made prematurely. After all, those who work as professionals certainly have knowledge in a particular area that is more pronounced than in other areas. Those who have spent their first professional years with large international auditing companies until passing the professional examinations certainly have particular specialized knowledge as these companies are highly specialized in all areas of activity. Professionals that work in smaller or medium-sized companies have done certain activities more often than others. Anything else would be unusual. However, the crucial question that every professional must ask themselves is: Do I want to build up expert status for myself? If the answer to this question is in the affirmative, then the 10,000-hour rule may very well serve as a rule of thumb.

Everyone must find a strategy that fits their situation. Professionals should check whether specialization in a particular field of activity is the more successful strategy.

This applies equally to professional services providers. As part of the situation analysis, it is important to determine at the company level whether the law firm or auditing company is perceived as a "specialist" in a particular field of activity. The bottom line is that only those professionals who work for the company can be perceived as specialists in the market. In the case of an auditing or law firm, clients expect the typical services of an auditor or lawyer. And there are plenty of these, as is well known. The positioning of an auditing or law firm as a specialist for a specific field of activity as part of its service strategy is practiced by only a few firms in this country. These firms are often

TIP

Building up expert status and the associated competence in a particular field of activity is done through professional practice, external training, and a lot of self-study. With an eight-hour day and an average of 220 working days in Germany, a professional has 1,760 working hours in a calendar year of time capacity to work on their expert status through professional practice. After about five and a half years of exclusive professional practice in the specific field of activity, they have accrued the required 10,000 hours as an expert provided that this is a company in which they are professionally active exclusively in this particular field. This will not always be the case.

Through further training measures and self-study, i.e., through diligence and discipline, every professional can train for one hour a day in the field of activity in which they later want to work as an expert. However, this further training is only useful if the professional can be active in this particular field of activity again during their working hours. For example, a professional who works on two to three practical valuation cases a year, which takes up 400 hours of their time, could invest an additional 365 hours of time in their expertise as a valuation expert through self-study. In this example, the professional comes to 765 hours in one year, with which they intensively deal with their special field. Although it now takes the professional about 13 years to invest as much time in the specialty area as the professional colleague who has been exclusively involved in a specific activity for five and a half years, the qualification perceived in the market could even be greater due to the seniority in the latter case.

referred to as "boutiques." They are far more common among lawyers than among auditors.

The fundamental decision to position an auditing or law firm towards a specific field of activity is associated with corresponding consequences. The biggest one being that the company must consciously decide against accepting assignments in connection with other services in the future. There may be weighty economic reasons against this. Many will argue that their fixed cost structures prohibit such decisions. This might lead to the false assumption that companies should only perform orders in a specific area of activity from one day to the next. That is not a claim I am making. Service strategy is about positioning the company. As my own example of a newly founded company showed, this cannot be done in a hurry or without proper lead time. For me, it is more a matter of professional services providers asking themselves the positioning question. Up to now, this question has been answered in favor of the broadest possible range of activities. The larger the firm, the more likely it is that it will resemble

EXAMPLE

I founded today's IVA VALUATION & ADVISORY AG Wirtschaftsprüfungsgesellschaft on December 6, 1999, as part of a joint venture with a regionally well-known medium-sized auditing company. At the time of its foundation, the company had already focused its activities on corporate finance consulting. Annual audits and tax consulting were not offered. After two years, the strategic decision was made to further narrow down the business consulting to the activity focus of business valuations. It took about another four years until in 2006, for the first time, sales revenues were generated exclusively from business valuations and valuations of intangible assets. There are numerous occasions for company valuations. In the further development of the company, we were able to specialize to the extent that today we realize significant revenues in connection with company valuations in structural measures that are not subject to stock corporation law. There are a total of 3,013 auditing companies in Germany as of January 1, 2022. I am aware of only one other German firm that also realizes revenue predominantly from business valuations.

a general store rather than a boutique. The problem here is that really only the Big Four and a few Next Ten firms are able to consistently provide services in all disciplines at the highest level. Depending on the team composition and the consulting project, I dare say that only very few companies can consistently offer and provide excellent services at the highest level. If the management of the respective companies communicate honestly internally, they know this. For all other companies, it is not possible anyway, because there is a lack of suitably qualified experts from the outset. However, there are good reasons for both the professional in the individual practice and for auditing and tax consulting companies for why they should specialize in one or more specific areas of activity.

 ## PRICE STRATEGY

The price strategy results from combining the brand and the service strategy. Those who are positioned as experts receive higher remuneration than generalists. Professional services providers with experts in certain practice areas can achieve higher remuneration. The pricing strategy therefore depends to a considerable extent on whether a professional or a firm operates in a niche or offers the very typical highly competitive services of a professional.

Professionals usually have the following options for realizing fees for their services:

- Time-based fee
- Fixed fee
- Regulated fee
- Performance-related fee

Professionals will charge their fees largely on the basis of the hours worked. Different hourly rates are agreed upon with clients depending on an employee's qualifications. Many companies simplify the procedure by setting a uniform hourly rate for a fictitious employee based on the experience levels of various employees. This hourly rate includes the hourly rates of assistants as well as seniors, managers, and partners. The disadvantage of this uniform hourly rate is that whenever the time share of a manager or partner is higher than planned, the uniform hourly rate will tend to be too low. However, since larger companies typically have partners and managers less involved in service delivery, the risk of miscalculation appears manageable. Performance-related fees are not permitted for all professionals and, moreover, not in all countries, which is why they are not discussed in detail here.

If you have positioned yourself as an expert or specialist and also offer your clients activities which, from the client's point of view, are of higher value than a professional's classic services, you can realize far above-average hourly rates. Thus, achieving expert status has a direct fiscal impact on the professional or their firm.

There are a large number of activities for which fixed prices are commonly agreed. Under certain conditions, this also includes the audit of annual financial statements. A trusting and cooperative relationship between a professional and a client should be based on a fair business relationship. A fair business relationship is given in a win-win situation for both business partners although this will rarely be the case with a fixed price.

A professional who agrees on a fixed price has calculated the work to be done in advance in terms of time. Either they have multiplied an hourly rate of a fictitious employee, as described before, with the times estimated for the activity and determined the fee. Or, they have multiplied different hourly rates corresponding to different qualification levels of the employees with the respective times and added the individual fees to a total fee. If the competitive situation allows, they may have included a risk buffer for unforeseeable times and increased the fee by this item.

At the end of the project, three case constellations are conceivable:

Case 1: The estimated times correspond to the times actually incurred.
Case 2: The estimated times are lower than the actual times.
Case 3: The estimated times are higher than the actual times.

In the first case, the project has generated the projected contribution margin and no further explanation is required. In cases 2 and 3 there are always winners and losers depending on the size of the miscalculations.

In the second case, the average calculated hourly rate is reduced more depending on additional time spent. Already during the project, the professional and their employees might lose motivation for the project with every additional hour that was not planned. Depending on the respective quality requirements, it could be that certain activities are not conducted because they are not remunerated. To what extent a client is then actually a winner because they have to pay less due to a fixed price than they would have if all times were invoiced, may be doubted. In particular, if quality losses are to be expected in this context because certain activities are not completed, the fixed price is counterproductive from the client's point of view. If the professional's

TIP

In a fair business relationship, both business partners should be winners. From the previous explanation, I advocate fixed prices for the classic activities of professionals only in exceptional cases. Experience shows that professionals can eliminate a fixed price agreement with a simple question. A professional should ask the client that wants to agree on a fixed price the following question: "Why do you want either of us to lose?" Now the professional must wait until the client answers. They might have to repeat the question if the pause is too long. It is important that the client answers this question! Normally the client should answer to the effect that they do not want anyone to be a loser. At least the conversation should go in this direction, and the professional should be sure that the client agrees on a win-win situation.

If you are dealing with a client who doesn't care if you lose out on this fixed-price project, you should strongly consider whether you want to enter into this client relationship. In general, the above question will take the issue of a fixed price off the table, and you will be able to reach a fee agreement that takes into account the actual time spent. Nevertheless, the client will want a fee estimate for the project, to which you should also adhere. In my lectures and seminars, I explain what you should do if this fee estimate cannot be met.

quality standards remain high, the fee will be significantly too low. Irrespective of the possible liability risk – because not all activities have been finalized – the professional services provider loses because of the significantly lower contribution margin generated.

In the third case, the professional is the winner and the client loses, because they pay too much for the service compared to the usual hourly rates.

 ## MARKETING ACTIVITIES

Marketing strategy is the part of the marketing plan that is used to achieve certain sales targets in the medium term through specific behavior. Marketing activities, on the other hand, are the compass for day-to-day activities. I do not consider a distinction between online marketing and offline marketing activities to be purposeful for our profession. Certainly, individual marketing activities can be assigned quite clearly to online marketing and offline marketing. In a digitalized world, however, where online and offline are increasingly merging, marketing activities would be categorized in a way that no longer reflects the spirit of the times. Rather, two worlds would be created mentally that no longer coexist but have long since become one through the use of smartphones and virtual technologies.

It is much more appropriate to divide marketing activities into those from the perspective of a professional and those of the company.

 ## MARKETING ACTIVITIES FOR PROFESSIONALS

In the US, people are called "Rainmakers" who bring their companies new customers, orders, and ultimately profits. "Rainmakers" have knowledge and skills that are distinctly different from other professionals. In essence, every time an order is placed, there is only one question at stake: Why should you receive the order and not your competitors? If you can answer this question clearly and unambiguously, you are one step ahead of your competitors. So, it's all about the question of selling. One or the other professional will probably think that having passed the necessary exams to become a professional, they have enough professional competence that they do not need to sell. After all, as a professional they are not working in sales as a salesperson, but as a consultant for highly qualified services in a specialized field.

NOTE

By the way, anyone who has negative associations with the term sales should remember that everyone is a salesperson. Whenever you "sell" yourself or an idea to someone else, you are acting as a salesperson. Many people are not at all aware of this. This process already starts when you choose a partner. Because that's where you often sell your "best" side. If you are courting another person, you rarely talk about your weaknesses and faults on the first dates but always present yourself at your best. Even within companies, you sell yourself to colleagues and superiors. You sell your work performance and your ideas within the company, and you have to convince superiors and colleagues in the process. And when you come home from work in the evening, you have to convince your family – even during vacations and leisure activities. Anyone who has children knows that "selling" certain things (going to bed, studying, brushing teeth, etc.) can be particularly difficult. In this respect, it is advisable and expedient if they see themselves as salespeople, both professionally and privately, in order to identify with this role.

It is worth remembering that with around 670,000 auditors and approximately 1.3 million lawyers in the US, there are more than enough qualified professionals available to clients. In many cases, both in small, medium, and large international companies, the workload situation in our profession has been particularly good for many years. There is enough to do, so that many do not realize how important sales is. Since there are even professional colleagues who no longer accept new clients in the field of tax consulting because of a lack of suitably qualified specialists to manage the cases, one or the other professional fails to realize how important sales is if one wants to be successful in business in the long term.

In other areas of activity, such as annual audits, competition is fierce and new clients are largely won only by dumping prices. The professional with a vision knows that ultimately the Rainmakers of a company who can acquire new engagements make the decisive contribution to the company's success for all others. After all, it is only through new and existing clients that cash flow is generated that covers the company's personnel and material costs and provides for employee bonuses. Any highly qualified expert will now immediately retort that the service can only be provided through high professional competence and that this is nevertheless at least as important as the sales competence of a professional who can acquire new engagements. It is certainly up to each professional to weigh the importance of professional competence and sales competence. However, I would like to point out: What good is the professional competence of a highly qualified specialist if they have no clients to use this competence in their work?

TIP

If you want to make employees your partners, you should make it a prerequisite that they can acquire engagements themselves. Targets should be agreed upon over a longer period of time (12–18 months), and it should be observed whether the employee is able to acquire clients themselves. If the professional does not succeed in repeatedly and reliably winning new clients, then they might lack a decisive qualification for a partnership: the ability to sell oneself, the services, and ultimately the company to new clients. This does not mean that the company should part with these employees. Especially not if they are highly qualified professionals. These professional colleagues are important to provide qualified services. For a partnership, however, there is (still) the risk of a lack of an important skill or valuable soft skill: Sales!

The following sequence should be observed (see Figure 7.5):

First, the professional always sells themselves first. Only then does a professional sell the services and the company. Many partners of large international companies or even second tier companies will vehemently disagree with this and propagate exactly the opposite order. With the shining logo and

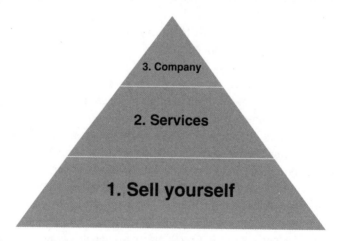

FIGURE 7.5 Sales pyramid

the international brand recognition, the professionals sell the services of the company. Undeniably, the brand recognition or the logo can be an important confidence-building measure. Just by taking a look at the logos of the Big Four international accounting firms, you can see that they are equally confidence-building. Therefore, differentiation can only be achieved by the individual professionals of the firms. It follows that the basis of the sales pyramid is first of all the ability of the professional to sell themselves.

Since the acquisition of clients involves the sale of an order or the sale of a service, the first step is to gain the client's trust for the services offered. This absolutely requires the involvement of the personality of the professional. It is not only a matter of being competent, but also of being likeable and convincing. It calls for skills that professionals have neither been taught at traditional universities nor can be found in the relevant specialist literature. A good salesperson possesses the following qualities, among others:

- can listen and asks the right questions
- has a pleasant and trustworthy voice and has rhetorical skills
- has empathy and gives feedback during the conversation
- knows the customer's needs and does not want to sell standard products
- is reliable and keeps appointments
- only promises what they can deliver
- is able to articulate themselves clearly and to present their results
- is friendly, truthful and has integrity
- can build and maintain a relationship with their clients
- is a good "networker"

These are all qualities that, for the most part, can be learned. They apply to people who can sell themselves well, both in their professional and private lives. Individual characteristics can be trained in targeted training sessions. A Rainmaker, i.e., a particularly good seller of professional services, if they want to, can learn these qualifications through study, training, practice, and professionalism to a certain degree. However, the principle from Chapter 4 "Leverage Strengths" must be observed. Someone who is introverted, that is, who prefers to deal with the factual problem rather than with the person who is to place the order, will have a tough time developing into a good salesperson. For them, the factual problem will always come before the person. Since humans, as described before, sell themselves permanently and privately as well as vocationally, it should be completely in each professional's own interest to further develop their sales abilities. Even if it's "only" for dealing with family and their circle of friends. This is part of personality development and acquiring relationship skills in dealing with other people. After all, for all those professionals who aspire to a partnership, it is part of their job to develop their sales skills anyway.

The following are some of the qualities that distinguish Rainmakers:

- They can "sell" themselves, their services, and their company.
- They have rhetorical skills.
- They are excellent "networkers."
- They have a natural authority.
- They are convincing and trustworthy.
- They have integrity, authenticity, and truthfulness.
- They are self-confident, but not arrogant or overbearing.
- They are outgoing and extroverted.
- They care about their customers and their potential new customers.
- They treat everyone as if they could become a customer.
- They are relational.
- They exceed their customers' expectations.
- They are reliable and appreciative.
- They are professional.
- They are self-reliant.

Anyone who is active in sports knows that championships are only won through practice. In the meantime, it is also widely known that in addition to physical training in a particular sport, mental training is also an important – in my opinion, the decisive – factor for success. However, the word "conditioning" is important. Many of the above-mentioned characteristics can be learned and trained. With this, it is important not to disregard individual hereditary factors and genes. As the saying goes, "A plow horse does not become a racehorse."

Those who are introverts and have strong analytical strengths will prefer to be in their office and will rarely have the urge to interact with potential clients. In a Rainmaker, however, being able to make contact is an important quality. We don't get new business by sitting behind our desk. You can solve problems and write expert opinions there, but you won't find potential clients that way. The same applies to the operationally fully occupied manager. If you work almost exclusively on orders, you won't have time to acquire new customers.

I would like to highlight three aspects of a Rainmaker's rhetorical skills:

- Empathy
- Conversational skills
- Presentation skills

Behind every company as a customer are the respective employees. These employees – no matter if they are top managers or clerks – are first of all "only" human beings. And these people all have "problems." You can also use the positive term "challenges" for the word "problems." By this, I primarily mean the tasks that the respective employee has to cope with. Accordingly, in a positive sense, every employee is also a problem solver; and the employee who does not solve problems, but causes more, will rarely advance on the corporate ladder. I would like to give an example of empathy.

EXAMPLE

Imagine a typical business valuation project in the first few months of a new fiscal year, taking place during the preparation of the annual financial statements and the subsequent annual audit. The head of a company's accounting department, in addition to their day-to-day business, deals with the auditors, the consultants for the business valuation project and – if necessary in the case of a structural measure under stock corporation law – an additional auditor in their company who takes up their capacities. Anyone who does not have the necessary empathy here and perhaps even finds words of admonition when a deadline for the submission of documents is first exceeded, possibly made public via a large e-mail distribution list, does not necessarily endear themselves to the manager concerned, but also sells their company badly in the long term.

In such cases, it is certainly necessary to apply a sufficient sense of proportion as to whether the entire project plan is called into question by the omission; even though, this will rarely be the case. Positive and constructive questions and honest understanding are characteristics of an empathetic consultant. Incidentally, the less than empathetic and admonishing consultant must face questions about their time buffers in project planning. This would at least show self-responsibility as another characteristic of a Rainmaker.

The way a Rainmaker conducts a conversation differs significantly from other professionals, and starts with the preparation of the conversation. A Rainmaker prepares their conversations in detail and meticulously with clients as well as with potential new clients. They gather all the information available to them about their conversation partner and the company in advance. The proper conversation is characterized by active listening. This means that they summarize the points made by their interlocutor in their own words in order to establish that they understood their conversation partner correctly. Both the correct questioning technique and objection managing appropriate to the discussion situation are important success instruments of a Rainmaker. The Rainmaker is quick-witted, and quick-wittedness can be learned, as shown in Chapter 15, Rhetoric.

In contrast to leading conversations in one-on-one meetings or conversations in small groups, Rainmakers also possess strong presentation skills in front of a larger auditorium. When presenting interim or final results in consulting projects, it is necessary to convince a larger group of participants of one's own or the team's achievements. Matthias Pöhm impressively shows in his book "The PowerPoint Fallacy: Still Presenting Or Already Fascinating?" the dangers of using PowerPoint for presentations. Rainmakers present excellently and know exactly if, when, and how to use PowerPoint. The ability to present is something that can be learned as well. We will look at this in more detail in the tools in Chapter 15, Rhetoric.

 ## NETWORKING SKILLS OF RAINMAKERS

Networking is one of the most important success factors of Rainmakers. However, networking requires that you be relationally capable. You are relationally capable if you are likeable. But how do you become likable? Tim Sanders devotes an entire book to the "likability factor." For him, the most important sympathy factors include empathy, truthfulness, and interest in the other person. All of these are qualities that are included in the previous list. In addition, friendliness is also an important sympathy factor for Sanders. Sanders shows impressively that these are all qualities that can be learned and trained. They are therefore by no means hereditary traits. Brian Tracy and Ron Arden show in their book "The Power of Charm: How to Win Anyone Over in Any Situation." Here, too, the authors show that charm can be acquired. Likeability and charm are important qualities when building networks. Networks usually work whenever both can derive benefits from the relationship. However, this is a lengthy process. Building a personal network takes time. And you have to do it all by yourself, because your relationships are the result of lived contacts. And you have to live these contacts yourself. Relationships are only bad if you don't have any.

The process of networking can be divided into three phases:

1. Making contacts
2. Maintaining contacts
3. Using contacts

Only when there is clarity of purpose, the next question to ask is what the possibilities and ways are to get new contacts. A Rainmaker knows their potential clients or target groups exactly. They specifically establish contacts that lead to orders.

Making contacts alone is not enough unless they are maintained continuously. Potential problems in this part of the process might be deciding which contacts are worth cultivating and which are not. The Rainmaker knows the answer to this question. They focus on cultivating the important and essential contacts with regard to their professional goals. These are the people who have considerable influence in placing orders. Only those who take care of their contacts will be able to use them one day. The Rainmaker uses a variety of tools both in making contacts and in maintaining them. This includes, among other things, taking notes on established contacts. They gather information from both the professional environment and the private environment of the contact.

Networks tend to be dynamic rather than static entities. This means that people can join and leave networks. Sometimes leaving a network is the right strategy to be able to enter a new network. In either case, Rainmakers have excellent networks and strive to maintain them permanently.

MARKETING ACTIVITIES FOR EXPERT POSITIONING

If a professional has recognized that a specialization strategy to become an expert gives them significant competitive advantages over professional colleagues, the first step is to credibly acquire this qualification. As already described, this requires a combination of several years of professional experience in a specific field of activity, a great deal of self-study, continuing education, and other proof of qualification. However, this does not automatically make it visible in the market that someone has expert status.

EXAMPLE

In one of my keynotes, I asked the participants in connection with the topic of expert positioning, how an expert becomes visible in the market for potential clients? The participants were predominantly experienced and older professional colleagues (CPAs), and I was all the more surprised that I created a so-called stop situation with this question and initially a stifling silence fell in the room. None of them could answer this question. A renowned university professor in the field of auditing and accounting then gave an answer. He said that the expert would make their expertise visible in the market by publishing articles.

Professionals have only a limited choice of activities to make their expert status credibly visible in the market, as Figure 7.6 shows.

The multiplication marketing cycle illustrates the marketing activities of a professional within the framework of expert positioning. On the one hand, the cycle is intended to vividly illustrate that the individual marketing activities are interconnected and, on the other, that a professional can start any marketing activity at any time as part of their positioning strategy. In his book "Become a Recognized Authority In Your Field – In 60 Days Or Less," published as early as 2002, Robert W. Bly dealt in detail with individual marketing activities in connection with positioning as an expert. Based on Bly's thoughts, the illustration Multiplication Marketing has already been created in another presentation by me in the context of my Rainmaker essays and has now been expanded in a contemporary way. Expert positioning can take place on two levels. (See Figure 7.7.)

The starting point of any expert activity is several years of practical professional experience in the specific activity or in a sector, as well as extensive self-study. The professional gains valuable knowledge during the course of their assignments as well as from discussions with clients. Frequently, file notes or other internal documents are created in the course of order processing. These documents can serve as basic material for publication. Professionals who have positioned themselves as experts always document this through a corresponding number of publications. Incidentally, this applies equally to the profession of doctors and lawyers. Anyone searching for an expert on Google today can easily check whether someone actually has the relevant knowledge by looking at the publications of an expert. In particular, the choice of medium provides valuable information about an expert's standing.

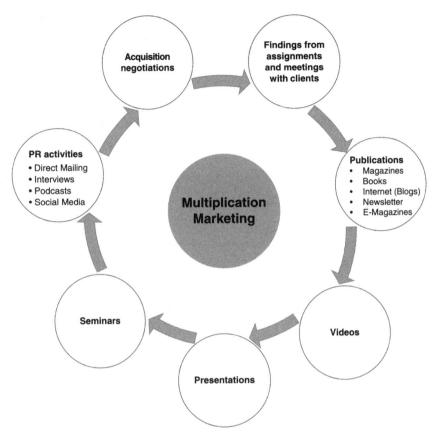

FIGURE 7.6 Multiplication marketing

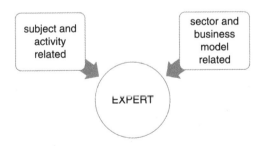

FIGURE 7.7 Subject-matter expert and industry expert

Those who publish in renowned journals regularly had a greater expert status than those who publish on their own blog on the internet. It is worth noting that especially in the academic journals in the field of economics, there are almost no practitioners who publish there. So, if you base your search here on whether someone has a publication in a high-ranking international journal, you will find almost exclusively high-ranking international academics, but fewer experts who can help solve practical problems. To position oneself as a professional who wants to underline one's expert status in a certain field or area of activity with one's publications, it is therefore necessary to find the appropriate platforms for publications.

In doing so, one should analyze in advance whether one wants to publish a professional article in a trade journal or an article in a newspaper or magazine that is read by potential new customers. The most effective way to acquire new customers is to publish in media outlets that are read by people who demand your services. Ideally, these should be issues that outline practical solutions to specific current customer problems. Depending on whether you are looking for potential new customers regionally or nationally, it is essential to find the right media. The goal of all these marketing activities is to sustainably increase your level of awareness.

All other publications of a professional are only indirectly aimed at potential clients in the case of subject-related expert positioning. This is because the main consumers of these publications are not potential new clients, but other professional colleagues who want to expand and deepen their knowledge. Please note that this is also the case in other professional groups, such as lawyers and doctors. Let's find out why this is so.

In the first step, a specialist expert always acquires the status of an expert within the circle of their professional colleagues. Only in the second step, through the recognition of the expert status by the professional colleagues, does the status become sustainably visible to potential clients on the market. Clients turn to accountants, tax consultants, or lawyers because they want to have problems solved. Patients go to doctors because they want to get better. What all these cases have in common is that a professional is sought out to solve a problem. If clients could solve their problems themselves, they would not need professionals. This is true for all services provided by professionals. If we disregard statutory audits and the typical reserved tasks of an auditor, what all other services have in common is that clients are generally unable to really assess the problem-solving competence of a professional or the commissioned auditing/accounting practice. This is because in order to be able to assess the problem-solving competence, the clients themselves would have to be in a position to provide the requested service in a professionally correct manner. If the service is provided not only to take advantage of a professional's liability or professional indemnity insurance, but because the problem-solving competence of the professional is at stake, then in most cases it will only become apparent to the clients, more or less long after the service has been provided, whether the professional has actually solved the problem.

In this context, the publications of a professional positioned as a subject matter expert take on a "gatekeeper function." In the case of recognized professional journals, the professional article is reviewed by an advisory board to ensure a certain level of quality. Thus, anyone who publishes professional articles that have been approved by an advisory board is certainly already part of an exposed circle of experts. Based on the publications or the positioning as an expert on the market, clients can be confident when awarding contracts that the professional is among the best in their field. They have clearly distinguished themselves from other professional colleagues through their positioning as an expert.

In the case of industry experts, the publication of articles offers the opportunity to establish direct contact with potential new customers, because these articles deal with solutions to problems within an industry. These publications are perceived far predominantly in industry magazines by decision makers. Here, the positioning as an industry expert takes place directly with potential clients.

Many experts also publish in their own blogs on the internet. Although there is no quality control by third parties here, articles can be published quickly and flexibly on a regular basis, which may achieve a significantly greater reach on the internet than a specialist article in a trade journal or an industry article in an industry magazine. Newsletters and e-magazines are also not subject to quality control and can therefore be easily used for publications. In so-called white papers, new clients become aware of the professional by using the report directly as a promotional tool. This can be done via direct mailings as well as websites (landing pages). The white paper as well as company-related research do, however, often require the support of employees, so that these instruments are presented during the marketing activities of the companies.

The publication of a book is certainly associated with the greatest time expenditure for positioning as an expert. It is clearly superior to all other publications. If you can convince a well-known publishing house to publish your book, not only wins you the support for the selling, but you must be equally convincing of the economic success by an appropriate demand of the respective target group. The publication of a book in a particular field therefore most strongly documents the expert status of a professional. Perhaps this makes you ask yourself, why write a book if a topic has already been covered in other books? Yes, do write a book. Because your book is your very own perspective on the subject. It is unique. Your uniqueness based on your experiences will make the book special, something no other book has offered before.

In the age of digitalization and the high reach of videos on YouTube, this medium is likely to take a weighty place in the future in positioning yourself as an expert in a particular field. Currently, there are only a few professionals who have a corresponding reach with their videos, so that they could be awarded the status of an expert. Entering the term "lawyer" on YouTube leads predominantly to videos about job descriptions, income, or image films of law firms or professionals. One lawyer in the US, however, uses YouTube exceptionally well. It's Devin James Stone, better known as LegalEagle. With more than 2 million subscribers, he has an impressive number of followers. The "Real Lawyer Reacts to Suits" episode currently has around 7.4 million users watching. His YouTube channel has been in existence since January 2017, and his videos have been viewed more than 315 million times.

EXAMPLE

For almost 20 years I have had teaching assignments in the field of business valuations and have lectured on topics in the field of business valuation as part of the training for the CVA. For this reason, I immediately notice when a particularly good speaker talks on the topic of business valuation. Aswath Damodaran is the world's best-known university professor on business valuation (https://pages.stern.nyu.edu/~adamodar/). For decades, he has made it possible for anyone to access his lectures on the internet. Unlike his contemporaries, he knows how to describe complicated issues in a way that not only students but also others without academic background can understand well. He has penetrated business valuation so deeply that he can teach people the subject in a motivating and exciting way even if they don't have a background in business valuation.

Both subject matter and industry experts are asked to share their expertise with a live audience during presentations. This can be at conferences during keynotes or technical and industry presentations. Anyone who regularly appears as a speaker at a recognized professional conference is indisputably one of the experts in a particular field.

EXAMPLE

The European Association of Certified Valuators and Analysts (EACVA) holds a conference for valuation professionals once a year (www.valuationconference.de). Over two days there are four keynotes and often up to 28 workshops. Valuation professionals who have made a name for themselves both nationally and internationally appear there. Many of them have been regular speakers there for many years. This goes hand in hand with a special position within the business valuation profession. The positioning as an expert is thus visible in the market.

Seminars are another variant of speaking activities. Anyone who has made a name for themselves as a specialist or industry expert is also booked as a speaker for seminars. Seminars differ from lectures in that they are longer. As I understand it, a seminar starts at three hours of lecturing. Sometimes seminars can last several days. Both lectures and seminars can, of course, be recorded and thus, be used several times. In contrast to publications, lectures require completely different soft skills than a good author's. If you can write well, you do not automatically have to be a good speaker. What both marketing activities have in common is that both a good author and a good speaker are experts in their field. And if they have properly penetrated their field, they can also convey the content in an understandable and simple language. This is a prerequisite for them to be able to present convincingly as a speaker as well. The decisive advantage of any speaking activity is that a professional can make direct contact with potential new clients at the event before, during, and after. The professional does not know who specifically will read their publication.

There are a variety of activities that can be subsumed into PR activities. Examples in the figure include direct mail, interviews, podcasts, and social media activities.

Direct mailings require that the recipient is known and that the mail provides a benefit to the recipient. The publications of professional articles are just as suitable here as current information about the field or the industry even if the extent to which these direct mails attract attention in the multitude of daily mails may be questioned. It requires a good subject and the overcoming of various (spam) filters by the recipient in order to be noticed at all; in addition, the requirements of data protection must be observed. If this is done successfully, the professional can attract the attention of potential new customers or be remembered by existing customers.

A newspaper, radio station, or television interview clearly sets the expert apart from other professionals because the request usually comes from the media. The extent to which staged interviews on YouTube gain a comparable reputation depends on the awareness of the channel and the interviewee. They can create an image-building effect.

Producing a podcast is time-consuming. In German-speaking countries, podcasts are not yet as widespread as in the US. A successful podcast has followers that listen to it regularly. The publication should therefore take place at certain intervals. Podcasts can be produced in a block and then published over a longer period of time. The extent to which the time required for production is in proportion to the goals in positioning the company as an expert is not yet foreseeable. But since podcasts are becoming increasingly important for us as well, you should not lose sight of this PR tool when positioning yourself as an expert. Especially because a podcast can contribute to customer loyalty and be noticed easily by potential new customers.

The social networks (social media), such as LinkedIn, Facebook, and Instagram, have developed impressively in recent years in terms of their published user numbers. LinkedIn had 756 million users worldwide, of these around 180 million from the UA. Facebook has around 2.9 billion monthly users, of which 300 million are from the US. And Instagram has around 1 billion monthly users worldwide, of which around 140 million are from the US. Data was retrieved in the third quarter 2021.

For positioning as an expert, only LinkedIn currently seems recommendable to me. The presence on Facebook and Instagram may be important for recruiting employees, but I currently see support for positioning as an expert as at least questionable. Using the search function on LinkedIn, a large number of decision-makers of potential mandates can be identified quite quickly. LinkedIn's Sales Navigator is a paid tool that supports professionals in their search for new clients.

The most important marketing activity in the multiplication marketing cycle is the acquisition negotiation. This is ultimately about the professional convincing a potential new client about themselves, their service offering, and their company. This can be a one-to-one conversation or a presentation by the professional and, if applicable, their employees to a potential new client. A distinction must be made between the following acquisition discussions:

- Occasion-related acquisition talks
- Acquisition meetings not related to an event

An occasion-related acquisition meeting goes hand in hand with a pitch to other competitors. A client makes an RFP or asks specifically for one or more particular services in connection with a specific occasion, e.g., a corporate transaction. A non-occasion-related acquisition meeting can be, for example, in the context of a technical lecture or a company presentation to a potential new client. Since these acquisition calls are without a specific occasion, the goal is to be competent and personable in the hope of winning a contract if there is a subsequent need for a service from the professional.

MARKETING ACTIVITIES FOR COMPANIES

Corporate marketing activities refer to those activities that tend to be carried out by larger companies because they have the financial strength and sufficient human resources so that they can be put into practice. But the decisive differentiation criterion in comparison with marketing activities in the positioning of professionals as experts is that these activities are completely independent of a specific positioning. They can therefore be conducted by all companies and no expert positioning is required for this. The marketing activities for companies are listed below:

- internet presence
- advertisements
- newsletters
- research
- corporate events
- sponsoring
- Public Relations

The individual marketing activities for companies will only be dealt with briefly because they will not be equally feasible for all professionals for the reasons mentioned previously, and it would go beyond the scope of the book to deal with them in more detail.

An internet presence may be taken for granted. Anyone who does not have a web presence today is living in the Stone Age and will be even less likely to deal with digitization. Anyone who has ever actively helped design an internet presence knows that this always goes hand in hand with strategy questions about the company. This is equally true when revising the internet presence.

If advertisements are to have a certain marketing effect, a larger capital investment is usually required. This applies at least to advertisements in newspapers, magazines, or on billboards. Ads in the print media no longer fit into a digital age. On the internet, ads can be cheaper and more target group-focused with less wastage. For a certain sustainability, appropriate financial resources are also necessary here. It is important that ads be placed regularly over a longer period of time, otherwise they will fizzle out.

Newsletters or client circulars are probably created and distributed by most professional services providers. They are a medium to stay remembered or can be used for direct mailing campaigns.

Research in the form of white papers or certain studies are an excellent marketing tool. However, this usually requires considerable human resources, which often only the exceptionally large companies have. These companies then make clever use of their research to disseminate the results in the media and to their clients. The media coverage also attracts the attention of new potential clients to the company.

Company events can take place on a large or small scale. The election of the Entrepreneur of the Year or sustainability awards for companies also achieve a high media reach. Small company events in the office space with good external and internal speakers, with a welcome drink and a small snack afterwards serve the client relationship care and give the opportunity to invite potential new clients.

The sponsoring of sporting, cultural, or other events often also involves considerable financial resources and serves to cultivate the company's image. This applies equally to professional PR work, as this requires the company's own qualified staff or external employees.

CHAPTER EIGHT

Setting Goals

A CENTRAL TASK OF EFFECTIVE self-management and external management is goal clarity. Goal clarity is an essential prerequisite for a successful professional and personal life. In this regard, most people overestimate what they can achieve in one year and underestimate what they can achieve in the medium term, for example in five years. This applies to both professional and private life.

> **NOTE**
>
> Today, most passenger cars have a navigation system. Google Maps is installed on every smartphone. Therefore, most people today take it for granted that in order to get to a destination, they enter the exact address into the navigation system or Google Maps. If you don't know exactly where you're going, you won't get there. If a ship or airplane changes course only minimally, it will arrive at a completely different place depending on the length of the route. These findings may seem trivial at first glance. However, they can be directly applied to your professional and private life.

The principle of focus goes hand in hand with concentration on a few things. This applies equally to setting goals. The principle applies: less is more. We almost always take on too much and too many different things. This applies equally in professional and private life and leads to stress as a result. Effective professionals therefore ask themselves the following questions repeatedly:

- Does it really matter?
- What happens if I/we don't do this?

The tool "setting goals" is a soft skill that is just as important in professional life as it is in private life. Professional and private goals are always the personal goals of a professional. To be distinguished from these are the goals of the company. Leading employees with goals (management by objectives) goes back to Drucker and is used by many professional services providers. However, the procedure for effectively "setting goals" is always the same. It does not matter whether the goals are personal goals or company goals. Since the book is entitled "Soft Skills for the Professional Services Industry," the task of "setting goals" is presented from the perspective of a professional. In this respect, we are dealing with personal goals. These are both professional and private goals. Only when there is clarity of purpose at the personal level will a professional be able to contribute their full potential to the achievement of corporate goals. The process steps that a professional goes through in personal goal setting are the same steps that are gone through in goal setting in a company.

The task of "setting goals" is therefore first presented from a professional's perspective. Then the topic is briefly outlined from the perspective of professional services provider. This chapter is about understanding the importance of the task of "setting goals" and about a professional internalizing the process of goal setting. Once a professional has internalized this process, they can also bring their knowledge to the company. Particularly in the case of larger companies, other shareholders or partners often also decide on the goals, so that a professional does not usually decide alone on the goals of the company anyway, unless the professional is a sole proprietor.

 ## SETTING PERSONAL GOALS

Effective professionals limit themselves to the few essential and important goals. In the principle of action orientation, we had dealt with the topic of extrinsic and intrinsic motivation of people in addition to the various life motives according to Steven Reiss. This basic knowledge is important if we want to deal with the task of "setting goals" on a personal level in a meaningful way.

FIND YOUR PURPOSE IN LIFE

Exceptional success is possible when you know your life's purpose, set clear priorities and live productively. A productive life of a successful person is determined by what is not visible. It is like the tip of an iceberg. The starting point is your life purpose or life meaning, and both terms are used interchangeably. If you now think that we are leaving the path of effective management and losing ourselves in the philosophical, you are mistaken. The question of the purpose or meaning of your life is closely related to your life motives and to your strengths. Only those who know their life motives and their strengths will find the purpose and meaning of their life. For only those who live in harmony with their life motives and their strengths will develop their personality to the fullest and make the greatest possible contribution to society. Those who are less socially minded are welcome to substitute the previous sentence that only then can they achieve their own greatest possible profit in their lives. For, those who do not live in harmony with their life motives and their strengths will often feel a sense of dissatisfaction in both their professional and personal lives. Burnout syndromes, lack of energy, and often unhappiness then become a permanent part of a professional's life. Figure 8.1 shows the correlations.

We already discussed the importance of the principle of ONE Thing in the principle of focus. Your ONE big task is the purpose of your life or your meaning in life. Your ONE (small) task is the priority on the basis of which you act every day. The more productive a person is, the more they are driven by their life purpose and priorities. Who you are and where you are aiming determines what you do and what you achieve? When you know the meaning of your life, you gain clarity more quickly when making decisions. Happiness and contentment set in when you act in accordance with your goals and your life purpose. A sense of life is the most direct path to power and the ultimate source of personal strength, the power of persuasion, and the power of perseverance. A sense of life without clear priorities is powerless. Those who say they don't have time really mean they don't want to do a certain thing. Because ultimately, everything is a matter of priority. And if you don't do certain things, it's only because other things are more important to you. The starting point is your long-term goals, which determine your daily actions. Figure 8.2 goes back to Keller and Papasan and shows the connections

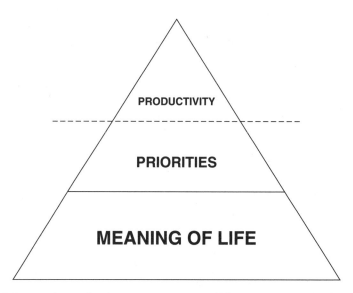

FIGURE 8.1　Relationship between meaning of life, priorities, and productivity

between long-term goals or visions and daily goals based on the principle of ONE Thing.

In the principle of focus, we presented different areas of life in Chapter 3 and asked the question in this context, "what's the ONE Thing I can do such that by doing it everything else will be easier or unnecessary?" Closely related to your different areas of life are your different life roles. Because within the different areas of life, you take on different life roles.

When the term "role" is used, some professionals probably immediately think of the profession of an actor. An actor plays a role in a movie or on a theater stage. Perhaps one or the other of you may feel like an actor in his various roles in life? Then he is indeed playing a role. Accordingly, he is by no means authentic! For me, the concept of life role is about the fact that you take a role in each of the individual areas of life, with which certain tasks and duties are connected. In this case you do not play a role but take responsibly the task or role in this certain area of life.

In the mindmap shown in Figure 8.3, you can see my different life roles that I currently perceive as an example. You can use this as a starting point for defining your own life roles.

I perform my professional roles in my capacity as CEO of several companies. I have deliberately separated the roles between being a corporate

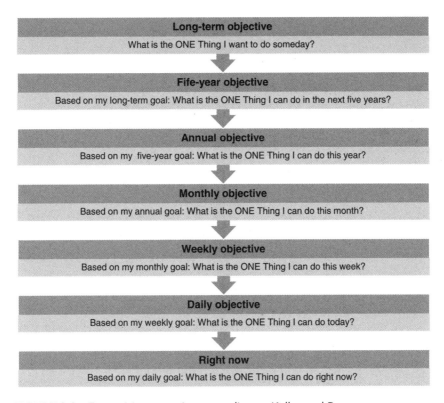

FIGURE 8.2 From vision to action according to Keller and Papasan

person at the companies and being an auditor. As CEO of two auditing companies, I have the role of entrepreneur and manager. As a professional German CPA and CVA, I leave the role of entrepreneur and manager and assume the role of professional who has other duties and responsibilities independent from those of an entrepreneur and manager. My other professional roles are the chairmanship of the board of a professional association for business valuators with currently about 900 members, which I perform on an honorary basis, and the deputy chairmanship of the supervisory board of a service company in the legal form of a joint stock company in the field of telecommunications. In addition, I have been active as a speaker for more than two decades, including 20 years as a lecturer at various universities. I also teach as part of the Certified Valuation Analyst (CVA) training program. Finally,

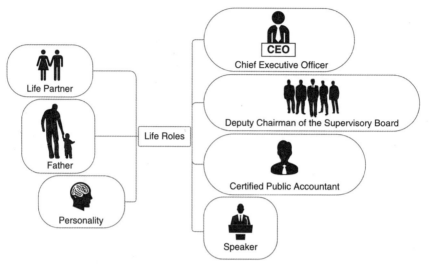

FIGURE 8.3 Life roles

I give keynotes, lectures and seminars on marketing and management of professionals as well as on topics related to business valuation.

My private roles are no less important. I have a life partner and two now grown-up children. Accordingly, I have the role of life partner and father. Furthermore, I have defined my personality as my own role. My personality affects my private life as well as my professional life. I see it as a life task to grow and learn from year to year with regard to my personality. For this reason, I have also written a mission statement on my personality development.

There are certainly professionals who take on more or less life roles. However, if you consciously deal with your different life roles, you will realize at the latest how important it is to always focus on ONE Thing. Depending on the importance that these life roles have for their life, even if you concentrate on the ONE Thing in the different areas of life or life roles, many different things come together quite quickly, which they all have to focus on equally more or less. The moment you focus on the ONE Thing in the various areas of your life – in terms of your goals – you inevitably have to answer an important question for yourself: What should I and do I not want to do in the future? Because by focusing on them, they will inevitably have to give up many other activities.

Many years ago, I formulated so-called mission statements or mini-mission statements for each of my individual life roles. They give me a concrete orientation in everyday life and serve as a valuable tool for setting priorities. These mission statements are formulated in the present tense and describe an ideal state. Since I am "only" a human being and not a machine, I do not always succeed in reconciling the target image of a life role with the actual image of a role. Nevertheless, these individual mission statements serve as a central guideline for my actions and I can easily determine whether or not I am living up to my own expectations and ideas in certain situations. To give you an idea of how you can formulate your own mission statements, here is an example of my mission statement as an auditor.

EXAMPLE

My actions in my profession are directed toward being an exceptionally successful professional who maximizes the benefit of my clients. The goal of my work is always to provide the best possible quality of service to the client. I am a valuation expert and am perceived as such by my clients and the public. The goal of my activities is to achieve the highest possible client satisfaction. I observe the professional principles and standards of my occupation: independence, personal responsibility, neutrality, confidentiality and conscientiousness as well as my professional oath as a German certified public accountant.

Many people absorb information more easily visually than auditorily. This is one reason, among others, why you will find many illustrations in this book. You may be familiar with the saying that "a picture is worth 1,000 words." Already during my studies of business administration at the University of Mannheim, I had my first contact with a method called mindmapping. Mindmaps can be traced back to the British psychologist Tony Buzan, and the first ideas for them were developed by him as early as 1971. It was not until the end of the 90s that software products came on the market that made it easy to create these tools. I have been using them for more than 20 years, both professionally and privately. The life roles shown before are represented as such.

I have summarized both my professional and private goals in writing in various mind maps. It is important to keep the principle of writing in mind. People who put their goals in writing are more successful than other people who don't. Gail Matthew, a professor at Dominican University of California, found in a study that people who put their goals in writing are more successful than others. The people who achieve the highest level of goal attainment are

> **NOTE**
>
> If you want to deal with mindmapping in more detail, you can find numerous hints and examples about it on Google. The fields of application are manifold. For more than 20 years I use software from Mindjet (www.mindmanager.com). For just over a year, I have also been using a collaboration tool in the cloud from Mindmeister (www.mindmeister.de), which is very suitable if you want to share a mind map with other people. Mindmaps ideally connect the right and left hemispheres of people's brains and summarize essential thoughts and information in one picture. For this reason, I use the tool for both my professional and personal goal setting.

those who share their goals with family or friends and share their progress in terms of goal attainment. For the professional environment, this means that a professional should make a commitment to their goals to their partner and manager colleagues. The principle of writing is too rarely followed in goal setting. Only when goals and subgoals are put in writing are they not only in the professional's mind, but they become materially visible.

In addition, the time frame for achieving the goals must be specified. A goal without a time when it should be achieved is like a voyage on a ship where it doesn't matter when the ship arrives. Goals are usually about achieving subgoals or even "milestones" in specific time frames. Goals should be formulated SMART. This means that they should be specific, measurable, action-oriented, realistic and terminable (see Figure 8.4).

Formulate goals as precisely as possible. This means specific. Goals are often unspecific and therefore they are unclear. Incidentally, this is just as true with work instructions to employees. The more precisely you formulate what result you want, the more likely it is that the employee will also implement the task in your sense. With regard to professional and private goals, this means that you must be clear and unambiguous. In most cases, goals will also be measurable. For professionals, numbers are often their lifeblood, so quantifying goals should not need to be explained in detail here. In the German translation of the SMART acronym, the A is often translated as "action-oriented" in German. In the English version, the A stands for either "achievable" or "attainable" and thus means "attainable." Since the principle of action orientation is central to goal achievement, I can accept the variating German translation. This is because the English original of attainability of goals automatically adds a valuation. However, if you consider a goal unattainable, they will discard it

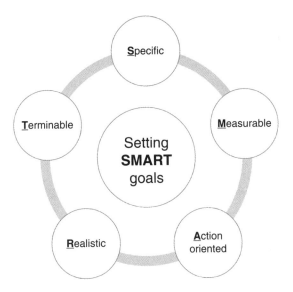

FIGURE 8.4 Setting goals SMARTly

according to the SMART formula. However, since I pointed out earlier that you should set goals that are as big as possible, I like the German term "aktions-orientiert" (action oriented) better. After all, perhaps much more is possible than you yourself consider achievable at the time you set the goal. And against the background of the highest possible intrinsic motivation, goals that are as large as possible are clearly better. The R stands for realistic and, as I understand it, is closely related to the T for terminable. Often goals are unrealistic against the background of when they are to be achieved. For example, a goal can be achievable and realistic, but only if the time frame for achieving the goal has also been set realistically. In this respect, I like to repeat myself. Many professionals overestimate what can be achieved in one year and underestimate what can be achieved in five years. The SMART formula helps you to formulate goals correctly with regard to goal clarity.

 ## CORPORATE GOALS

The previously outlined approach to personal goal setting for professional and private goals can be applied to the corporate goals. There are both quantitative and qualitative goals in a professional services provider. Quantitative goals can be formulated according to the SMART formula. Typical quantitative goals are based on the value drivers of a professional services provider or the "key performance" indicators. Typical key performance indicators and value drivers are, for example:

- Sales revenue and sales growth
- Turnover per employee
- Personnel costs per employee
- Contribution margin per employee
- EBIT and EBITDA (absolute figures)
- EBIT and EBIDTA margins (relative figures as return targets)
- Operating result before partner compensation
- Number of new mandates
- Average revenue per new mandate

A company's size determines the quantitative targets that are well known to professionals. For them, it is obvious to quantify as many targets as possible. After all, anything that can be measured is also easier to monitor in terms of target achievement. For this reason, professionals are often extremely interested in making every goal quantifiable. We also recommend this to our clients. Peter Drucker said, "If You Can't Measure It, You Can't Manage It." This quote has stuck in the minds of many managers and professionals and has been considered an important management principle since the introduction of the Balanced Scorecard.

More than 25 years of professional experience have shown me that there is still a large number of qualitative goals that often cannot be measured at all. For example, I consider it an important goal for a partner and manager to create a work environment that enables their employees to perform exceptionally well. This includes, primarily, the way employees interact with each other. Closely related to this is team spirit. Although the level of turnover in the team or in the company can be a first indication of the quality of the working environment, there are many cases where an intact working environment exists but employees still leave the company for completely varied reasons. So how do you measure the quality of the work environment, or the conditions in which employees are working? It seems to me that quantifying this is much more difficult than expressing a revenue target.

The quality of services provided by a professional should also be at the highest possible level and is often not measurable either. A successfully passed peer review by an external quality control auditor may give an initial indication of the quality of an accountancy practice, but experienced professional col-leagues know the limits of a positive judgment in a peer review. This is because it is quite easy to see that a peer review passed without any deficiencies in an individual case says nothing about the actual quality of a tax consulting ser-vice or a business consulting service. This is because the peer review essentially examines the quality control system or the processes in seal-bearing engage-ments to determine whether they function or not. The recognition by the tax authorities in the context of a tax audit says nothing about the actual qual-ity of a tax consulting service. This is because it does not show whether there might have been a more advantageous arrangement.

These are just two of many examples that show that not all goals can be quantified. Qualitative goals are also important and should also be formulated in writing.

CHAPTER NINE

Planning and Organizing

THE TASK OF PLANNING and organizing is another key task of a professional. In this context, planning and organizing refers to the following levels in a professional services provider:

- Project tasks
- Management tasks

In addition, planning and organizing naturally also relates to a professional's self-management. However, as I understand this to be a tool for a professional because it is about their own management and not about the management of employees, this is not discussed in further detail here, but in Part Three, Tools.

Not every professional has management tasks in a professional services provider. Management tasks are reserved for executives. On the other hand, comparatively young employees have to cope with project management tasks relatively early in their professional life. This applies at least in part to projects. Ultimately, project responsibility lies with the partner or senior manager responsible for the assignment. In any case, far more professionals participate in project management than in the management of a professional services provider, which is why the key task of planning and organizing from a professional project manager's perspective is presented as follows.

Planning is often understood as the mental anticipation of future action. In this sense, the ability to plan a project properly stands for the mental anticipation of the individual project steps. This is the starting point for calculating the time required to conduct the activities. However, this in turn presupposes knowledge about the execution of the individual steps as well as the time required for them. Without practical experience in the execution of many projects in a particular field (for example, execution of audits, business valuations, and so forth), the probability of submitting a bid for the execution of a particular project resulting in a loss order is extremely high.

Thus, the ability to plan is an important task for any professional who is also responsible for job costing. This includes the ability to assemble an appropriately qualified team for the project task. Delegation of individual tasks and proper prioritization are other sub-activities that must be considered during planning. Again, the top priority is to get the planning in writing.

Closely related to planning is organizing. Projects require regular internal and external meetings, the involvement of specialists, the procurement of data and information, the deployment of staff from quality assurance departments, and much more. Effective professionals do not wait to be organized, they do it themselves, for themselves and their tasks and areas of responsibility. Accordingly, in addition to the ability to plan, the ability to organize is part of a professional's job.

Larger projects are best worked on in teams. The prerequisite for the successful completion of such projects is effective and efficient project management. If one follows the semantics of the word project management, the term can be broken down into two parts as Figure 9.1 shows.

According to this, a project is characterized as being a one-time process with a complex structure, predefined goals, a specified completion date and

FIGURE 9.1 Project management

limited costs. The term management in this context means taking responsibility for the planning, coordination, steering and control of the project.

Effective and efficient project management is based on the objectives. For example, in a business valuation project, the essential objective is to determine the value of the company for a specific occasion on a specific date. Business valuation projects are effectively "managed" when the team does the right things. Efficient project management is characterized by the team doing things right. This raises two central issues for effective project management (see Figure 9.2).

The project manager must always be able to answer both questions in every phase of a project. The requirements for effective project management and an effective manager can be deduced directly from the answers to these two questions. In the following, effective project management will also be understood synonymously as successful project management. A critical success factor and thus a minimum requirement for effective project management is the project manager's knowledge of the processes themselves. A professional who has not himself already successfully completed a large number of projects in a particular field (for example, final audits, business valuation projects, and the like) might not necessarily have the knowledge of the processes of these projects. In principle, this applies to all other projects that need to be managed. It is crucial for project success that the professional knows the processes as well as the expected results at the end of the process chain.

If a professional does not know what the results are to look like, they cannot intervene in the project in a controlling manner if problems become apparent on the way to achieving the goals. If, for example, there are problems with information procurement or if, the planning calculation is not plausible in the case of a business valuation, measures must be taken at an early stage to ensure that a high-quality result is achieved at the end. In addition to process knowledge, the professional must also know the activities to be performed.

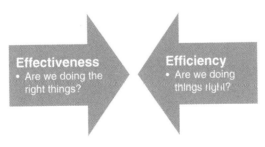

FIGURE 9.2 Effectiveness and efficiency

It makes sense that a professional who does not know what activities are to be performed during the project will, at best, accidentally produce high-quality results. If the person responsible for the project is different from the project manager and the project manager does not have knowledge of the processes and activities to be performed, it is advisable to bring in external professionals in compliance with professional principles.

Closely related to process knowledge and knowledge of the activities to be performed is estimating the time required for the activities as accurately as possible. Certainly, the qualification of the employees in the team plays a decisive role here. Only qualified employees will deliver the expected results within the time budget given to them. Therefore, it is the responsibility of the project manager to correctly assess the skills and abilities of the employees. If the assessment of team members' qualifications is incorrect, the project manager himself may have to be able to intervene in a supportive manner. In turn, he will only be able to do this if he has accomplished a large number of activities himself as part of an assessment project.

In particular, a project manager must have the ability to demonstrate certain activities to team members. For example, someone who has certain ideas about reporting and documenting a project should be able to show that they are capable of performing these activities themselves. Incidentally, a corresponding role model function increases the credibility of the project manager.

In order not to create a false image of effective project management at this point: The project manager does not have to be the best employee. It should be self-evident that there will most likely be members of the team who are more qualified than the project manager in certain areas. It is important that the project manager themselves acknowledges this and does not demonstrate that they are above the team, as it were, on the basis of their function. An essential requirement for effective project management is therefore that the project manager sees themselves as part of the team with a special role assigned to them. So, it is not only the employees who have to be team players, but also the project manager.

The principle of result orientation states that effective project managers should already have the end in mind at the beginning. In an audit, that is the audit report and the audit opinion. In business valuation projects, the end is the documentation of the business valuation result in an expert opinion. Effective project planning is therefore geared not only to ensuring that the audit has been conducted properly and professionally, or that the enterprise value has been determined appropriately, but also to ensuring that the reporting provides conclusions about high-quality work. The project manager must have clarity about the project objectives and results. He is responsible for the quality of the results at the end of the project. Key questions to ask during project planning are:

- What is the goal?
- What should the result look like?
- How do we achieve the goal?
- When must which results be available?
- Who is responsible for what during the project?

Starting with a precisely worded engagement letter that aligns with the client's expectations, the project manager creates a plan about how the assignment will be conducted. A project manager who does not have a clear idea of the activities to be performed during valuation project will only randomly assign the right activities to team members.

With regard to scheduling and deadline coordination, it is important to correctly assess the available human resources. Anyone who incorrectly assesses employees in terms of their performance or does not have or plan for sufficient personnel capacities should not ultimately blame the employees for poor project results. The principle of personal responsibility applies to all team members. This also applies to the project manager.

A central task of the project manager is to ensure that key milestones are clearly defined in terms of time and that the envisaged goals are achieved by these dates. This requires an important characteristic of an effective project manager: They must possess so-called leadership qualities. An essential leadership quality is that the project manager has appropriate control mechanisms.

Another task of the project manager is to ensure that the project goals are achieved at the desired quality level. For this reason, they must identify possible obstacles to achieving the goal at an early stage in order to initiate appropriate countermeasures. To achieve both, he must control. The subject of controls can be the intermediate results or milestones (result control), the process as such (procedure control) as well as the behavior of the team members (behavior control)

However, the decisive question in connection with outstanding leadership quality is the fourth question: How does the project manager control? The basis of control is trust in the other team members. Trust in the performance and in the willingness to perform of a team member. The starting point of any control is self-control. This is in line with the principle of self-responsibility. Employees are responsible for the results they themselves have caused. The project manager is responsible for the success of the project as a whole. A good project manager sees their task and role in a coaching function.

An effective and efficient project manager gets the right things done right et vice versa. They already have the end in mind at the beginning and are thus, highly characterized by the principle of result orientation. They have a clear idea of what the results should look like at the end of the project. In the case of financial statement audits, this is the audit report, and in the case of business valuation projects, it is the expert opinion. Without precise knowledge of the activities to be performed and the processes during the project, effective project management is not possible. Only then can he intervene in a supportive manner during the project if there is a risk of failure. In cases where the person responsible for the project is not identical with the project manager, it must be ensured that the project manager has the expertise required to manage the project. A project manager who has not himself already conducted significant activities in the context of company evaluations will in the rarest of cases be able to successfully manage an audit or any other project. Failure is preprogrammed here.

CHAPTER TEN

Decision Making

A N IMPORTANT TASK OF professionals is decision-making, and all professionals make a large number of decisions every day. This applies to both their professional and private lives. Professionals with employee responsibilities also make decisions that are relevant for the team or the entire company. Malik reduces the task of decision-making to managers. He claims that this shows the difference between a manager and a clerk. A person who does not decide is not a manager. In decisions, everything comes together, everything comes to a point. Deciding is not the only manager's task, but it is a critical one. Certainly, decisions in the management of employees have a greater significance than decisions made by a professional in the context of their factual tasks without direct reference to employees. However, since every professional, regardless of whether they are a manager or not, makes a large number of decisions every day, it would be too short-sighted to view the topic of "decision-making" exclusively from the perspective of a manager.

In many cases, professionals make decisions too quickly. This is especially true when they think it is clear what has to be decided. In many cases, however, it is not clear from the outset what has to be decided, but it has to be found out first. The greatest possible sense of reality on the part of a professional helps here, because often facts are either made worse than they are or presented better than they actually are.

Effective professionals make few decisions, but they make them carefully and deliberately. They know that decisions are associated with risks and that they will have consequences – both desired and undesired. Correcting decision errors often costs a professional much more work, energy, and time than would have been necessary if the decisions had been made carefully in advance. Every decision involves risk. Many professionals think that when they make quick and spontaneous decisions, they can justify this with their intuition. The problem with intuitions is that a professional does not know from the beginning which intuitions are correct and which may turn out to be wrong in retrospect.

Gerd Gigerenzer is director emeritus of the Harding Center for Risk Competence at the Max Planck Institute for Human Development in Berlin and has been involved in research in the field of decision making for many decades. He has written a large number of publications on this subject. His books "Risk Savvy: How to Make Good Decisions" as well as "Gut Feelings The Intelligence of the Unconscious" are bestsellers and well worth reading. Central thoughts from these two books follow.

At their core is the question of what role the mind or gut feeling (intuition) plays in decision-making. Intelligence is often described as a superior and conscious activity governed by the laws of logic. But much of our life takes place unconsciously, as already shown, and is based on processes that also have nothing to do with logic. Gigerenzer defines intuition as felt knowledge,

■ which quickly appears in our consciousness,
■ whose deeper reasons we are not aware of, and
■ which is strong enough to act upon.

Intuitions, in his view, consist of two elements:

1. simple rules of thumb, which
2. make use of evolved capabilities of the brain.

He uses the colloquial term "rules of thumb" synonymously with the scientific term heuristics. A rule of thumb tries to pick out the most valuable information and disregards the rest. In the context of intuitions, he has identified three fallacies:

1. Intuition is second-rate, conscious deliberation always better.
2. Complex problems always require complex solutions.
3. More information, calculation, and time are always better.

Gut feelings are often based on surprisingly little information. That's why they seem so untrustworthy to the superego. Most people have internalized that more is always better. But experiments have shown that less time and less information can lead to better decisions. Less is more, as he understands it, means that there is a certain range of information, time, or alternatives where smaller amounts are more beneficial. However, it does not follow that less is more in every case. "Less is more" contradicts two central beliefs of our culture:

1. More information is always better.
2. More choice is always better.

Less is more only when the following conditions are met:

▪ *Useful Level of Ignorance:* recognition heuristics show that gut feelings can outperform a considerable amount of knowledge and information.
▪ *Unconscious Motor Skills:* Gut feelings of experienced experts are based on unconscious skills whose execution can be impaired by too much thinking.
▪ *Cognitive Limitations:* Our brains protect us from the danger of processing too much information by having innate mechanisms, such as forgetting and the tendency to start small. Without cognitive constraints, we would behave far less intelligently.
▪ *Paradox of Free Choice:* The more options one has, the greater the possibility of conflict, and the more difficult it is to compare options. From a certain point, more options, products, and choices hurt.
▪ *Benefits of Simplicity:* In an uncertain world, simple rules of thumb can predict complex phenomena as well or better than complex rules.

Gigerenzer currently sees a risk-incompetent society. He calls for risk intelligence as a basic prerequisite for finding one's way in a modern technological society. By risk competence, he means more than risk intelligence. For him, risk competence means the ability to deal with situations in which not all risks can be known and calculated. Making good decisions, he believes, requires two distinctions:

▪ When risks are known, good decisions require logical and statistical thinking.
▪ When some risks are unknown, good decisions also require intuition and wise rules of thumb.

When making decisions under uncertainty, he recommends the following four rules, which can also be applied to professional services provider:

1. To make good decisions in an uncertain world, one must ignore information and use rules of thumb.
2. Implement positive error culture in professional services provider for management decisions: If the courage to decide or plan is lacking because you may be held responsible for a mistake, you have a negative error culture in the management of the company. Not deciding or planning in order to avoid responsibility is defensive decision making.
3. Robust instead of "optimal" solutions.
4. Good intuition cannot be replaced by "Big Data."

In any project, a professional has to make a variety of decisions. These include:

▪ Judgment about contract risk and bidding
▪ Calculating the time required (and the average hourly rate)
▪ Job planning and the selection and deployment of staff
▪ Determining the activities during the execution of the assignment
▪ Delegation of individual sub-activities to employees and identification of the essential tasks to be performed by the employees themselves
▪ Method of communication of the project results
▪ Scope and content of reporting against the background of the respective group of recipients.

Accordingly, decisions on factual tasks and management tasks have to be made permanently during the entire project. The extent to which these decisions are right or wrong is shown in retrospect by the reactions of the customers. In Part I, Chapter 5, the method of mindstorming is presented, which is also very well suited for decision preparation. In this method, each task or problem is formulated as a question and at least 20 answers to the question are to be found. Effective leaders then demonstrate accountability for implementing their decisions. They make sure that the essential things are actually done. Professionals with many years of professional experience know that intuition plays a significant role. This also includes many years of experience in a specific field of activity.

EXAMPLE

Auditors with many years of professional experience in the field of auditing routinely have good intuition when selecting samples. I still remember my time as an audit assistant at a Big Four accounting firm. A more experienced colleague had selected exactly those cases in his samples that were objectionable. As a young audit assistant, I could not explain at the time why he had often selected from a large number of documents precisely those that led to audit findings. Today, I know that this was related to his many years of professional experience and good intuition.

A key insight for me from Gerd Gigerenzer's two books was that good decisions are based both on intuition and on consciously weighing information through analysis and reason. For many years, I have made it a habit that before I make decisions, I analyze whether I have considered all the options or alternatives that are available. Successful professionals always assume that there are more alternatives than the ones they know about. Furthermore, many professionals are not aware that not deciding is also a decision. The principle of personal responsibility implies that a professional can decide for something, against something, or not at all. In any case, they bear the responsibility for their decision.

Successful and effective professionals make realization part of the decision-making process itself. Their idea of a good decision does not end with the decision making, but it also includes the realization phase. Often, while the decision per se is difficult, its realization in many cases is much more difficult. And even the best decision can become wrong in the implementation phase and through the way it is implemented. It can be misunderstood, distorted, and sabotaged by colleagues. Successful professionals therefore always think ahead to the later realization at every single step of a decision process. They think through in advance which people in the professional services provider will be confronted with the decision in the implementation phase. Furthermore, they anticipate what their colleagues need to know so they can understand the decision and then implement it correctly. Therefore, it makes sense to a high degree that you also involve the colleagues in the process of decision making. Not only is it motivating for colleagues and employees to already be involved in decision making, it is a necessity to ensure that implementation will be as effective as possible.

Many professionals believe that it is important to have as much consensus as possible within the professional services provider when making decisions. This has to do with the fact that many professionals believe that this would give them a greater chance of realization when implementing decisions. Especially since many professionals have a pronounced desire for harmony. However, Malik correctly points out that it is not consensus that is really important, but dissent. Truly sustainable consensus, namely the consensus that really holds when implementation difficulties arise, does not result from a general striving for harmony, but only from a well-founded dissent. And this dissent should always be openly expressed! Successful professionals therefore tend to be uncomfortable when a quick consensus is reached on decisions. And especially among professionals there are often many different opinions on certain topics. However, if dissent is not openly expressed until the implementation phase, it is usually too late. It therefore makes sense to present provocative arguments more often during the decision-making process in order to encourage dissent.

Malik recommends the following approach for good decisions:

1. Precise definition of the issue or problem
2. Specification of the requirements that the decision must fulfill
3. Elaboration of all alternatives
4. Analyze the risks and consequences for each alternative
5. Decision itself
6. Realization in the decision
7. Establishment of feedback: follow-up and follow-through

The **first step** in any decision-making process is a thorough and complete determination of the facts or the real problem. If the facts have not been accurately determined or if there is an incorrect understanding of the problem, decisions cannot really be made well. This requires overcoming limitations in thinking and implementing a thinking-out-of-the-box philosophy. This raises the question of whether decisions are being made about an individual case or whether a problem of principle exists. Because problems of principle require decisions of principle.

The **second step** is to work out as precisely as possible what requirements the decision must meet. The crucial question is: What would be right? Closely related to this is the handling of compromises. First, however, it should be thought through what would be right and what would really solve the problem. What would be right in this situation for the professional services provider? Few things distinguish good from bad and competent from incompetent professionals as much as the ability to separate important tradeoffs from the wrong ones. The key is to determine an ideal situation accurately and conscientiously.

The **third step** in the decision-making process is the search for alternatives. Here, according to Malik, two mistakes are made. First, professionals settle for the first few alternatives that are found. Effective professionals, however, know that there are always more alternatives, and they force themselves and their employees not to immediately settle for the first few alternatives. The second mistake is to exclude the status quo as an alternative. However, sticking to the status quo is also an alternative. Sometimes sticking to the status quo is a better alternative than doing something different or new. However, there are professionals who allow their environment to pressure them into making decisions and changes. Sometimes new alternatives look like they will eliminate difficulties. However, this is not always the case. The term "aggravation" expresses this.

The **fourth step** is to analyze the consequences and risks associated with each alternative, and beforehand each alternative should be thoroughly and carefully thought through. In particular, it is important to consider whether or not the decision is reversible. Since in many decisions it is often de facto impossible to really consider everything, this is where the intuition outlined earlier comes into play. Many decisions are based on future assumptions. These assumptions can be right or wrong. Therefore, it is necessary to determine when circumstances occur that a professional is willing to accept as a mistake. If this is not clear in advance, a professional will miss the moment to make possible course corrections.

When a professional has carefully and conscientiously taken the first four steps, they can decide. The decision is the **fifth step**. At this point, further analysis, and consideration of the previously examined points is no longer useful. Some professionals do not dare to decide. This is a sign of their own indecisiveness. Especially if the decision is a management decision, this is an indication that a professional is not yet suitable as a manager. So, if you have gone through all the steps presented before, have intensively dealt with a problem, and have analyzed all the available information, intuition comes into play when deciding. If your inner voice clearly says that something is not right here, even after you have thoroughly dealt with a decision, then you should take every opportunity and start all over again. This is not always possible, but in many cases it is. Nor should this be a welcome opportunity to use the excuse for your lack of resolve. As previously illustrated, good intuition is based on a considerable degree of experiential knowledge. If your inner voice advises you not to do something, then listen to your inner voice! So, if you have analyzed everything and a further examination of the matter would not bring any additional information, then intuition is often more helpful and reliable than if you follow the first spontaneous intuition.

The **sixth step** is the realization of the decision. Steps six and seven are the crucial part of the decision-making process. Experienced professionals know that it is often difficult to decide in the first place, but realizing it is even more difficult. Successful professionals are therefore strong in implementation. In realizing the decision, the critical success factors must be determined and put in writing. In addition, the responsible persons who are to implement the decision must be determined, and deadlines must be set for when each milestone is to be realized. Decisions are realized by the deadline-related execution of measures by the respective professionals or employees of the professional services provider. Without these measures, one has no decision. One merely has good intentions. In connection with the determination of the individual measures, the following questions must be answered:

■ Who must be involved in the realization?
■ Who must be informed about the decision by when at the latest and in what way?
■ Who needs what information, what tools, and what training to understand the decision, its realization, its consequences, and to actively contribute to its realization?
■ How should the realization of the decision be monitored and controlled?
■ What should the reporting on the decision look like?

Successful professionals establish clear and unambiguous responsibilities. This means that the name of the person responsible for the action should be written after each individual activity. To what extent the respective person then needs other colleagues to implement the measure is another matter. This measure is in line with the principle of self-responsibility. In this context, it is important to consider what this person must know and be able to do and what competencies they need in order to actually be able to take on the responsibility. The right timing and good planning are essential elements of any decision. It is a wise decision to set tight deadlines. The reason is simple: you can extend a deadline, but you cannot shorten a deadline. A professional who extends tight appointments will be welcome in any professional services provider. However, a professional who shortens appointments often creates stress and chaos in the firm. So, the sixth step is an action program: what, who, by when?

The **seventh step** is to establish feedback. Successful professionals get permanent reports on the realization progress and difficulties as well as on the results. In particular, they monitor themselves on how the realization is progressing. They operate a consistent "follow-through" until the job is done. They keep themselves informed about the status of the project. In addition, they make results and successes visible. Because they know that one of the greatest motivators is visible success. Effective professionals talk to their employees themselves. They want to see things with their own eyes and, as far as possible, grasp them with their hands. This gives them expertise at every stage of implementation.

TIP

In a professional services provider, there are colleagues on various levels. These can be partners, but also professionals and other colleagues. The question therefore arises as to who should be involved in which decisions. There are certainly clear and unambiguous rules in every practice, depending on the scope of the choices. Strategic and investment decisions above a certain level are made by the shareholders or partners. However, there is a multitude of other management and factual areas within and outside the respective order processing, which are the responsibility of a professional. Ultimately, a professional who is able to choose for themselves is responsible for every choice they make, in accordance with the principle of self-responsibility. Nevertheless, it would be negligent if colleagues were not involved in all discussions at an early stage. This is particularly true if the colleagues are to implement the decisions. In this respect, I have a long-established practice to involve my colleagues in all the important decisions. Simple questions help:

- ▪ How do you see it?
- ▪ What do you think?
- ▪ Are there other points that are relevant?

The point here is not that you shift to your employees the answers to the questions. That would be a sign of leadership weakness. It's about drawing on the expertise of your employees as part of the decision-making process and gaining valuable information that you may not have considered.

CHAPTER ELEVEN

Developing and Promoting People

A PROFESSIONAL SERVICES PROVIDER'S SUCCESS depends crucially on the qualifications of its employees. This applies to both professional qualifications and personal qualifications. Closely related to the personal qualification is the social competence of an employee as well as his soft skills. An essential and important task of a successful professional is therefore the professional and personal development and promotion of his employees. Anyone who wants to develop and promote other people should have two prerequisites:

1. He should have the willingness to develop himself professionally and personally.
2. He should be a positive role model.

A professional who believes that he has reached the zenith of his professional and personal qualifications after passing the exam to become a certified public accountant or lawyer has poor prerequisites for developing and promoting other people. Far predominantly they are not suitable for it. Because with the passed professional examinations a professional is only at the beginning of their professional career. This is true even if they already have many years of professional experience before passing the professional exams. Rather, the readiness for lifelong learning is inherent to professionals.

If you want to develop professionals, you have to demand something from them. Professionals develop with and through their tasks. For me, the principle is to encourage and challenge employees, but not to overtax them. Employees want to be encouraged and challenged according to their performance. And since this performance is very individual, there can be no uniform approach to employee development. This starts with the fact that employees absorb and process information in completely different ways. Some employees learn best by reading. Others learn best by listening. Other professionals learn best by doing.

The major accounting firms all have internal training programs. Employees go through a variety of training as part of their various career stages. Exceptional employees achieve exceptional performance. Since professionals go through various learning phases in their careers and advancement and development only occur by being assigned the right tasks at the right time, it is important to develop and promote people in a targeted manner according to their strengths profile. However, this requires knowledge of an employee's strengths profile, and often, employees' strengths are not known. Instead, internal training programs are run that have no relation to an employee's strengths profile. In the early years of an employee's career, this approach is often justified by the fact that internal training is basic knowledge that is assumed of every employee regardless of their individual strengths. However, the result may be exclusively technical knowledge. This is because only technical qualifications in specific areas can be passed on to each employee in a standardized manner. This ensures that every employee has a certain basic technical qualification. Of course, this only applies as long as the employee actually acquires the knowledge in the internal training courses. Often, there are no tests after the technical training courses to check whether the specialist knowledge has actually been acquired; only applied knowledge is actually acquired knowledge.

The starting point for employee development are the principles of successful professionals outlined in Part One. These principles form the basis for the personal development of employees. A professional who is responsible for employees should exemplify these principles in their day-to-day work. As a positive role model, they have the opportunity to ensure that their employees internalize these principles in their actions.

The principle of using strengths is of particular importance in employee development. A professional's existing strengths must be further developed – both

> **NOTE**
>
> A large auditing firm (Big Four) decided years ago that the majority of its training courses in the field of business valuation should no longer be conducted internally, but that all its junior employees should be sent to EACVA as part of an external training program. At the end of their training week, they have to pass a two-part exam to become a Certified Valuation Analyst (CVA). The first part of the exam consists of a multiple-choice test lasting five hours. If part I is passed, the participant has to work on a practical business valuation case in part II. For this, they have to perform a business valuation of a stock-listed company according to different methods and have to submit their results in a written valuation report. This approach has several advantages for the Big Four company:
>
> - Employees not only learn theoretical knowledge during the CVA training week, but they also have to prove to their employer in a two-part exam that they can apply the knowledge.
> - The internationally recognized CVA qualification certificate documents the employee's qualifications to clients and competitors.
> - The employee has also acquired a qualification certificate and title in a professional services provider, where titles and professional examination are an important qualification criterion.
> - The external costs are not significantly higher than the internal costs since, if the professionals cannot generate revenue, the largest cost item is the loss of revenue for the professional services provider anyway.
> - Since many employees of potential new clients are also present during a CVA training week, there is a considerable chance of making valuable contacts during the CVA training week.

the strengths that have already been identified or recognized and the strengths that can be suspected on the basis of certain indications. Employee development must therefore be strength oriented. Many employee development systems, on the other hand, are weakness-oriented and aim to reduce or eliminate weaknesses. However, professionals will never be successful in an area where they have weaknesses. They will usually not be successful in that area even if they have eliminated the weaknesses. Professionals will only be successful in those areas where they can do something. So, they have their strengths, and success will come much faster there and will be more visible. A professional with management responsibility should therefore recognize the strengths of his employees and use them where they can play to their strengths and develop them further. This raises the question of how professionals with leadership responsibility recognize the strengths of their employees.

Two cases need to be distinguished here:

1. New hires
2. Existing employees

 ## AD 1: NEW HIRES

Employee development and advancement already begins when employees are hired. Since at this point only recruitment interviews have been held and/or tests and possibly assessment centers have been conducted, the strengths of most new employees can only be assumed. There are two tests that can at least give you valuable clues about an employee's potential strengths and important insights with regard to managing employees:

1. Profile XT Test
2. DISC Personality Test

An internationally recognized test is the Profile XT. It helps to get to know strengths and to become more aware of one's own development areas and those of the employees. Profile XT is the joint result of developmental psychologists from PROFILES International and scientists from the University of Texas. With more than 400,000 job applicants and job holders participating in its development, the tool illustrates a representative cross-section of occupational and income groups, education levels, companies, and industries. "Profile XT is one of the most technologically advanced, three-dimensional online leadership tools. It can be performed from any computer connected to the internet, with online processing available worldwide in over 30 languages. There are various providers that can be easily found through Google.

The goal of "Profile XT" is to achieve the optimal "job match." For this purpose, the success-relevant characteristics of a person (e.g., behavioral traits, professional interests, thought patterns) are compared with the requirements of their job and checked for their accuracy of fit. As a result of its prominent level of scientific validation, the procedure is now used worldwide in all industries and professions. The system comprises:

Requirement profile	⇒	WHAT are the requirements of the job?
Thought patterns	⇒	CAN the person do the job?
Behavioral characteristics	⇒	HOW will the person do the job?
Job interests	⇒	WILL the person do the job?
Job match	⇒	DO the person and the job match?

The areas of application go beyond personnel selection for new hires:

▪ Potential analyses
▪ Coachings
▪ Trainings
▪ Promotions

The requirement profile is just as important as the personal profile. Because only if you know exactly which employee you need, you will know when you have found them.

The Profile XT Test and the DISC Personality Test are not exclusively designed for new hires, but also provide valuable information about professionals who have been with your company for some time. The DISC Personality Test leads to a specific personality profile. The personality of a professional is reflected in how they behave in certain situations. Successful professionals know their behavioral tendencies. They learn to adapt their own style so that they can act more effectively in a wider range of situations. The DISC Personality Profile helps you improve your self-knowledge and develop greater adaptability to other people.

All of a person's traits make up their personality. Parts of these characteristics are visible while other parts are not immediately visible. What is visible to us is behavior. Other characteristics, such as unexpressed thoughts or feelings, remain invisible. In DISC, what is of interest is what is visible from the outside, namely people's behavior. DISC is therefore even more a behavioral profile than a personality profile. Every professional should question their own behavior. Those who do not learn to adapt their behavior to their professional (and private) environment will soon feel like a foreign body. Those who never question their behavior will in all likelihood have a hard time. This applies to both the professional and private environment.

DISC is an acronym for D as in Dominance, I as in Influence, S as in Steadiness, and C as in Conscientiousness. It originated with William Moulton Marston, an American psychologist who graduated from Harvard in 1921. The four original terms Dominance, Inducement, Submission, and Compliance were then further developed by John G. Geier at the University of Minnesota into the DISC model recognized today.

The aim of the DISC model is to name certain personality types, to make their core characteristics clear and, based on this, to recognize their "typical" communication behavior. Once a professional has identified the communication behavior of an employee, they can specifically adjust their own communication behavior to the employee. The same applies to professionals vis-à-vis their superiors. The following illustration shows the four different personality types and their central characteristics for identifying a type. Each type is assigned a color (see Figure 11.1):

- Dominance = red
- Influence = yellow
- Steadiness = green
- Conscientiousness = blue

The personality model based on D, I, S, and C describes the behavior of a professional, which is always a combination of all four behavioral tendencies. The behaviors that are more intensely present, you use more often. There is no such thing as the "best" profile. All behavioral styles can be more or less effective. Each professional also often has behaviors of different behavioral styles. Lothar Seiwert and Friedbert Gay in their book "Das 1x1 der Persönlichkeit" have several good and short tests to determine your individual personality profile and your expressions of D, I, S, and C. One behavioral tendency will be more pronounced than all other behavioral tendencies. Professionals are most effective when they can understand their own behavior and the behavioral style of others, assess the requirements of the situation at hand, and adjust their behavior accordingly.

The success or failure of professional services teams is determined by the personal behavioral style of each member and the interactions between individual team members. In order to reduce friction among each other, it is necessary to understand, respect, and appreciate the individual differences within the team. Those who wish to study the DISC personality model and its application in practice more extensively will find valuable information in "The 1x1 of Personality." Figure 11.2, which is only excerpted here, is taken from the book and shows how the DISC personality profile can be used in teams.

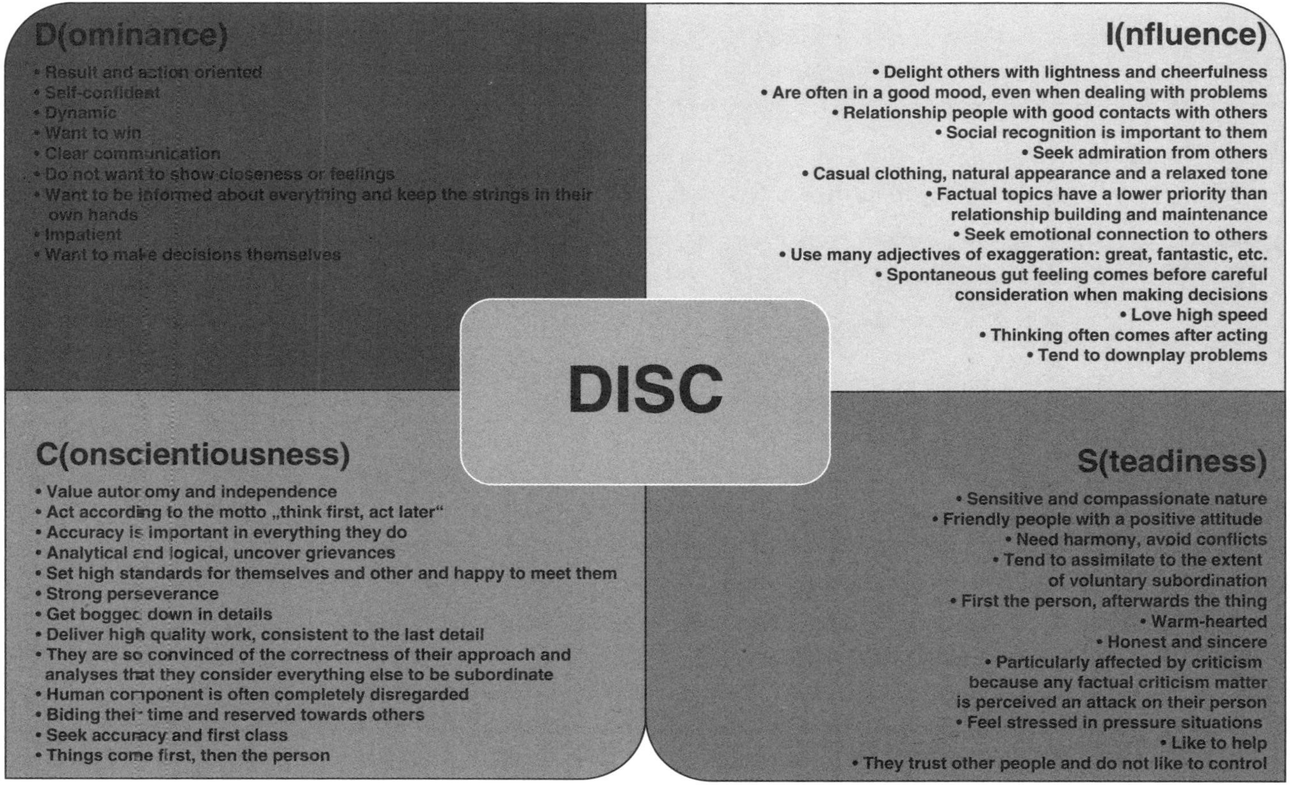

D(ominance)

- Result and action oriented
- Self-confident
- Dynamic
- Want to win
- Clear communication
- Do not want to show closeness or feelings
- Want to be informed about everything and keep the strings in their own hands
- Impatient
- Want to make decisions themselves

I(nfluence)

- Delight others with lightness and cheerfulness
- Are often in a good mood, even when dealing with problems
- Relationship people with good contacts with others
  - Social recognition is important to them
    - Seek admiration from others
- Casual clothing, natural appearance and a relaxed tone
  - Factual topics have a lower priority than relationship building and maintenance
    - Seek emotional connection to others
- Use many adjectives of exaggeration: great, fantastic, etc.
  - Spontaneous gut feeling comes before careful consideration when making decisions
    - Love high speed
    - Thinking often comes after acting
      - Tend to downplay problems

C(onscientiousness)

- Value autonomy and independence
- Act according to the motto „think first, act later"
- Accuracy is important in everything they do
- Analytical and logical, uncover grievances
- Set high standards for themselves and other and happy to meet them
- Strong perseverance
- Get bogged down in details
- Deliver high quality work, consistent to the last detail
- They are so convinced of the correctness of their approach and analyses that they consider everything else to be subordinate
- Human component is often completely disregarded
- Biding their time and reserved towards others
- Seek accuracy and first class
- Things come first, then the person

S(teadiness)

- Sensitive and compassionate nature
- Friendly people with a positive attitude
  - Need harmony, avoid conflicts
    - Tend to assimilate to the extent of voluntary subordination
- First the person, afterwards the thing
  - Warm-hearted
    - Honest and sincere
- Particularly affected by criticism because any factual criticism matter is perceived an attack on their person
  - Feel stressed in pressure situations
    - Like to help
- They trust other people and do not like to control

DISC

FIGURE 11.1 Characteristics of people according to the DISC personality model

Teamwork	D	I	S	C
Value for the team	Directional, takes the initiative, booster	Makes contact with people, influences others	Works continuously, specialized work, creates relationships	Focuses on details, pays attention to standards
Strengths	Goal and result oriented, persevering, solves problems quickly	Enthusiasm, motivates and wins over others, advocates	Gets along well with others, good team member	Thorough, persistent, analyzes all data with precision
Possible weaknesses	Insensitive to feelings of others, impatient, authoritarian	Impulsive, does not like to focus on facts and details	Sacrifices results for harmonious relationships, reluctant to take initiative	Very careful, overly thorough, forgets deadlines
Motivated by	Results, challenges, deeds, actions	Recognition, approval, applause, need to be seen	Relationships, recognition, understanding, appreciation	Quality consciousness, confirmation of being able to do things "right"
Potentially more effective by	Listening	Giving themselves a pause for reflection and including data	Taking the initiative, responding positively to changes	Communicating own ideas to others

FIGURE 11.2 How teamwork succeeds according to Lothar Seiwert and Friedbert Gay from "The 1x1 of Personality." (© 1996–2022 persolog Management GmbH, D-75196 Remchingen. All contents protected by copyright. All rights reserved).

It is obvious that C-types will often be found among professionals and that there are many conscientious people in a professional services provider.

TIP

Use your DISC personality profile knowledge when hiring employees and during the probationary period. Several years ago, I hired a young assistant who was absolutely unsuitable for the job as an auditor and tax consultant. For professionals, accuracy is important in everything they do. The goal should always be to work coherently down to the last detail. If you don't want to work accurately, you are not in the right place in an auditing firm. I had a conversation with them towards the end of the probationary period and was able to use the DISC model very well to justify to them why I had strongly advised that they work in another industry.

The DISC model is also well suited for analyzing existing employees. Those who have weak expressions in the area of dominance and initiative have a tough time with employee management. Some professionals do better as experts without personnel responsibility.

 ## AD 2: ALREADY EXISTING EMPLOYEES

For already existing employees, the Profile XT test and the DISC Personality Test can also be performed. However, a much better and reliable assessment are the tasks, performances, and results the professional has achieved so far. An experienced manager should usually be able to tell after three to five assigned tasks whether or not the employee is suitable for a particular job. Therefore, when working with a new employee, I can tell within the first few weeks of the probationary period whether or not there is potential for a professional in the field of business valuation.

Effective professionals multiply their professional expertise in the field of personal development. Knowledge sharing should be a maxim of every professional. Those who hoard knowledge know that they may be able to perform exceptionally well on their own, but exceptional performance by a team is prevented. Those who know this will work to develop and promote their employees.

Although people can ultimately only develop themselves, and virtually all skilled professionals were self-developers, most of them had role models and mentors who encouraged them and provided impulses for further development. It cannot be emphasized often enough that people develop with and on their tasks. Therefore, the tasks should not overwhelm the employees, but should be challenging enough so that the employees will grow with them. Accordingly, they must be larger and more difficult than the previous tasks.

An integral part of developing people is providing feedback, which they should receive as directly as possible in connection with the completion of tasks. Most managers and entrepreneurs are usually sparing with praise and generous with criticism. Too seldom is it considered that the employee does not need to be told what they have done wrong. As a rule, they are usually aware of this after a misstep. Feedback is much more important in terms of how they can do better in the future. This is a real contribution to the development of people.

TIP

Integral to any quality assurance system in an accounting practice are annual employee performance appraisals. This institutionalized feedback is also important for employees in the first three years of their career. During this time, an employee has many opportunities to demonstrate their professional and personal competence. Their strengths should be known at this time and the employee's further development should be based on them.

Regardless of the length of time an employee has been with the company, I believe that immediate feedback is much more important in certain situations than institutionalized, standardized appraisal interviews at a later date. My employees receive feedback immediately after conference calls, meetings, or after completing specific tasks. It is not uncommon for me to call an employee after a conference call and express my appreciation if they were able to convey complex issues to a client in easy-to-understand language.

This applies equally to completed tasks. If something was done poorly, especially in light of an employee's professional experience, I also tell an employee this directly. For most observers, this address would then be too direct and not a few would claim that the manner of communication could be demotivating.

My point of view is: If something is rubbish, it is legitimate to say so. To wrap this up in flowery, pretty words makes little sense, because it would not be authentic for me. Of course, in all of these feedback discussions, the employee must be respected and given support for their professional and personal development directly in the feedback. You can only learn from mistakes if you know how to do things correctly. I consider this immediate positive and negative feedback to be much more effective than an appraisal interview conducted at a much later point in time.

CHAPTER TWELVE

Control

THE LAST TASK IS controlling. Talking to an auditor about control is like carrying water into the sea. Control is the DNA of an auditor. However, I am not concerned in this chapter with controls in the context of an audit or with the four-eyes principle in the context of carrying out the professional activities of an auditor or tax advisor. I am concerned here with the task of control in the context of the management of the employees of an auditing practice. This also includes all employees who do not work within the scope of auditing, legal, or management consulting.

Many will now spontaneously think of quality control and peer review. Perhaps some people will skip this chapter because they no longer want to deal with quality control issues, since they do this all the time in the course of their professional activities anyway. Much of this is written in the quality control manuals of an auditing practice, and it makes no sense to write about the quality controls that are subject to peer review in a book on soft skills for professionals. However, only certain activities of auditors are subject to peer review quality control. Lawyers, M&A advisors, and management consultants, on the other hand, are not subject to peer review. To that extent, there are professionals who are less deeply versed in the subject of quality control and quality control manuals. In any case, professionals are more or less intensely familiar with the topic of control, which is why I write more about the "how" of possible controls than the "what" in this chapter.

If you want quality, you have to control! Quality assurance systems and quality controls are for this reason in the absolute best interest of every professional services provider. If a professional is interested in quality in the management of employees, they cannot see the topic of control only from the perspective of their professional activity but must apply it to all other areas in the management of a professional services provider.

However, the basis of control should be trust towards the employees. Trust in the performance and in the employee's willingness to perform. If a professional cannot trust in the performance and willingness to perform of an employee, then they do not have a control problem, but a problem in filling the position. Besides, nothing can be accomplished anyway if an employee is not capable or willing to perform.

Therefore, the crucial question is, "How should a quality assurance and control system be structured?" It should definitely contain elements of self-control. This is why the principles of "self-responsibility" and "results orientation" outlined in Part One are so important. Employees are responsible for the results they themselves have caused. Without clarity of purpose and a mutual understanding of guidelines accepted by all, as well as structures and systems that support these processes, quality control based on the principle of self-responsibility will not work.

This approach has implications for the controlling professional. In fact, their role shifts from "big boss" to coach. The following questions to their employees will help them to continue to live up to their new role:

■ How are things going?
■ What are you learning right now?
■ What are your goals or what are you trying to accomplish right now?
■ How can I help you?
■ How good am I as a helper?

Without mutual trust and accountability, such a system will not work. Use the following questions for guidance:

■ Why is it being controlled?
■ What is being controlled?
■ Who is being controlled?
■ How is it controlled?

There are two important tasks of controls:

■ Quality assurance measure
■ Identification of obstacles on the way to the goal

All measures for quality assurance within the scope of order processing are not discussed further here. The IDW as well as the AICPA have published a large number of standards and literature on this subject, which deal with the topic extensively. With regard to the identification of obstacles on the way to the goals, however, it is important to continuously monitor the employees by means of questions and visual inspections.

NOTE

Many professionals control their employees with regard to their recorded times on orders. Depending on a professional's level of control awareness, this can be daily, weekly, or monthly. For many years, I have trusted my employees to work effectively and efficiently. However, this trust requires a certain level of experience on the part of a professional. An entry-level employee cannot yet work effectively and efficiently per se but must first learn to do so. Therefore, you cannot proceed as described below in the case of young professionals.

My actual control of the rendered times takes place only in the context of invoicing and accounting of orders. In the meantime, I have been working as an entrepreneur for about 20 years and, with a few exceptions, I have not had any problems with the billing of the times of my employees. If I considered that the times for certain activities were too extensive, after consulting with the employees, I either did not charge for them or charged them at reduced hourly rates. In this context, it is important to talk to the employee concerned. I then asked for the reasons for the additional time required. If I could understand the reasons, and if the time was also spent by other professionals with comparable professional experience, I charged them. It is also important in this context that the respective controlling professional has sufficient experience for the time required for certain activities. This is only the case if they performed many of the activities to be controlled themselves once in the course of their professional career. So, in essence, I am advocating self-responsibility and self-control for my employees.

I often ask my employees whether they would be willing to pay the fee for the time they have spent working instead of the client. Then I first have the employees themselves propose how much of the hours they provided they would bill the client for. In most cases, the staff has a particularly good feel for what can be billed in such cases. In the end, however, as the responsible partner, I decide how much to charge for the hours. I always have a market price in mind for the service in question. This procedure leads to the fact that the employees are sensitive with regard to the services rendered by you and when recording their times, they already think about the invoicing to the client.

What is controlled and how says a lot about a professional services provider. The control of persons should be as individual as possible. There is a difference if and how a professional services provider controls a long-serving employee who has always worked reliably and conscientiously, or new employees who have yet to prove themselves. There are professionals who are prime examples of correctness and reliability. If you start to control such employees all of a sudden, this is not only a withdrawal of trust for them, but also demotivating to a high degree. On the other hand, it would be negligent if you did not control the work of an employee who is still in the probationary period so intensively that you can dismiss them again in the event of poor work results while they are still in the probationary period.

Since every control serves the purpose of quality assurance and errors are to be avoided, the control in a professional services provider is closely related to how the company wants to deal with "errors" of employees. The error culture and how employees deal with errors says a lot about the corporate culture of a professional services provider and the management philosophy of a professional. Where people work, mistakes happen. This is what distinguishes us humans from machines, although even machines are not always error-free. The crucial question, however, is how does a professional or a company deal with the mistakes of its employees?

Closely related to the task of controlling is the controlling of a professional services provider. Controlling is understood to mean the planning and management as well as the control of companies. A professional services provider often uses certain key figures to control its firm. Ideally, these are value drivers or so-called "key performance indicators" (KPI). Such key performance indicators can be, among others:

- Revenue per employee
- Billable hours per employee
- Contribution margin per employee
- New clients per partner
- Newly acquired sales per partner
- Result before partner compensation

Depending on how open these key figures are and on which levels they are communicated in the company, they can be motivating or demotivating for employees. My point here is not to evaluate individual metrics and discuss the

EXAMPLE

The employees of our companies work in a family business. I always emphasize this when hiring new employees. I have been a member of the association DIE FAMILIENUNTERNEHMER for almost 30 years. Family businesses strive for long-term cooperation and decisions are made with sustainability in mind. Family business owners are often committed to their employees.

During recruitment interviews, I talk openly with potential new employees about the subject of lying. In many industrial companies, it is not uncommon for employees to lie to each other. In particular, they cover up their own mistakes. Covering up mistakes and lying are an absolute "no go" for me. This is what I bring up during job interviews and immediately point out that even the first lie would be grounds for dismissal, regardless of whether or not it would be valid under labor law.

In my home region, there is a saying "When the milk is spilled, it's spilled!" This proverb is meant to express: When something has gone wrong, you can't change it; you have to accept it. I quote this proverb in hiring interviews and tell the employee that covering up mistakes would permanently disrupt a working relationship and that the consequence of termination is to be expected. Then I tell the respective potential new employees that, in the case of mistakes, my sole concern is how they can be avoided in the future. After all, once a mistake has been made, it is an unalterable fact. The only thing that can be done then is to eliminate the mistake and to respond appropriately to ensure that the same mistake does not happen again in the future.

Why am I so tough and direct in job interviews? I want to achieve two things:

I want employees to know right at the start of their job what the consequence in my family business would be if they lied.

I want them to know that a mistake will not have a negative consequence, as long as it is communicated openly.

By mistakes, by the way, I mean mistakes related to a professional activity. This must be distinguished clearly from things that are relevant under criminal law. Anyone who makes mistakes in the criminal law sense must, of course, also bear responsibility for them.

associated pros and cons of each metric. Anyone who wants to promote team spirit in a professional services provider should be aware that not every key figure is conducive in this sense.

EXAMPLE

If, for example, an employee's turnover is the focus of a key figure, then only those activities that bring them the highest possible turnover are desirable for an employee. However, there are a number of activities in all areas of a professional services provider that are important but do not generate revenue. In addition, the billable revenue of an employee also depends on the particular assignment. There are assignments that generate higher average billable hours or a higher contribution margin than other assignments. Especially with clients who have been loyal to the professional services provider for many years, hourly rates are sometimes agreed upon that are lower than for one-time new clients. If, for example, an employee performs excellently for a long-standing client, but for strategic reasons the employee subsequently generates lower revenues for the client due to lower hourly rates, it would be inequitable if the employee were to receive a reduction in their annual bonus, for example.

In addition, there are a large number of activities in a professional services provider that do not result in billable hours anyway but are important for the development of the firm. However, if revenue per employee is a key metric for a professional services provider, few employees are willing to take on truly important and strategic tasks for the firm. It is important to keep this in mind for other metrics as well.

PART THREE

Tools

THE LAST PART DISCUSSES the tools for managing and successfully accomplishing tasks. If you want to successfully manage yourself and others, you should master the tools described in the following chapters. Effective management stands or falls on the proper use of tools. Professionals usually think of tools as their computer and software applications (apps) or their smartphone and tablet. The following chapters will only mention technical tools, not cover them. The pandemic, in particular, has led to collaboration tools like Microsoft Teams or Zoom changing a professional's day-to-day life. Rather, the tools for effective management presented here are about self-management, the psyche, in the form of mental strength, rhetoric and the way professionals communicate, and communication tools. Finally, I present a tool with the Work-Life-Balanced-Scorecard, which helps you to bring balance into your life and thus combine the aspects of professional success and private happiness.

For a top athlete it is a matter of course to train on a regular basis. Only through repeated practice do they reach mastery. Anyone who wants to learn a new language knows that they will only succeed through regular practice. What is natural for an athlete or a person who wants to learn a language should also be natural for a professional. There is only one way to master the following tools: regular practice! Professionals often have a penchant for perfectionism.

Sometimes, perfectionism can prevent people from starting to act. Therefore, it can be useful if professionals are not always perfectionistic. However, when using the following tools, professionals should definitely aim to apply them as perfectly as possible in their everyday professional and private lives.

The following tools require no special talent. Every professional can learn to incorporate these tools and to apply them better and better from day to day. Nevertheless, it is important to point out that the starting conditions will not be the same for all professionals. This is because both rhetorical skills and mental strength, in particular, depend heavily on what experiences, role models and conditioning a professional has had in the past. For example, those who grew up in a home or environment in which one or both parents or other family members had strong rhetorical skills clearly have advantages over a professional whose parents or family environment were less rhetorically strong.

The daily application of the following soft skills is important. If you want to take a big step forward in your personal development, you should not only deal intensively with these tools, but also integrate them into your everyday life. These soft skills were not on a syllabus during training, studies, or a professional exam. Therefore, many things will be new for most professionals. If you always eat the same thing at a buffet and never try anything new, you will never get to experience what other dishes taste like. That's why I want to encourage you to try the tools that follow. A professional who always does the same thing will always get the same results. Only if you change something, will something change in your life. If you want to improve, apply these tools. Surely there are professionals among you who have already identified these tools as important and who use them in their professional and personal lives. If this is the case, use my recommendations to optimize your use of the tools. The tools presented here are key to a successful professional life and happy personal life.

CHAPTER THIRTEEN

Self-Management

YOU ARE THE STARTING point of effective and successful management. If you cannot manage yourself, you cannot manage others. That is why your personal work methodology and productivity is so important. Self-management is closely related to the principles of focus and results orientation. In addition, self-management is the bridge to your goals. Figure 13.1 shows the connections.

Focus and results orientation are the principles that should be at the core of a professional's self-management. Their personal work methodology is focused, designed to get results, as well as professional and personal goals. Setting and attaining goals are the key tasks of a professional. Self-management serves to realize these goals. Figure 13.1 shows that the principles of results orientation and focus are the starting point for a professional's actions. If you do not know exactly what results you want to achieve and do not focus on them, you will not accomplish your goals. Goal clarity is the prerequisite for a professional to direct their self-management activities in a result-oriented, focused manner towards their goals. Focusing helps to concentrate on the essentials. Every professional should already have the end in mind at the beginning. It is always important to have the targeted result in mind within the framework of self-management and the planning of professional and private activities. Accordingly, all activities should be directed towards the desired results.

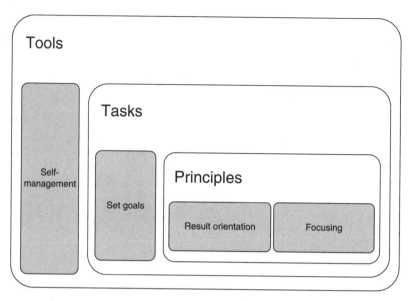

FIGURE 13.1 Relationship between self-management and tasks and principles

NOTE

During my studies of business administration at the University of Mannheim, I was already entrepreneurially active in financial consulting, first part-time and later full-time. Even as a student and young entrepreneur, I quickly realized that personal work methodology and productivity would play a decisive role in my later professional success. At that time, I bought the first books by Lothar Seiwert, the German "Pope of Time Management." All his books left a lasting impression. In the meantime, we have known each other personally for many years and are on friendly terms. Today, I am still interested in everything about effective and efficient self-management. The continuous improvement of my personal work methodology remains important to me. Therefore, I am continually interested in everything that helps me become more productive. Improving personal work methodology is a lifelong learning process.

Very few people can spontaneously answer how many hours a normal calendar year has. With 365 days in a year, that's 8,760 hours. This means that everyone has the same number of hours available in a year. The crucial question, however, is what do you do in these 8,760 hours? Assuming you need an average of seven hours of sleep a day, you can subtract 2,555 hours from the 8,760 hours to arrive at 6,205 hours of awake time. Why am I calculating this for you? My point is to make you aware of how many hours you have in a year that you can spend productively, usefully, and happily. What are you doing during that time, and does it align with your plans?

Conscious planning and effective and efficient self-management are the beginning of a successful and happy life. In the principle of focusing, I have already presented why it is so important to concentrate on a few things. I introduced the extreme Pareto Principle and the concentration on ONE Thing. Focusing is the central key to professional and private success. If you want to achieve professional and private goals, you will find the way by applying the "the ONE Thing" life principle. Keller and Papasan give valuable advice on how to manage yourself excellently. In their book, they begin by clarifying the following six misconceptions (see Figure 13.2) when it comes to personal productivity. In their opinion, these six misconceptions prevent professional and personal success. Therefore, the first thing to do is to recognize that these

FIGURE 13.2 Six misconceptions of success according to Keller and Papasan

misconceptions might be getting in the way of your professional and personal success.

1. **Everything Is Equally Important.** In the principle of focusing, I have already shown that not everything is equally important. In self-management, you must always keep this in mind. Instead of using to-do lists, I advocate that you better keep success lists that are based on your goals and targeted results. Not all activities are equally important to your professional and personal success. Successful people can distinguish essentials from non-essentials. Success lists are short and focus on the essential activities. Successful people know the priorities that lead to their success. However, this requires the right decisions. In essence, then, it is a question of how everyone chooses the right activities in their different areas of life so that, step-by-step, a successful and happy life emerges. If you want to achieve more, you must reduce to the essentials. To the ONE Thing. If you want to be successful, you have to do what matters most. Keep looking for the most important activity until you find the ONE Thing that matters. Not everything is equally important.

2. **Multitasking to Get More Done.** Believing you will accomplish more with multitasking is a misconception. In his book "Hyperfocus: How to Work Less and Achieve More," Chris Bailey has dealt extensively with multitasking, among other things. He outlines how we deal with external and internal distractions and why hyperfocus is so important. He sees multitasking as a trap of constant interruptions. When we try to get several things done simultaneously by multitasking, we are constantly stopping ourselves from doing and finishing the ONE Thing. By hyper-focusing on one important thing, we can maximize our productivity.

3. **If You Want to Be Successful, You Have to Live a Disciplined Life.** If you want to be successful, you have to do the right things. For many people, being successful is related directly to always and constantly being very disciplined. If you are never disciplined, you will certainly not be successful. However, it is much more important to develop habits of success. Selective discipline is necessary for this. Researchers at University College London have found that it takes an average of 66 days for a person to incorporate a new habit. When doing this, you should always focus on one habit that you want to acquire anew. Mental training as well as autosuggestions support the change process here. You can be successful if you apply the principle of selective discipline. Find the right success habits and be disciplined until your subconscious mind automatically applies

this success habit. It is a misconception to think that to be successful, you always have to be disciplined in everything and everywhere.

4. **Willpower Can Be Produced at Any Time.** If you want to achieve excellent results, you need sufficient energy to do so. However, willpower cannot be produced at any time. Those who are exhausted have significantly less willpower and energy. Illnesses, burnout syndromes, as well as states of exhaustion considerably reduce the willpower to pursue your goals and lead a successful life. Therefore, it is important for everyone to determine exactly what is the most important ONE Thing for using your willpower. Eat healthy and regularly and make sure that you always have enough energy and power reserves. This also includes sufficient sleep. Every person has different sleeping habits. Determine your individual sleep requirements. Always do the most important things first during the day when your willpower is still unused. Ensure you have enough energy and willpower with a healthy diet. Maximum willpower means maximum success. It is a misconception to think that you can produce willpower at any time. The right conditions are necessary. Mental training helps to strengthen willpower.

5. **A Good Work-Life Balance Is a Prerequisite for a Successful Life.** If you want to be exceptionally successful, you have to focus all your time and energy on the ONE Thing that leads to success. That a life must be in balance to be successful is a misconception. Life purpose and life meaning are the things that make a successful life. Those who know their life purpose and life meaning will pursue those things they are in harmony with. Extraordinary results require focused attention and time. Having time for the ONE Thing means not having time for another thing. And that makes balance an impossibility.

EXAMPLE

Anyone who wants to become a lawyer or CPA knows that they can only succeed if they are focused. During the preparation period for the professional exams, a balance in life is rarely possible. This is especially true during the time when a professional is still involved in day-to-day work and is not yet on special company leave (given during periods of exams). Even in the later course of a professional's life, there will always be phases in which a balance with other areas of life is difficult to achieve if professional success is the focus of their activities. In these phases of life, a professional spends most of their time on the job. Time with family and friends as well as other private activities take a back seat during these phases and sometimes do not take place at all.

Successful people always have phases of life that make a work-life balance impossible. If you want to be successful in your career, you have to be prepared to sacrifice balance in your life. This does not mean that you should focus exclusively and at all times on your professional life. You do need your private life for a balance. You lead a happy life when your life is in harmony with your life's purpose and meaning. However, if you permanently neglect your private life, you should not be surprised if you lack the necessary balance and energy to achieve your life's tasks.

6. **Big Is Bad and Scary.** If you want to be exceptionally successful, you need big and ambitious goals. Big is bad and scary is a misconception. Many people don't have the courage to think big because they don't believe in achieving immense success. However, those who think small will never achieve big. None of us really knows our own limitations. That's why you think big. Setting ambitious and big goals is an essential characteristic of success. Big stands for the outstanding, for the extraordinary result. Therefore, formulate ambitious and big goals. Set a goal that is so far above your actual expectations that you must develop a plan that virtually guarantees your actual goal. In doing so, it is important to leave well-worn paths. Visualize your goal and imagine the way to achieve it. If you don't succeed, look for people who have already achieved their goal. Learn what these people did to achieve their goal. Ultimately, you will no longer fear failure. Failures are a part of your path to extraordinary results and success.

 ## EFFECTIVE AND SUCCESSFUL SELF-MANAGEMENT

At its core, effective self-management is about how everyone chooses the right activities in their different areas of life so that a more successful and happier life gradually emerges. Exceptional success depends on the choices we make and the activities necessary to achieve them. The answer to this question is not always easy. The ONE question aims to keep the "Big Picture" in mind. On the other hand, you can stay focused on a daily basis by asking, *What's the ONE Thing I can do right now such that by doing it everything else will be easier or unnecessary?* Asking "right now" will keep you focused on the most important activity in the present.

To achieve extraordinary success, it is necessary that you are as productive as possible. You will be as productive as possible if you master the tool of self-management. Thus, high personal productivity goes hand in hand with effective self-management. However, effective self-management is not an end in itself. Effective self-management is a building block to a successful and happy life. Therefore, personal productivity only makes sense in your life if you know why you should be productive. The starting point, therefore, is to know the purpose of your life. This is where the interaction between the tool of self-management and the task of setting goals becomes particularly clear. Keller and Papasan have detailed the following six steps in their book *The ONE Thing* because they see this as the key to an exceptionally successful life. Figure 13.3 summarizes the central ideas of Keller and Papasan.

The starting point to personal productivity is your meaning in life. Who you are and where you are aiming determines what you do and what you can achieve. That is why the start of any goal setting should be knowledge of the meaning. Only through knowing the meaning of your life do goals get a meaning. This applies both to the "corporate" and your personal meaning of life. The question of why must therefore be clarified. Once you know the "Why," the next step is to ask about the "How" and the priorities. Priorities come from your goals. We have already covered the point of "setting goals" in the tasks, so I will not go into it further here. With self-management, I am concerned with your personal productivity and how you can best combat the thieves of productivity.

Particularly successful professionals are also particularly productive people. If it's true that time is money, then perhaps the best way to judge the quality of your time management system is by how much money you make from it. Particularly productive people get more done than others. They get better results and earn far more than others because they spend the maximum amount of time doing their highest priority, their ONE Thing with maximum productivity.

Successful people make appointments with themselves for that ONE Thing and protect those blocks of time with all their might. *What's the ONE Thing I can do today for my ONE Thing such that by doing it everything else will be easier or unnecessary?* To achieve extraordinary success, it is necessary that you firmly schedule blocks of time for three items (see Figure 13.4) by making appointments with yourself for this purpose.

TIME BLOCKS FOR DOWNTIME

Rest is just as important as work. If you want to achieve extraordinary success and top results, you need time off. Rest periods and times of regeneration in which you can recharge your batteries. That's why reserving a block of time for downtime comes first. This includes free time, vacations, and recovery times.

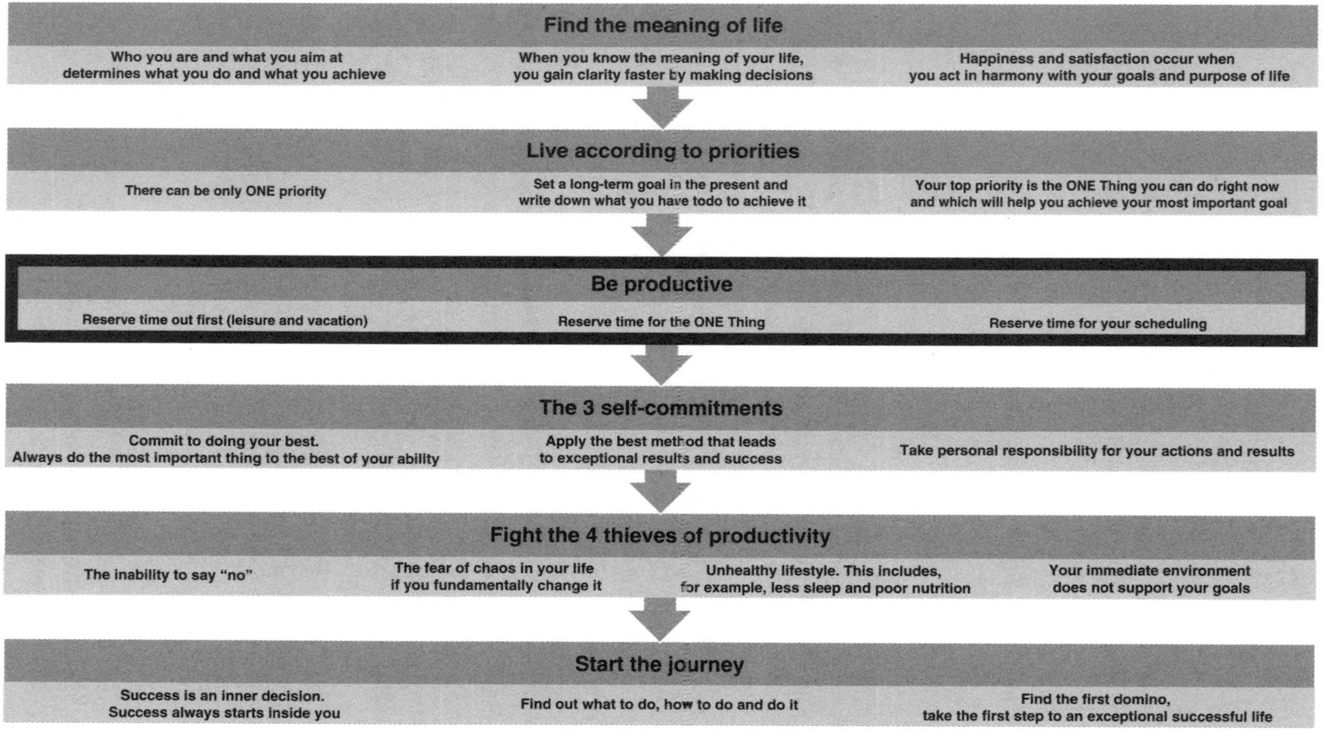

Find the meaning of life

Who you are and what you aim at determines what you do and what you achieve

When you know the meaning of your life, you gain clarity faster by making decisions

Happiness and satisfaction occur when you act in harmony with your goals and purpose of life

Live according to priorities

There can be only ONE priority

Set a long-term goal in the present and write down what you have todo to achieve it

Your top priority is the ONE Thing you can do right now and which will help you achieve your most important goal

Be productive

Reserve time out first (leisure and vacation)

Reserve time for the ONE Thing

Reserve time for your scheduling

The 3 self-commitments

Commit to doing your best. Always do the most important thing to the best of your ability

Apply the best method that leads to exceptional results and success

Take personal responsibility for your actions and results

Fight the 4 thieves of productivity

The inability to say "no"

The fear of chaos in your life if you fundamentally change it

Unhealthy lifestyle. This includes, for example, less sleep and poor nutrition

Your immediate environment does not support your goals

Start the journey

Success is an inner decision. Success always starts inside you

Find out what to do, how to do and do it

Find the first domino, take the first step to an exceptional successful life

FIGURE 13.3   Six steps to extraordinary success according to Keller and Papasan

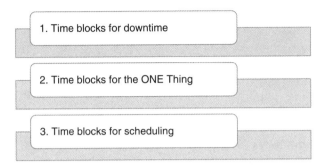

FIGURE 13.4   Three keys to personal productivity according to Keller and Papasan

Top athletes can only achieve peak performance in competition if they have sufficient time for regeneration between competitions. This is equally true for successful people in other professions. Particularly successful people start a new calendar year by determining their time off in advance.

Presumably, many auditors will now object that they schedule a large number of annual audits at the beginning of a calendar year because that is what the job of an auditor entails. However, this does not change the fact that an auditor can also schedule blocks of time off. Time off can also be extended weekends.

NOTE

Oliver Kahn writes in his book "I. Success Comes from Within" that he doesn't understand why top managers pride themselves on working as many hours as possible, seven days a week. Professional soccer players would only be able to deliver absolute top performances if they used the time between games optimally for regeneration. Some professionals, on the other hand, believe that they can perform around the clock. However, the more stressed a professional is, the more likely they are to make mistakes and overlook important things in their professional activities.

Professionals should schedule time off to regenerate. Scheduling time off at the start will likely be met with resistance by some professionals. Especially since for many, their profession is also their vocation, and they enjoy doing it. However, if professionals want to do their job particularly well, they need time off.

TIME BLOCKS FOR THE ONE THING

After setting aside blocks of time for downtime, make appointments in your schedule with yourself for your ONE Thing. Your most important work comes second. After all, you can't achieve sustainable professional success if you don't take time off.

Peter F. Drucker said, "Efficiency is doing things right. Effectiveness is doing the right things." Especially successful people know this and plan their day around their ONE Thing, working in the morning like an entrepreneur to create things and in the afternoon like a manager to oversee and delegate things. Their most important appointment each day is the appointment with themselves. The most productive professionals work with a focus on results. They don't stop until the ONE Thing is done.

> ## NOTE
>
> Many professionals will object that they have to perform a multitude of factual tasks every working day. Younger professionals in particular do not perform the role of a manager and cannot delegate tasks. They only perform factual tasks that are assigned to them. Experienced professionals, on the other hand, are in the role of a manager on a regular basis. However, those who understand the principle of the ONE Thing apply this to their factual tasks as well. In this respect, the principle is independent of whether or not a professional performs a management task. Because every task can often be broken down into several subtasks. And it is always necessary to concentrate on the ONE Thing that makes the greatest possible contribution to the fulfillment of the respective task.

If a professional does not set aside time each day to devote to the ONE task, they will never get it done.

 ## TIME BLOCKS FOR SCHEDULING

The third item you reserve a block of time for is your planning time. Reserve a block of time each week for your time planning by scheduling an appointment with yourself. During this time, review your weekly, monthly, and annual goals and assess your status quo for each. Determine the activities that will lead you to the ONE Thing that will make everything else easier or unnecessary. During this time, a professional is dedicated to determining their position. They consider whether they are on track to achieve their goals or have lost their way. Look at your goals and ask yourself if they are on the right track. Reserve one hour each week to review your goals and make your plan for the next week in writing. Good weekly planning is the foundation for your professional and personal success. A weekly plan is also useful to determine if you have balance in your life.

The following mind map (see Figure 13.5) shows the framework of my weekly planning. I have not shown my concrete activities, on the one hand for

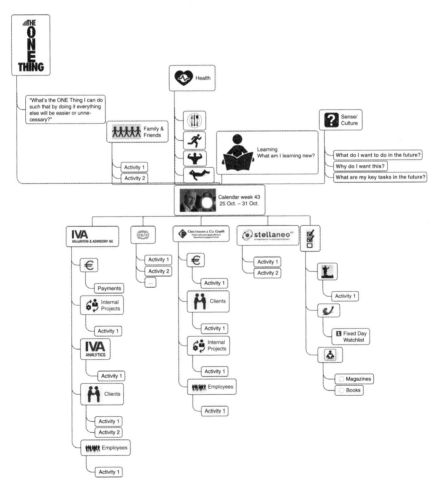

FIGURE 13.5 Exemplary structure of a weekly planning

reasons of confidentiality and on the other because they also include private activities.

TIP

For more than 20 years, I have been taking the time – mostly on weekends – to plan my week. I use a mind map because it gives me an instant overview of all my weekly activities. I can prioritize individual activities and highlight them visually. By including additional images, the individual activities become deeply engrained in my mind and help me stay focused. If certain activities remain undone, I can carry them over to the next week. This is equally true if appointments are postponed or activities need to be completed at a later date.

The mind map contains activities relating to my factual tasks as a professional as well as management activities. It also serves as a control. After all, a weekly plan is documentation of what I accomplish toward achieving my professional and private goals.

 ## FIGHT THE FOUR THIEVES OF PRODUCTIVITY

Along with focus comes the fundamental decision that you don't want to do certain things. The following four thieves (see Figure 13.6) of productivity are important to keep in mind if you want to live a particularly exceptional successful life.

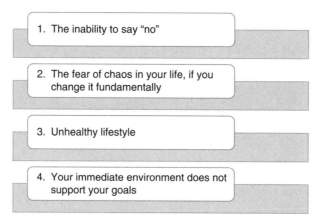

1. The inability to say "no"

2. The fear of chaos in your life, if you change it fundamentally

3. Unhealthy lifestyle

4. Your immediate environment does not support your goals

FIGURE 13.6 The 4 thieves of productivity according to Keller and Papasan

THE INABILITY TO SAY "NO"

If you want to be extra successful, you need to focus on the ONE Thing. Saying "yes" to the ONE Thing means, conversely, that you have to say "no" to many other things far more often. Saying "yes" to any- and everything means you have to say goodbye to your actual goals. The more you get bogged down, the less successful you will be. If you try to please everyone, you will fail to please one person in particular: yourself. The key to a professional's failure is trying to please everyone. A professional who is not able to say "no" often, will never really be able to say "yes" to achieve their goals. Successful people in particular have said "no" much more often in their lives than they have said "yes." The ability to say "no" is focusing on action. Focusing is saying "no."

 ## THE FEAR OF CHAOS IN YOUR LIFE IF YOU FUNDAMENTALLY CHANGE IT

Focusing on the ONE Thing has one consequence: other things are left undone. This can easily lead to chaos in your life. This kind of chaos is inevitable. Learn to endure it. If you always do the same things, you will always get the same results. Only when you change things will you get different results. So, if you follow the principle of focus in your life, other things will inevitably fall by the wayside.

 ## UNHEALTHY HABITS

Unhealthy lifestyle habits and poor nutrition put your health at risk. If you are in poor health, you will not be able to perform at your best. This prevents you from being exceptionally productive. We often want health for ourselves and others first. However, we often put so much strain on our bodies that we put our health at risk. There are three elements at the heart of a healthy life:

1. Sufficient sleep
2. A healthy diet
3. Enough exercise

Those who are permanently sleep-deprived cannot be productive. The ability to concentrate decreases and with it the performance. A healthy diet is a prerequisite for having enough energy to complete our tasks. Accountants and lawyers have a predominantly sedentary job in their profession. Evolutionarily, we were hunters, and our bodies are designed to move on a daily basis. Movement or rather sporting activities leads to vitality and gives us reserves of strength. Healthy habits are the basis for high productivity.

Very productive professionals use the following sources to recharge their batteries (see Figure 13.7).

A successful and productive professional has reserves of energy. They have sufficient energy to cope with daily tasks. From what or where a professional ultimately draws this energy is irrelevant. Due to a person's uniqueness, the five energy sources presented below are probably not

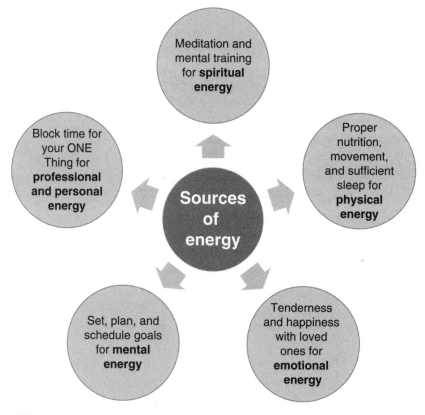

FIGURE 13.7 Energy sources based on Keller and Papasan

identical in terms of importance in any one person. The importance of an energy source is individual. For me, for example, physical energy has a special meaning. For me, a healthy body is the prerequisite for mental peak performance, therefore, I eat consciously, make sure I get enough sleep, and exercise regularly.

As a professional, you have experience in preparing spread sheets. Draw up your energy balance sheet. The asset side lists your energy sources, and the liability side your energy thieves. Maximize the energy sources and minimize the energy thieves. Live in energy surplus. Check if you can make an energy thief an energy source or a neutral item. In the sense of polarity, there could also be a positive energy in every energy thief.

YOUR IMMEDIATE ENVIRONMENT DOES NOT SUPPORT YOU IN YOUR GOALS

Unless your environment supports your goals, you will significantly lose productivity. Your environment is all those you see every day, with whom you spend time. These are the people you are familiar with in your immediate environment. However, in order to achieve extraordinary results, these people must support your goals and not counteract them. Therefore, you should surround yourself with people who have the same mindset as you. Ideally, surround yourself with people who motivate you. Any person can become a time thief at any moment. They can divert your attention from your most important work and take away productivity. For you to achieve extraordinary results, the people around you must support you and your goals.

If you live in an environment that negatively influences you and does not support your goals, goal achievement becomes much more difficult. Every professional who has passed the demanding exams knows how important it is to have a supportive private environment to pass those exams. Any distraction from the private environment can be an obstacle and prevent you from passing the exam. But the colleagues you take a professional exam with should also have the same mindset as you. Successful people surround themselves with successful people. If you surround yourself with successful people, you can learn from them, and the likelihood increases that you too will become successful. When professionals surround themselves with ambitious, motivated, and high-performing people, it strengthens their motivation and increases their performance.

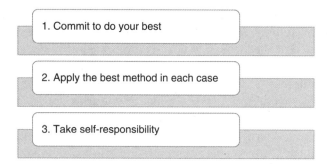

FIGURE 13.8 Three self-commitments according to Keller and Papasan

 ## THE THREE SELF-COMMITMENTS

It takes three "commitments" to achieve extraordinary results by reserving blocks of time or appointments with yourself. The above three self-commitments are required to achieve extraordinary results (see Figure 13.8).

Commit to always doing your best. Always do your most important thing to the best of your ability, with the goal of becoming the best in a particular field. In doing so, apply the best method that leads to exceptional results and success. "Thinking out of the box" will help you do this. Disruption is currently a topic in almost every industry. Use the thought in identifying the best method to achieve your goals. Avoid well-trodden paths. If you always do the same thing, you will always end up where you have already been. Take personal responsibility for your actions and results. The principle of self-responsibility is important. There is undoubtedly a relationship between your actions in the past and your current life situation. Always take personal responsibility for your life. Only those who take responsibility for their lives are proactive and in the role of the actor. All others can become victims of circumstances. Find a mentor or a coach who will support you on your way to extraordinary success.

 ## START THE JOURNEY

Start the journey by taking the first step. Focusing on the ONE Thing is the beginning of a complete shift in thinking. Failure is buried in versatility. Extraordinary success requires that you focus on the essentials. Think big in the

process and your life has a chance to grow. Action builds on action. Habits build on habits. Success builds on success. The right domino sets off a whole chain of dominoes that fall over one by one when you do the ONE Thing that leads to success. Live your life in such a way that you have as few regrets as possible at the end. Success is an inner decision. Success starts inside of you. You know what you need to do. Effective self-management is the basis of a successful and happy life and a prerequisite for being able to manage others.

CHAPTER FOURTEEN

Mental Training

M ENTAL TRAINING WITH THE objective of becoming mentally strong is one of the most valuable tools of a successful professional. Perhaps it is the most valuable tool of a professional, as Figure 14.1 shows.

Mental training is the central tool for programming a professional's principles. It also helps to achieve professional and private goals. Adherence to the principles is an important prerequisite for the success of a professional. The mental training helps you to learn these principles and to keep them. It also supports you in attaining your goals. In the principle of result orientation, I have already pointed out how important mental training and mental strength is for athletes. Athletes have competitive goals, and they want to reach them. They want to win. Professionals also have professional and personal goals that they want to achieve. Now, here's how you can use mental training in your professional and personal life as a professional to accomplish your goals.

Mental strength is the basis for professional and private success. Only those who are mentally strong in critical life situations win. Winning or losing in certain life situations is decided in the mind. In professional life there are regularly situations in which one must react mentally strong as well

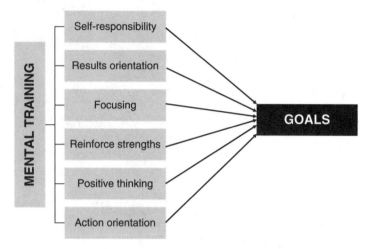

FIGURE 14.1 Relationship between mental training and principles and goals

as calmly and confidently. These can be negotiation situations, employee meetings, presentations, speeches, job interviews, exam situations, and the like. The number of situations can be extended many times. What has long been recognized in top-class sports is still not common in professional life.

NOTE

Why is mental training so important? For many people, programs, beliefs, and behavior patterns have been formed since birth, mostly unconsciously. They are often the decisive causes for failures in professional and private life. Changing these programs, beliefs, and behavior patterns is a process that does not happen overnight. It usually requires a training program that takes place over a longer period of time. The time period depends on the intensity of the programs, beliefs, and behavior patterns as well as the individual's willingness to change.

Mental training makes a professional mentally strong. Mental training comes from the psychology of top-class sports and is used there to optimize learning and performance. According to Eberspächer, mental training is defined as the scheduled repetition and conscious visualization of a movement without its simultaneous practical execution. The mental training is to be understood thereby also as a kind of simulation, which can be quite identical with the actual experience, only that this experience takes place completely in the imagination. The goal in sports is to positively influence the execution of a movement or action by intensively imagining it.

According to Jan Mayer and Hans-Dieter Hermann, one of the challenges of psychological training in sports is that athletes often have difficulty concentrating on the essentials under stressful circumstances, such as in decisive competitive situations. When taking a penalty kick, it is important for the shooter not to engage in negative self-talk before taking the shot. The shooter must believe in themselves with confidence and be 100% convinced that they will kick the penalty into the goal. Anyone who doubts themselves even minimally is highly likely to miss. Golfers know this, too: After a failed tee shot, the ball lands in a bunker. Negatively soliloquizing on the way to the bunker, this golfer will very probably not hit the next shot optimally.

Professionals suffering from exam anxiety know these stressful situations. Anyone who once failed a professional or any exam, even though they had prepared extensively for it, was probably not mentally up to the pressure of the exam. A professional who is not convincing in a pitch for a contract or in a presentation in front of an audience, despite otherwise having the appropriate rhetorical skills, has probably also failed mentally. Mental strength is therefore not only important in the life of a top athlete, but also in everyday professional and private life.

Especially in important situations, many professionals occupy themselves with things that do not help at all in the current situation. These can be distractions on the smartphone. They can be thoughts of possible failure in that particular situation, or they can be distractions by colleagues, clients, family, and friends. This is another reason multitasking is not a success factor. When demands increase and top performance is expected from a professional, they must only be occupied with one thing and must be focused. During client or employee meetings, many professionals are preoccupied with potential future scenarios or with past events. These can be, for example, memories of comparable – positive or negative – experiences with clients and employees. The situational conditions are often the cause of a professional losing focus. Mental training helps a professional to learn the skill of actively shaping thought and imagination processes in certain situations. Through mental training, the conviction should grow that a professional can survive even in adverse or critical situations and can call up certain patterns of action.

In their book, "Mental Training," Mayer and Hermann transferred mental training in top-level sports to the professional and business spheres. They also systematically arranged the differences between training and competition. They summarized the following criteria of a competition-like situation:

■ A competition is always accompanied by a forecast, i.e., an expectation placed on the action and the result.
■ A competition or its result always has positive or negative consequences.
■ In a competition, the performance has to be delivered at an externally determined point in time.
■ In competition, one has no opportunity to repeat a failed action.

This distinction between training and competition is found not only in sports, but also in many performance situations in working life. In many situations in everyday professional life, you are expected to perform to the best of your ability (prognosis). The consequences of failing to perform a professional act can be serious (liability risk), the timing is often externally determined, and the non-repeatability is often self-explanatory when you consider the daily demands on professionals. These competition-like demands of professional life are perceived as a burden by many professionals. They feel under pressure because performance and performance orientation are often assumed in everyday professional life.

In this context, the terms "stress" and "strain" must be distinguished. The term stress actually comes from physics and means a specific pressure exerted on a certain material. In contrast, the term "strain" means the respective experience of this load. A load can be the same for two professionals, but they experience it very differently. This results in individual stress.

EXAMPLE

For one professional, the timely completion of an audit report or an expert opinion is an activity that causes him no stress. Another professional experiences stress during the identical activity simply because there is a given deadline.

A professional's perception of stress is highly individual. The emergence of stress is the result of a different interpretation of a particular event. While it might be a pleasure to present the audit results in front of the client for one professional, for another every presentation in front of an audience is a stressful situation. The extent to which a situation is interpreted as a threat or a challenge for a professional also depends on their individual assessment of the resources available to them. Many professionals need certain pressure situations to perform at their best. Other professionals break down as a result of them. Coping with stressful situations requires the following three skills:

▪ Factual competence (specialist knowledge)
▪ Social competence in dealing with clients and employees
▪ Self-competence in dealing with stressful situations

These competencies can usually be trained within the framework of training, education, quality assurance, and quality control programs. Mental training can be used as part of the training of professionals to automate everyday routines and to prepare for stressful situations. This should also improve the quality of decisions.

TIP

Self-competence in dealing with stress also includes the realization that stress often arises for two reasons, both of which can be controlled:

▪ Meeting the expectations of others.
▪ Meeting your own expectations of yourself.

In many life situations, professionals want to meet the expectations of others. These may be the expectations of superiors or clients, for example. But it can also be the expectations of your life partner in your private life. If you are aware that the expectations of others are just that and not your own expectations of yourself, you will be able to manage this kind of stress more easily.

If a professional has made it their business to always meet the expectations of others, this inevitably leads to stress. By the way, this does not mean that a professional should react indifferently to his environment. After all, the quality requirements and quality demands that exist within an accounting practice must be closely observed. My point is that a professional should always be aware that the expectations of others can only cause them stress if they want to meet them. Freeing oneself from the expectations of others to a certain extent is a big step towards freedom from stress.

The second point is much more crucial: Your expectations of yourself. If you should feel that you cannot meet or live up to your own expectations, this will certainly lead to stress. It is important to examine your self-image and know exactly whether your self-expectations are realistic or unrealistic. For example, someone who does not have enough professional experience in a certain field should not have the expectation to provide these services flawlessly.

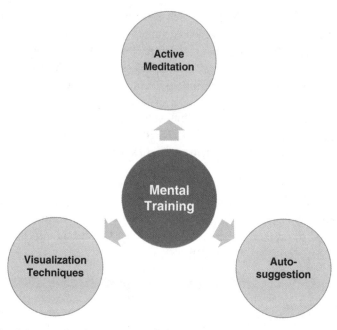

FIGURE 14.2 Levels of mental training

Mental training, with the goal of becoming mentally strong, consists of three components (see Figure 14.2):

ACTIVE MEDITATION

Meditation (from the Latin origin meditatio to meditari "to reflect, ponder, consider") is a practice designed to calm and collect the mind through mindfulness or concentration exercises.

Through the use of music and suggestions, active meditations aim to reach the alpha state, as in a state of relaxation. The starting point of meditation is the correct breathing technique. A distinction is made between abdominal breathing and chest breathing (costal breathing). In abdominal breathing, the diaphragm is moved downward during inhalation so that the chest cavity with the lungs is expanded downward. The organs in the abdomen are moved downward or forward and the abdominal wall bulges outward. In chest breathing, the inhalation primarily lifts and expands the chest by activating the muscles between the ribs.

It is remarkably effective and possible at any time to focus on our own breathing. Awareness of our breathing automatically guides us into our bodies, allowing us to notice signals that may have escaped us before. Another benefit is that when you pay attention to your breath, you are completely in the present. The sensation of breathing occurs only in the present. This may seem trivial to you now, but we spend much of our time with our thoughts not in the present but preoccupied with matters past and future. Conscious breathing can then be like a time out or provide an escape to free yourself from negative thoughts and coming to your senses in the present. By deepening your abdominal breathing, the goal is to get into a relaxed state.

If you can control your breathing, you can control your body state, your thoughts, and your emotions. It is not possible to breathe calmly, slowly, and deeply and be tense at the same time. In periods of stress, shallow breathing (chest breathing) often dominates.

NOTE

Check how many times you inhale and exhale in one minute and whether it is chest or abdominal breathing. Less is more: aim for six to seven breaths a minute with belly breathing. Place your hands on your abdomen and breathe in deeply and out slowly. Your abdominal wall should move up and down. The number and depth of breaths per minute also depends on the amount of oxygen you need. If you are lying down, you will need less oxygen than if you are exercising. The guideline of six to seven breaths refer to a relaxed state.

Conscious breathing is the easiest way to get into an alpha state. It is a particularly effective way to recharge your energy and the best way to reduce anxiety, nervousness, and hectic activity.

Abdominal breathing helps you get into the alpha state, a state of relaxation. In active meditation, in addition to abdominal breathing during mental training, a voice is added to suggest positive texts to you. Enkelmann has recorded a variety of such active meditations for mental training. The goal of these suggestions is that positive beliefs become deeply anchored in your subconscious. This is to replace negative beliefs with positive beliefs, if necessary. As a student, I regularly listened to the CD "I can do what I want." This mental training strengthens your self-confidence and belief in your own power. If you

TIP

For almost 30 years I have a ritual during my morning drive to the office. I practice the so-called psychogenic breathing and voice training according to Nikolaus B. Enkelmann (www.enkelmann.de), which I have expanded for many years with exercises by Patric P. Kutscher (http://mce-rhetorik. de). You can easily train abdominal breathing with the audio file "A positive day begins" by Enkelmann. By combining it with voice training, breathing training helps me train my voice. For example, after an intense inhalation, the vowels a, e, i, o, and u are spoken on exhalation. These are spoken until your breathing settles down to exactly six to seven breaths per minute.

would like to access web-based audio files in the age of digitalization, please send me an e-mail at andreas.creutzmann@creutzmann.de with the keyword "Motivation for Professionals." I will then send you a regularly updated playlist of English suggestions that I have compiled under Spotify and Apple Music. These suggestions often have more of a motivational character, whereas the suggestions of Enkelmann aim to program the subconscious in the alpha state. The Spotify and Apple Music playlists are therefore something complementary to Enkelmann's suggestions.

NOTE

It is understood that for both university and professional exams, learning and training are the primary prerequisites for any success. No top athlete enters a competition without having trained beforehand. Mastering the material or a certain activity is always a prerequisite for success. Mental training is ultimately about being able to perform at your best in a stressful work or exam situation, or as an athlete in a competition.

 ## AUTOSUGGESTION

The second component of mental training is autosuggestion. Autosuggestions are training sessions to increase self-awareness and focus on essential and important things. A mentally strong manager and businessperson appears confident and credible during presentations, negotiations with clients, speeches, and lectures. Mental strength is the foundation for persuasive rhetoric, which is another valuable tool of a successful professional.

While suggestion is about influencing others, autosuggestion is the art of influencing yourself. We hear a variety of external suggestions from the day we're born. These come from our private environment or from media. Many of these suggestions have become deeply anchored in our subconscious and are often negative. We often adopted them unthinkingly and they become negative beliefs. Autosuggestions are commands to the subconscious mind that help you to be mentally strong. This allows you to override and reprogram negative programming and extraneous programming. You can input objectives, and by doing so, you strengthen uplifting thought structures. You cannot rethink your subconscious mind. You have to talk to your subconscious. That is why autosuggestions only work when they are spoken. The spoken word has a much stronger effect on the subconscious than a thought. The more often you discuss your subconscious through autosuggestions, the faster you will succeed with it.

TIP

Speak autosuggestions loudly and clearly. If you have the opportunity to do this in front of a mirror: Use it! In this case, look into your eyes. Repeat the autosuggestion as often as possible. This can be in the car, while walking, in the bathroom, while exercising, or wherever.

There are two types of autosuggestions:

1. Short phrases (affirmations and beliefs).
2. Longer autosuggestions with several sentences.

The word "affirmation" includes the Latin word "firmare," which means "to confirm, affirm." An affirmation is an affirming, performance-enhancing sentence that – if you repeat it aloud or inwardly often enough – will guide your thoughts, beliefs, feelings, and actions. Affirmations are therefore short, simple, clear, positive, or affirming, easy-to-pronounce sentences in the present tense that always begin with "I." You can repeat these simple sentences several times a day. In contrast to the negative beliefs already presented, these are positive beliefs.

EXAMPLE

Here is a selection of positive affirmations and beliefs:

- I am a good lawyer, CPA, etc.
- I am a highly qualified specialist.
- I can develop good relationships with my clients.
- I can develop good relationships with my employees.
- I see revenue opportunities with my clients.
- I am on my way to becoming a partner in my company.
- I am reaching the next career level.
- I think it's great how I make a living.
- I love my profession.
- I am responsible for my life.
- I find my life exciting.
- I like myself.
- I am a likeable person.
- I trust myself and my intuition.
- I feel better from day to day and in every way.
- I am healthy.
- I am full of energy.
- I eat a healthy diet.

It is best to memorize the longer texts. It will be easier for you to remember sentences that already belong to your beliefs and with which you identify. In the case of new beliefs, which were previously foreign to you, it usually takes longer for you to memorize them. Use the present tense and positive phrases. The subconscious mind works with images. If I tell you not to think of a pink elephant, you will think of the image of a pink elephant anyway. The word "not" does not prevent the image of the pink elephant. Therefore, always use positive wording and avoid negations. Nikolaus B. Enkelmann has written a large number of positive autosuggestions in his books, and you will find enough suggestions there and at the Enkelmann Institute in Königstein. You can also find a large number of examples on Google.

In the written law part of my (German) CPA exam I had a poor grade. Since this written grade was weighted more heavily than the oral grade, I had to get a good grade in the oral exam in order to pass the law part of the (German) CPA exam. Since I had been practicing mental training through suggestions and autosuggestions for several years at that time, I had formulated the following autosuggestion and spoken it once a day four times in a row in front of a mirror in the weeks before the oral exam.

EXAMPLE

I am determined to make the most of my opportunities in the oral exam. If I want to achieve great goals, I must have a rock-solid belief in myself and have the confidence to perform at the highest level.

My examiners are convinced of my professional qualifications, and I will answer every question to their satisfaction. Whoever wants to be successful must be restrained in speaking and absolutely confident in the tone of their voice. I know that for the power of speech, inner confidence is crucial. It is a question of confidence in my own power.

I can be confident in speaking only when I am confident inwardly. I am sure, completely sure, and will fight to the end, no matter what.

I believe in my success and will pass the exam.

On the day of the oral exam, I was in a trance. Just before the start of the oral exam in law, after I had already been tested in auditing and business administration, I stared out the window of the waiting room outside the exam hall and was thoroughly focused. At the time of my oral examination, new legislation to improve corporate governance in German companies had been introduced and the legal concept of a "merchant" had been reformed. Actually, one would have expected that these changes in the law would provide enough material for a prospective auditor in an oral examination. Instead, I was presented with the following case at the beginning of the exam: A certified public accountant would be involved in AIDS relief and, in addition, had not trained any assistants in the field of auditing for many years. The state board of accountancy asked him to comment on this. The question to me was: What is your answer to the state board of accountancy? The second question also had nothing to do with the new law or the reformed "merchant" concept. It was about a comparative advertisement by a sports store that claimed that the competitor did not offer a certain product and that this could only be obtained from the sports store that advertised the product. In response to the first question, I initially replied, "A certified public accountant does have a very intimate and intense relationship with his clients, but I consider the risk of infection through transmission of the AIDS virus to be low." This was certainly not the answer to the question that the auditor had expected, but it earned me a laugh from several sides of the auditors. I then proceeded to talk about the Public Accountant Act and the professional statutes, but presumably this had nothing to do with the examiner's expected answer either. However, since my examination colleague next to me, a lawyer, also did not give a very sensible answer to the question, the flippant start was probably not harmful. However, I was able to answer the second question with a relevant ruling by the European Court of Justic, based on my many years of reading various daily newspapers.

I passed the exam with a good grade and could thus avoid a supplementary exam. Without the mental training and the autosuggestion presented earlier, I would have had no chance of passing the law subject. My will to pass the exam and my willingness to talk my head off led to success.

VISUALIZATION TECHNIQUES

The third component of mental training is the use of visualization techniques. In competitive sports, the power of visualization has long been used. Inner images can be used to replay past situations and lead to a positive outcome, as well as to relive new situations in advance and prepare for them in a positive way. Athletes use the power of their inner images, for example:

- to optimize movement ideas,
- to motivate themselves by recalling memories of moments of success,
- for psychological regulation, to induce lightning relaxation with restful images, or
- to visualize desired goals.

Visualization is all about your imagination and power of imagination. It has been scientifically proven that thoughts and inner images always have an effect on your emotions and your body as well as your actions. The medical term "placebo effect" has long shown that medication can have a healing effect even without active ingredients, if the patient only believes and imagines that the medicine will heal.

We have a multitude of images in our heads and have our individual "mind movies." These movies run almost constantly at all times of the day. A thought becomes an image and tends to materialize. We imagine something in our mind's eye. The more intense and clear the image is, the more energy it receives and the more likely it is that this image will be realized. Suggestions and autosuggestions have an immediate effect on the subconscious through the spoken word. With visualization, we now make these goals visible so that they become even more firmly anchored in our subconscious. Visualization of suggestions and autosuggestions lead to mental strength in mental training.

Your imagination depends on the following factors:

■ Ability to relax and concentrate
■ Daily condition
■ Number of performed visualization exercises (training intensity)
■ Belief in the method

The technical term for the phenomenon that the intense inner imagination of a movement tends to transfer to the physical level is "Carpenter effect" (ideomotor effect). In elite sports, target states are visualized. Athletes imagine in great detail how they will win the competition or the game. In addition to visualization, other sensory organs are also involved if this is goal-oriented, which includes hearing, feeling, smelling, tasting, and touching. The purpose of visualization techniques for athletes is based, among other things, on the following fields of application, most of which can also be transferred to professional and private life:

■ Learning a (new) technique
■ Refining and specifying already learned techniques
■ Stabilizing techniques
■ Recalling routine activities
■ Memorizing tactics
■ Learning behaviors
■ Recalling automatisms
■ Concentration
■ Introducing goals
■ Introducing endurance and strength training
■ Mastering challenges
■ General relaxation on a physical, mental, and emotional level

There are two different perspectives when visualizing:

1. Camera perspective or audience perspective (external perspective)
2. Actor's perspective (internal perspective)

In the camera perspective, a professional observes himself from the outside, whereas in the actor's perspective they are part of the scene and, so to speak, play a part in the film.

TIP

In professional life as well as in private life, there are always events that do not correspond to the objectives of a professional. These can be past negotiation situations, client meetings, presentations, or even employee meetings. During these events, you are part of the scene and often fail to take a camera or a spectator's perspective. However, the retrospective view of such events from a camera perspective helps you to achieve better results in the future. To do this, take the camera perspective, and observe yourself behaving in the corresponding situation. Then ask yourself the following questions in this context:

■ How could I have behaved differently in the situation?

■ What else could I have said?

■ What questions could I have asked?

■ What other options might there have been?

The answers to these questions could be a quantum leap in your personal development.

If you are able to take the camera perspective, you are also training yourself to put yourself in other people's shoes, and you are also practicing visualization. Taking on a unique perspective is an important prerequisite for empathic behavior. Those who cannot empathize with others will rarely establish good relationships. Visualization can also be done in slow motion (slow motion) or real time (real-time, normal pace).

Visualization combined with positive thoughts and positive images causes you to have positive feelings. These positive feelings are important if you want to achieve peak performance. Peak performance is not possible with negative feelings. Inner images of success, happiness, or health cause positive feelings. They activate energies and strengthen the immune system. From this feeling you can act successfully. They free you from negative feelings that might prevent you from success.

Autosuggestions depend on the choice of words and the exact target. With the visualization it depends on the clarity or the unambiguity in the imagination. Blurriness in visualization results in blurriness in execution. Enkelmann names the following six steps to build up pictures:

1. Colors
2. Objects
3. Fantasy pictures
4. Change
5. From picture to film
6. The film of the future

In the **first step**, imagine some colors in your mind. Think of different shades of red or different shades of green. If you have difficulty imagining certain colors correctly, search your memory for examples. If this doesn't help you either, get color sheets or search for assorted color scales on the internet.

In the **second step**, close your eyes and imagine an object in the room you are in. This can be a desk or a chair or something else. What color is the desk? How does the desk feel when you run your hand over it? Integrate internally everything into the image that you can recall. Use all your senses for this: eyes, sense of touch, and sense of smell. Now imagine that there is something to eat and drink on the table. Imagine eating the food and drinking the drink. What do the food and drink taste like? What is their smell? Imagine that there is a cut lemon on the table. Bite heartily into the lemon and eat the pulp. Pay attention to your body as you bite into the lemon in your mind. Unless your imagination is already strong enough, your body should react at the thought of biting into a lemon. This is a simple example of how you can evoke physical reactions just by thoughts and images.

In the **third step**, think of fantasy images. Imagine things that do not exist in reality or that you have never seen. In your mind's eye, create a spaceship, a fairy, or some other fantasy image. If you cannot imagine a fantasy picture, draw your fantasy on a piece of paper. Close your eyes again and imagine your fantasy images. Probably this step is the most difficult one for a professional who usually believes only in evidence and documentation.

In the **fourth step**, start changing the images. For example, turn a red wine bottle into a white wine bottle or a dining table into a desk. You can also turn a VW into a Ferrari. You are the painter of your paintings, the architect of your imagery, and the director of your imaginary movie.

In the **fifth step**, your paintings learn to walk. For example, see a dog walking, moving, smelling, greeting other dogs, running, or growling. Alternatively, imagine that you are making a movie about your last birthday. See all the details of how the day went. What time did you get up, what did you wear, who called you, did you have unexpected visitors or guests over? Your inner movie should be chronological.

By the **sixth step**, you are already on to mastering the imagination. Now you can start making future movies. You now are able to depict your goals in a film. For this you should develop a truly clear picture of your future. In a commercial by the company Nike, the example of Robert Lewandowski is impressively shown in practice how a professional soccer player visualizes to prepare for a game (query on 10/04/2021: www.youtube.com/watch?v=wB59Z3NFTrw, Nike Football Presents: Pro Genius Visualisation ft. Robert Lewandowski). All senses are used in the process.

EXAMPLE

Visualization is something professionals can incorporate into their working as well as their personal lives. Imagine in all detail how you conduct client and employee meetings. The more detailed your imagination, the better. Keep in mind that the conversation should be positive. This does not mean that your counterpart will always respond positively. Rather, be prepared for how you will respond if they react negatively. What do you say, and how do you say it?

You can also use the power of imagery in your partnership and in dealing with your children. Imagine exactly how you want to deal with your partner and what you would like your partner to do with you. Thoughts are forces and have the tendency to realize themselves.

When visualizing, your inner movie should be so embedded in you that it runs immediately when you think of your goal. Your autosuggestions must match your images. The image and the words must match. In a state of relaxation, visualization will come more easily to you. In "Jonathan Livingston Seagull," Richard Bach says, "You have to be there before you arrive."

If you don't believe in success, you won't achieve it. A goal that we are not able to see, not able to visualize, and not able to recognize as an image in front of our eyes loses the power of orientation. How should we be able to achieve something if we cannot even imagine it? Accordingly, an important prerequisite for mental training is a corresponding ability to imagine. Develop this imaginative ability through repeated training.

The mental training tool makes you mentally strong. Through suggestions, autosuggestions, and visualization techniques you will learn to control your thoughts and emotions. Breathing training helps you to get into a relaxed state. In the state of relaxation, you can positively influence your subconscious mind in a targeted way. This enables you to better deal with pressure in stressful situations. Mental training with the goal of becoming mentally strong is part of personality development. You change your self-image and gain self-confidence. You can optimize your behavior and beliefs. You process negative results better and believe in your success.

Mental training is designed to enable you to influence yourself through meditations, autosuggestions, and visualization techniques. However, there are things in life that you cannot influence. For these things, the principle of self-responsibility does not apply either. Mental training and mental strength are important tools to achieve your goals. Once again, it becomes clear why it is so important to be extremely focused on your goals. Because only through precisely defined goals can you clearly program your subconscious mind during mental training. If you have only vague ideas about your goals or live in a wishful world, you will not be able to program your subconscious mind unambiguously. Mental training is probably the most valuable tool on the way to achieving your goals. It is also the basis for the next tool of a successful professional.

CHAPTER FIFTEEN

Rhetoric

THE TERM RHETORIC COMES from ancient Greek and translates as "the art of speaking." The task of rhetoric is to convince the listener of a statement or to persuade him to take a certain action. It aims to provide the means necessary to establish a common ground and find out differences between speaker and listener.

Rhetoric is essentially about the "how!" How do I affect others, and how can I influence others through language? The extent to which influencing can be manipulation will not be discussed further, especially since it is an ethical question. With a knife you can kill a person or cut something. The same is figuratively true of rhetoric. How someone uses rhetoric is their ethical responsibility: Do they want to manipulate or influence people? Manipulating people, as I understand it, is covertly influencing people to their detriment. I distinguish rhetoric with the goal of positively influencing a person to their advantage through open communication from manipulation.

In rhetoric, the words do not always play the decisive role. A person's voice and body language frequently determine whether or not someone comes across as convincing. This is true both professionally and privately. Professionals want to convince their clients and employees. And in their private lives they also want to convince their partners, children, and friends. In this sense, rhetoric is a valuable tool for marketing, especially for how the professional sells themselves to clients and how they sell their company.

This requires a personality that inspires trust. Only those who win the trust of others will be convincing. They will be able to influence others and motivate them to follow their recommendations. Employees will also only follow a professional if they trust them and if they are convincing. Therefore, the tool of rhetoric is an important instrument for the successful mastering of the professional's tasks.

Researcher Albert Mehrabian, from the University of California at Los Angeles, conducted a study in the early 1970s to examine the impact factors of people. He was often quoted as saying that the impact of people would depend 93% on a person's voice and body language, and only 7% on the content of their words. Many have called this Mehrabian's 55-38-7 rule because supposedly the greater influence would come from 55% body language, and 38% voice, totaling 93%. Therefore, content would be comparatively insignificant. Mehrabian subsequently clarified in several interviews that his study was often misinterpreted. He did not mean to say that only 7% of a message is conveyed via the content, for example, the spoken words. For a professional it would also be fatal, since they "sell" their expertise to their customers after all, and the content of their statements is often also of great importance.

Regardless of the "correct" influence ratio of content, voice, and body language in rhetoric, every professional who has been part of an audience as a listener will confirm that a speaker with a boring voice and body language tends to have a soporific effect and it is difficult to listen to such a speaker in a concentrated manner.

In addition, unfortunately, few speakers have been trained in how people process information. Many teachers still do not know that pupils and students perceive information essentially through three sensory channels:

- ▪ Visual (seeing)
- ▪ Auditory (hearing)
- ▪ Kinesthetic (feeling)

The sensory channels olfactory (smell) and gustatory (taste) usually play no role in speech or conversation. For most people, one sensory channel is dominant, which is predominantly visual. Intuitively, many teachers seem to realize that things written on the blackboard or thrown on the wall by flip-chart or beamer are better remembered than just the spoken word. However, the speaker's choice of words also plays a crucial role.

A person who mostly processes information visually also uses images and visual expressions in their language and should receive information from speakers and interlocutors with the following expressions: "see, look, gaze, observe, eyeball, peek, shine, seem, visible, manageable, apparent, bright, dark, be far-sighted, overview, have a view, gain clarity, demand clarification, see in the light, illuminate/illuminate an issue, sham argument, transparent argument, clear layout of space, dark figures, opaque personality, unmistakable, be lenient, be cautious, be foresighted, have an overview, have charisma, provide insight, be insightful, shadow someone, have good powers of observation."

People who take in information primarily auditorily often use the following expressions and should have messages conveyed equally auditorily: "Loud, soft, that sounds good, being deaf to the ears, racket, trampy, rumbling, rattling, musical, unmistakable, dribbling, pounding, shrill, bleeping, dark, harsh, whimpering, screeching, snapping, hoarse, rasping, not being at a loss for words, not listening to others, deafening, hearing a pin drop, being in tune, having one's peace, being left alone, hearing the angels sing, sweet-talking, clucking like a chicken, it clicked, hearing the grass grow, mute as a fish, enduring silence."

For kinesthetic people, language addresses feelings. Terms used by people who process information predominantly kinesthetically: "floating in seventh heaven, falling on the ground, falling into a hole, floating above the ground, letting oneself fall, standing with both feet on the ground, feeling secure, the cold comes up in me, goose bumps run down my back, I feel elated, my heart beats with joy in my body, my heart beats up to my neck, my heart aches, my blood rushes through my veins, my stomach tightens, is doing summersaults, I feel dizzy, my ears buzz, my hands tingle, I break out in a sweat, my limbs shake, my heart laughs."

Knowing how people process information is equally important in speeches and in speaking with clients and employees. With clients and employees, a professional can specifically address the dominant sensory channel of their interlocutor by deliberately addressing the respective dominant sensory channel in the conversation. This is not possible in speeches to larger audiences, where it is important to address all sensory channels alternately in one presentation. The visual sensory channel is the most important because it is the dominant one for most people.

When a professional gives a speech or conducts a client or employee interview, they want the full attention of their counterpart. However, knowledge of how people process information is only the starting point for a good rhetorician. It is necessary to strengthen the persuasive power of a professional through effective rhetoric. This is done through training on three levels, as Figure 15.1 shows.

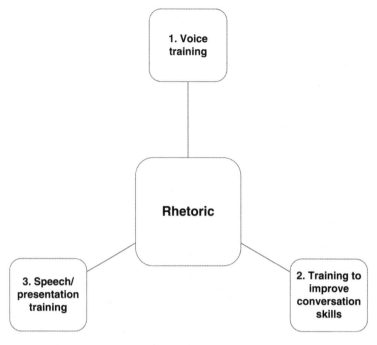

FIGURE 15.1   Rhetoric training

A professional learns to speak only by speaking. Many believe that they can speak just because many people listen to them. Bad examples of this are often politicians. Politicians often have the opportunity to speak in public. And just because they have the opportunity to speak in public, quite a few of them believe that they are particularly good speakers.

Professionals who have grown up in a rhetorically strong environment usually have an easier time with rhetoric. They were fortunate to have positive role models in childhood and adolescence and are usually more rhetorically adept than professionals who had less rhetorically strong parents or a rhetorically strong environment. The starting point of any rhetoric training should be voice training.

VOICE TRAINING

The first level is voice training. Nikolaus B. Enkelmann said, "Whoever works on the voice works on the core of his personality." Voice and speech are very closely related to your overall personality. The voice gives information and conclusions about your personality. We reveal ourselves through our voice. It relentlessly reveals our actual state of mind, our actual condition, our fears, our joy, and in the broadest sense, our mental state. We can smile at someone when we feel like crying. We can look petrified and not make a face when someone offends us. However, when we open our mouths, our actual attitude and condition can be heard in the tone of our voice.

EXAMPLE

Think of a phone call from someone familiar to you. This could be your life partner, your children, or even your parents. You can immediately tell by the sound of their voice how the person is doing. If you have worked with an employee for a longer period of time and you know them better, you can also recognize their emotional state by the sound of their voice.

When a professional suffers from anxiety, stress, or feelings of inferiority, this will often manifest in corresponding blockages of the voice. If you are internally agitated, then your voice will habitually react to this. Especially in critical client or employee meetings, when you do not want your counterpart to have insight into your emotional state, your voice will reveal this. Conversely, your conversation partners recognize your strength and self-esteem when your voice unfolds freely and according to its nature in your body and to the outside world. For this reason, voice training is always personality training. No "voice can be formed" and no rhetoric can be trained without you as a person also maturing inwardly. The work on your voice, the development and unfolding of your own voice potential always goes hand in hand with mental, physical, and spiritual development and unfolding. For this reason, speech exercises go hand in hand with the expansion of your own expressiveness.

Your voice is as unique as your fingerprint. Your presentation slides can be copied, and even your documents can be used by others. Your voice, on the other hand, is yours alone. It cannot be copied. Your voice and your way of speaking are always individual. With your voice you always give your presentation your very own style. It expresses your personality. The word "personality" comes from the Latin root "personare," which translates as to resound, to resound loudly, to let one's voice resound. Accordingly, your counterpart usually infers your personality from the sound of your voice. In addition, many people associate some character traits with certain vocal qualities. If your outward appearance does not match your acoustics, then you have a competence problem in other people's perception. And competence problems are not something a professional can afford.

The important thing, therefore, is how your voice is perceived. Have you ever recorded your voice with your smartphone and listened to it? Many people are surprised when they first hear their recorded voice. As stated before, people associate certain character traits with certain voices. For example, if someone speaks quite slowly and deliberately and makes long pauses, many people feel that such a person has no life temperament and fire. Often such a person is called "lame." In a conversation, the voice decides within a few seconds whether and how we reach the other person ... what mood, what tone, what echo we achieve.

Research results often show that people prefer hearing speakers with a warm and deep voice rather than those with a high, gushing voice. Low voices often enjoy an advantage of trust and are classified as competent, self-confident, and credible. In movies, for example, Santa Claus or other authoritarian figures usually have dark and sonorous voices. These voices are considered a mark of wisdom and power. Shrill squeaky voices, on the other hand, trigger unpleasant feelings in the other person. A lifeless and weak voice acts as a soporific. A professional will not radiate strong conviction and high competence if their voice is weak and thin. In this case, their listeners think that the professional must be quite indifferent to the subject and lacks qualifications.

The good news at this point is that your voice is changeable. Anyone familiar with "My Fair Lady" knows what Professor Higgins said, "When you give a person a new voice, you give them a new character." Voice training with simple and regular exercises can have a significant positive impact on voice development in a short period of time. The focus here is on improving breathing technique with the aim of obtaining a pleasant, confident, and convincing voice. The starting point is abdominal breathing. Psychogenic breathing and voice training was discussed in Chapter 14, Mental Training. The following voice exercise to improve your voice quality comes from Enkelmann and his audio file "A positive day begins."

After three months of practice, note what has changed in your voice and to what degree:

- Voice pitch
- Speech tempo
- Voice volume

TIP

Breathe out and breathe in, saying each letter in a loud voice until you run out of breath: I-E-A-O-U. Please keep the order. We start with the letter "I" at the highest frequency. Put your hand on your head and you will feel a slight vibration. By saying this letter, the head area gets better blood flow and more energy. The "E" activates the throat area. If you put your hands to your throat, you can feel this. The "A" with a wide-open mouth has a positive effect on the chest area. The "O" affects the upper abdomen. The "U" energizes the lower abdominal area. Speak this combination of letters five times in a row. If your voice seems too bright, speak the "U" several times a day. Also, you can read texts in a whisper to get a deeper voice.

Breathe out and in, humming softly with your lips closed: MMMM. When you run out of breath, repeat this exercise three times with more force each time. The third time, put as much force as you can into your MMMM. Do you feel the strong vibration in your chest and abdomen? This exercise trains that area.

The next exercise trains the pronunciation. It leads to powerful, expressive pronunciation. Exhale and inhale, and then speak the tongue R: RRRRRR. Speak the following words out loud with a totally exaggerated "R": rub, roll, riff, romp, rich, ribbon, rock'n'roll, weir, err, stray, etc.

Finish the voice training with the Tarzan exercise. This is not only a breathing and vocal exercise, but also suitable as a prophylactic against colds. You breathe out again and in deeply. Clench your hands into fists. Now slowly speak the letters of the first exercise. While speaking a letter, drum your fists on the upper base of your chest. Do not do this at shoulder level or too close to the neck.

- ◼ Speech volume
- ◼ Pronunciation
- ◼ Timbre
- ◼ Modulation
- ◼ Persuasiveness

If you want to combine voice training with mental training, I recommend the following autosuggestion by Nikolaus B. Enkelmann:

"I am determined to seize the opportunities in my life.

If you want to be successful, you have to be articulate in speaking and absolutely confident in the tone of your voice.

I know that inner confidence is crucial to the power of speech.

It is a question of confidence in one's own power. I can be secure in speaking only when I am secure inwardly. I am secure, completely confident, and free of all inhibitions!"

Breathing and voice training is the basis for successful conversations.

TRAINING TO IMPROVE THE CONDUCT OF CONVERSATIONS

For professionals, conversations with the following groups of people are to be distinguished:

- Client conversations
- Discussions with employees

In both cases, the successful conduct of conversations is important for professional success. For a successful private life, conversations with your life partner, family, and friends are crucial. Words can motivate or demotivate. Words can help achieve goals or miss them. Words can convince clients and employees, inspire them, or lead to the loss of the client relationship or the employee. Words can unite or divide people. Words can inspire employees to extraordinary performance or be the seed of failure. However, communication does not only consist of words. Silence, body language, action, or inaction also have a communicative character. Effective communication is particularly important when people want to achieve goals. Be it professionally or privately. But how does one communicate effectively? The focus of a successful conversation is on effective communication between people.

Distinguishing between Content and Relationship Levels

Effective communication is understood as communication that leads to a specific goal. This includes not only the acquisition or employee interview, but also small talk, which usually aims to establish a relationship between the interlocutors. In communication psychology, a distinction is made between the content or subject level and the relationship level (see Figure 15.2).

On the content level or subject level, "objectively" verifiable facts of rational content such as dates, length of employment, etc., are communicated. On the content level, the emotional interplay of the communication partners – in

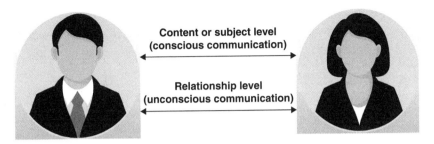

Content or subject level (conscious communication)

Relationship level (unconscious communication)

FIGURE 15.2 Content or subject level and relationship level in communication

contrast to the relationship level – is left out. In psychology, the relationship level is the quality of interpersonal cooperation in the sense of intuitive, emotional, and social inner connectedness that helps people feel connected outside of the content level. First of all, it is important to recognize that communication takes place on both a content and a relationship level. By far the greater proportion in communication occurs unconsciously at the relationship level. Those who believe that they are communicating exclusively verbally fail to realize that the person they are talking to also perceives body language, including the voice, both consciously and unconsciously. The saying goes, "It's not what you say, but how you say it."

Someone who has an image of humanity that is characterized by respect, tolerance, and acceptance will approach their interlocutor differently than someone who feels superior to them. Arrogance kills any communication. Those who believe that the listener does not perceive whether respect is being shown to them are mistaken. People who want to gain trust should be authentic. Authentic people are truthful and honest. They are who they are. It doesn't matter whether they are in a meeting with a client, giving a presentation, in an appraisal or job interview, or in their private lives.

An important principle of effective communication in conversation is goal or result orientation rather than problem orientation. The right questions help to prepare focused conversations. Anyone who answers the following questions in writing before an interview with (potential) clients or (potential) employees will have made a significant contribution to effective and efficient conversation.

1. **Determine the objective**
   - What do I want to achieve?
   - Why am I going there?

2. **Know the listener and their expectations (analysis)**
   - What does my conversation partner want to achieve and what are their goals?
   - What do we have in common?
   - Where do we differ?
3. **Determine the right approach (solutions)**
   - What am I talking about?
   - What is the best statement to achieve my goal?
   - Possible objections of my conversation partner?
   - Possible answers to my conversation partner's objections?
4. **Finding a hook to open the conversation**
   - How can I open the conversation?
   - What are the common interests?
5. **Call to action**
   - What needs to be initiated by whom and by when?
   - What are the next steps?

At the end of a conversation, the main results should be summarized, in business in writing, if possible.

Empathy as the Key to Success

Even Henry Ford said, "If there is any one secret of success, it lies in the ability to get the other person's point of view and see things from that person's angle as well as from your own." Communication psychologists today would refer to this as a person's ability to be empathic. Empathy is the term used to describe a person's ability to grasp another person from the outside as holistically as possible, to understand their feelings but without necessarily sharing them, and thus to be clear about their understanding and actions (cf. https://en.wikipedia.org/wiki/Empathy). One could also formulate it colloquially: Understanding the world of the other! Empathy is the key to success. If you can establish a relationship with your interlocutor, you will win the other person's sympathy. This also means taking an honest interest in the other person. Empathy is a central characteristic of people who can create a so-called win-win situation during a conversation.

Creating a Win-Win Situation

The core element of a win-win conversation strategy is addressing the interests of the other person. The result of this is that the partners conduct a discussion on the factual level and do not get caught up in their fears and anxieties or mutual slights and recriminations. Points must be found, which are to the advantage of both discussion partners. Those who are only concerned with asserting their own interests, who only see their own advantages, should not be surprised if no agreement is found at the end of a conversation. A central element of a successful win-win strategy is being able to create a "we" feeling. In the end, both parties must find themselves in the points that have been agreed upon.

Positive Language and Constructive Criticism

Who doesn't know people who see everything negatively? The corners of the mouths of these contemporaries are usually turned down. Smiling and laughing are often foreign to these people. The most prominent characteristic of these people is criticism. Not positive or constructive criticism, but negative criticism. This negative mindset shows itself in negative language. Negative language does not lead to effective communication. Positive language is an important principle for effective communication. Criticism should be constructive and forward-looking. Many people can spend hours discussing mistakes or negative events in the past. However, it is crucial to remember that mistakes or negative events in the past are clues for improvement in the future. A person who has made a mistake does not want to have this mistake pointed out to them constantly by their interlocutor. They know that they have done something wrong. Constructive criticism is therefore expressed by the interlocutors talking about how mistakes can be avoided in the future and what exactly needs to be done to achieve the desired result in the future. But what distinguishes exceptionally good communicators who have successes in conversations?

Practice Active Listening

You are particularly good at listening! Listening is the central task and characteristic of a professional who can communicate exceptionally well with others. Those who do not listen will hardly be able to find out the interests of the other person. Those who listen carefully will find the "win points" of the interlocutor, which are so important for the success of the conversation. But how can you learn to become a better listener? By practicing what is known as "active listening" during a conversation. A person who listens actively is able to reproduce what the conversation partner has said in their own words. If you then ask your conversation partner whether they have understood you correctly and wait for a positive confirmation, you can be sure that the other person feels understood.

Five Steps to Effective Communication

Some important characteristics and tasks of effective communicators have already been presented. The five steps shown in Figure 15.3 serve as a guideline for professionals who want to communicate particularly effectively and efficiently.

Step 1. In the first step, you must establish a relationship with the respective interlocutor. This assumes that the other person finds you at least likeable enough to listen to you. People with charm have an easier time of it than conversation grumps. Smiling connects. Basically, this phase is about finding the right rapport with the other person. Colloquially, people often say that if they get along particularly well with their conversation partner, they are on the same wavelength. In the course of a conversation, people who are in resonance take on the posture, gestures, and facial expressions, and sometimes also the breathing, the pitch, and the tone of voice of the person they are talking to. This usually happens unconsciously. Anyone who has ever observed a couple newly in love in public will very quickly notice that these couples often adopt an identical posture. In the jargon of Neurolinguistic Programming (NLP), this phenomenon is called "pacing" (mirroring) in the context of "rapport." When people come into contact with each other, their verbal and nonverbal communication usually adjusts to each other unconsciously. The more positively the individual evaluates the contact, the stronger is their adaptation to the other. To establish rapport, one can

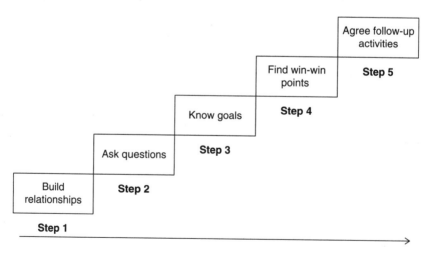

FIGURE 15.3 Five steps to effective communication

empathetically and respectfully adapt to the body language of the other, in other words, mirror their body language.

Step 2. Who asks, leads. The right questions are crucial to the success of the conversation. There are many distinct categories of questions, which will be discussed in more detail in a moment. Against the background of Steps 3 and 4, the questions should be formulated in such a way that you can clearly and unambiguously state the goals of your discussion partner and identify the decisive win points of your counterpart. So-called open questions, which cannot be answered with a simple yes or no, help here. It takes several sentences to answer an open question. The following are open questions that can be decisive for negotiation success, for example:

■ What exactly has to be in place for you to agree to this agreement or item? Or:

■ Under what conditions do you agree?

If you now listen carefully and really know all the points that lead to the agreement of your discussion partner, then it is only a matter of checking whether you can or want to fulfill these points. If so, you have achieved the goal of the conversation.

Step 3. You need to know the goals of your conversation partner in order to find the crucial win-win points in Step 4. Only if you know exactly what your conversation partner wants, can you prepare a win-win conversation strategy. However, the interlocutor does not always disclose the true goals of the conversation. Often people say one thing but mean something completely different. Sometimes people don't even know exactly what they want. Here you can see how important Step 2 is for the success of the conversation. Only those who ask have a chance to explore the other person's goals.

Step 4. Negotiations consist of compromises. If you stubbornly insist on your point of view, you should not be surprised if the other person blocks you. Effective communication is then no longer possible. The moment each party is satisfied with the agreed result, i.e., when the points that are decisive for the respective party can be realized, an agreement is reached. This is what is known as a win-win situation.

Step 5. At least in business, written documentation of the agreement reached between the contracting parties is usually required. This means that the agreed results must be translated into a contract. But also, in employee meetings or in the context of projects, what has been agreed should lead to (follow-up) activities. An effective and successful discussion can be recognized by the fact that a follow-up activity is agreed upon. A conversation that does not lead to an action was not successful. This is because nothing follows from the conversation.

Those who communicate effectively and efficiently use figurative language and get to the point. This includes simple, clear, understandable, and concise language. Anyone who thinks in a complicated way usually also expresses himself in a complicated way. If you use a lot of foreign words and technical terms in conversations that your interlocutor doesn't know, you shouldn't be surprised if you are not understood. So, if you want to be understood, you should speak the language of your conversation partner. And this does not only apply to conversations abroad.

Quick-Wittedness in Critical Conversational Situations

Most of us have had situations in our professional or private lives where a quick-witted answer was not immediately obvious and then, in retrospect, we suddenly think of the sentences and questions we should have said. Training to improve conversational skills also includes training to increase repartee. Quick-wittedness helps to bring critical conversation situations or negotiations to a successful conclusion. Matthias Pöhm focused on the topic of repartee as a rhetoric trainer in the 1990s. In his book, "Das NonPlusUltra der Schlagfertigkeit: Die besten Techniken aller Zeiten" (The NonPlusUltra of repartee: The best techniques of all time), he distinguishes between three areas of repartee:

■ Reply
■ Wit and
■ Discussion

In the reply skill, a verbal attack is followed by a hidden counterattack. We make witty remarks about statements or in situations. When a person succeeds in selling themselves confidently in a negotiation, meeting, or discussion, we also perceive that person as quick-witted and Pöhm calls this discussion skill. This is the most important type of repartee for professionals. In his book, Pöhm shows a variety of techniques that help a professional become more quick-witted and successful in conversation with others, both in their professional and personal lives. First, he sets up four simple rules of repartee, equating repartee with aplomb:

Rule 1: Repeat the name of the interlocutor or attacker: You reinforce a response if you repeat the name of the attacker again. This comes across as confident.

Rule 2: Look your counterpart in the eye with a steady gaze. A steady, confident gaze alone makes you look like a winner nonverbally. After you have answered the question, you stop looking at the aggressor. You are effectively cutting him off nonverbally.

Rule 3: Hold yourself upright. Straighten up "tree trunk-like."

Rule 4: Speak loudly. If you speak your mind out loud, you come across as self-confident and confident.

In order for your answer to appear confident, you should speak loudly, hold yourself upright, look intensively at your counterpart, and immediately pull your gaze away after your answer. However, this only applies to conversational situations in which you are replying to attacks and several other participants in the conversation are present.

Much more frequently, however, there are individual conversational situations for professionals vis-à-vis clients and employees in which you want to convince the other person for a certain cause. This can be acquisition talks with clients and employees or talks where you want to inspire and convince a client or employee for something else. In the following, I have transferred selected techniques from Matthias Pöhm to typical conversation situations of professionals, which you can use for a successful and quick-witted conversation. Figure 15.4 shows an overview of possible techniques:

These techniques are intended to contribute to effective communication, where effective is synonymous with successful in the sense of results-oriented conversation. Training to improve conversational skills is not only important in everyday professional life. Think of the many conversational situations with your life partner, children, friends, and generally in everyday life. The right words and questions are critical to the outcome of a conversation. A good technique to motivate children is the so-called alternative question. You give certain alternatives that always lead to the same result. For example, if you want your child to go to bed at night, but the child still wants to play, ask the following question: "Do you still want to play with X or with Y before you go to bed?" In both cases, it's off to bed for the child afterwards. The same works if you want to go out to eat at a restaurant with your life partner. "Would you like to have dinner with me tonight in an Italian or a Korean restaurant?" In both cases, you will go to a restaurant and the goal of going out with your partner is achieved.

You can, of course, use the alternative question in professional situations. You want the client to place an order in any case. For example, it could be about a business valuation. Depending on the scope of services, the fees vary. For example, a full expert opinion is more expensive than a short opinion on so-called indicative values. In this case, the alternative question would be

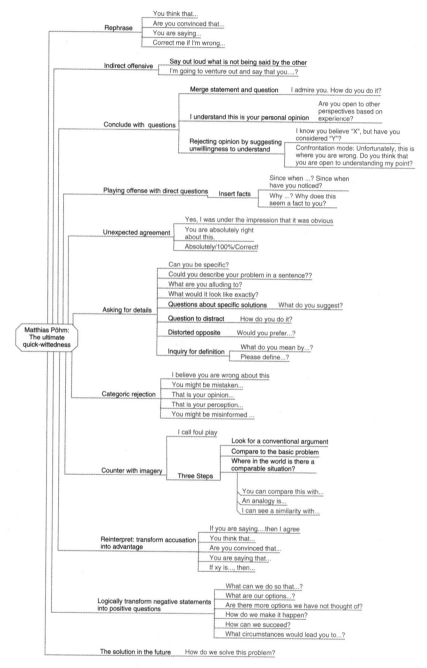

FIGURE 15.4 Selected techniques of repartee by Matthias Pöhm

EXAMPLE

Clients frequently raise the following objections during acquisition discussions:

- Your offer is too expensive!
- You do not have the necessary expertise for this task in your company!
- Your company is too small for this assignment.
- You do not have the necessary capacities for this engagement.
- Competitor XY is cheaper than your company!

For all of these objections, you can respond with the following techniques, for example:

- Rephrase or reinterpret:

    You mean, if the offer were a good value from your point of view, you would accept it?

    You mean, if we could show you that we have the necessary expertise, you would place the assignment with us?
    Or

- Solution-oriented:

    What would the offer have to be like for you to accept it?

    Exactly what expertise are you looking for?

    How big would the contractor have to be for you to place the order?

In both cases, the goal is to find out the exact structure of the offer so that the client accepts it. If possible, it is important that you know or find out all objections. Often "expensive" is only pretended and there are further objections. Therefore, you should then always ask the following questions in these discussion situations:

- If we could prove the necessary capacities, would you assign the project to us?
- Are there any other preconditions that must be fulfilled for you to place the order with us?
- Find out all the preconditions that have to be fulfilled for the order to be placed and then finally, ask the following question:
- If all these requirements are fulfilled, do we get the mandate?

The client must now say yes. If they do not, repeat the question. Only when they agree do you start to explain how you will fulfill the requirements. If there are unfulfillable conditions, check whether you can fulfill the conditions by cooperating with other colleagues.

as follows: "Do you want to commission a full expert opinion or is a rough estimate of the enterprise value on an indicative basis also sufficient?" The answer to this question is an engagement in either case. Only the scope of services varies.

I got to know the technique of the alternative question during my studies. My girlfriend at the time worked as a manager in a hotel bar. Since she received more tips with larger turnovers, I suggested that she ask her guests "Would you like another glass of beer or might it be a whisky this time?" when their glasses were empty. She varied the technique with any type of drinks. In each case, the outcome was already decided beforehand. The guests ordered one more time. Her tip and income increased substantially thanks to the technique of the alternative question. You might want to pay attention to this when you next visit a restaurant or bar. Most waiters simply ask if they can bring something else. You can answer with yes or no. A clumsy question if you want to sell something.

 ## SPEECH AND PRESENTATION TRAINING

The third level concerns speech training in the true sense. Experienced speakers know that you only learn to speak by speaking. The well-known sports motto "practice makes perfect" also applies here. A good rhetoric training course therefore gives participants sufficient opportunity to improve their speaking technique through practical exercises in the seminar, in addition to voice training and training in conversational skills.

Successful managers and entrepreneurs have above-average rhetorical skills. In a few rare cases, these skills have been unconsciously adopted by excellent rhetoricians through positive imitation; in most cases, continuous and regular rhetoric training is behind them. A positive side effect of rhetoric training on these three levels is that you learn to structure your thoughts more clearly and better. For unclear thinking produces unclear speaking and is usually a defining cause for poor results.

PowerPoint Presentations

Nowadays, PowerPoint slides are habitually used by presenters in business meetings, trainings, and speeches. Many companies have established precise rules on how the slides must be formatted. Meticulous care is taken to ensure that the logo is in the right place and that the font size corresponds exactly to the company's internal specifications. The focus of the presentation is the optimized slide and not the speaker. The occasions for presentations based on PowerPoint slides are manifold for professionals. These include, among others:

- Order acquisitions
- Presentations of results during audits or other consulting projects
- Training courses
- Lectures
- Speeches
- Staff meetings
- Advisory board and supervisory board meetings

The crucial question in connection with whether a speaker should use PowerPoint for these presentation occasions is: What function should the PowerPoint slides have? For example, anyone who wants to provide information about their business valuation results during a valuation project will find: Shortly after the PowerPoint slide set is distributed as a so-called "hand-out," participants will flip through the printout and immediately focus on the assessment results. By then, most professionals will not succeed in having the participants listen attentively slide by slide to what the presenter has to say.

On the other hand, anyone who specifically uses PowerPoint as part of an order acquisition process to explain in detail their company, its services, and the reasons why the company's services are better than those of its competitors should not be surprised if they do not win the mandate. After all, in this case, the presenter has deflected attention from themselves to the company and thus, failed to recognize that they are the decisive person for winning the assignment and that the company presented on the slides is often only secondary.

It is the same with presentations, speeches, and staff meetings. In these cases, the aim is to motivate, inform, and ultimately initiate behavioral changes or activities on a regular basis. Effective presentations that achieve the desired goals often succeed better without PowerPoint in these cases.

It is not intended at this point to create the false impression that I am against PowerPoint on principle. I only want to sensitize that PowerPoint often does not lead to the desired result of a presentation. Since you probably haven't experienced a presentation that wasn't supported by PowerPoint for a long time, for years this has led to a certain herd instinct among all professionals. Everybody uses PowerPoint; therefore, PowerPoint is state-of-the-art, and I also use it for presentations. But not always! I am more interested in using PowerPoint correctly.

But how can you recognize an effective presentation? First of all, it is useful to examine the essential characteristics and features of an effective presentation and of the speaker. These include:

- Effective presentations are memorable and compelling.
- They are interesting and entertaining.
- They appeal to the left and right hemispheres of the listener's brain.
- They are delivered freely and not read.
- They contain many personal examples.
- The speaker is authentic and personable.
- The speaker generates a laugh, at least a smile.
- The audience listens attentively from beginning to end.
- The speaker informs and motivates.
- The speaker appeals to the emotions of the audience.
- The speaker is the focus of the presentation, not the PowerPoint slides.

Overall, effective presentations depend on a multitude of individual characters and characteristics. I repeat: In the end, you only learn to speak by speaking. Practice makes perfect. Video recordings and feedback from trainers with proven speaking experience can help. However, if you consider the following points in your speeches and presentations, you will quickly achieve much more impact in your presentations than in the past.

Figure 15.5 shows the seven steps that lead to effective presentations.

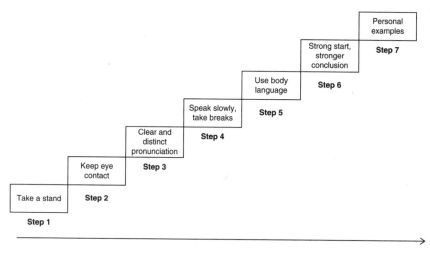

FIGURE 15.5 Seven steps to an effective presentation

Step 1: Take a stand. The nervousness of many speakers causes them to walk "long distances" during a presentation. They walk back and forth and from left to right. They are constantly on the move. True to the motto, "Don't stand still; a thought you're presenting might settle on the listener." If you want to present effectively, you should take a stand. This doesn't mean that you should remain in one place for 45, 60, or even 90 minutes. If you start a new topic, you can certainly move to another position to increase the effect. Constant running back and forth creates restlessness.

Step 2: Keep eye contact. All exceptionally good speakers maintain eye contact with their audience. They linger in the eyes of their audience. In doing so, they indirectly address all other audience members as well. Depending on the number of participants, this can be everyone present during a speech or only certain different people in each of the four areas (front, back, left, and right, respectively) of the venue. If you want to make sure to lose the attention of your audience, use PowerPoint and conduct monologues with the screen on which the PowerPoint slide is projected.

Step 3: Clear and distinct pronunciation. If you want to be heard, you must be able to articulate clearly and distinctly. You must speak loud enough to be understood by everyone. If you swallow endings or speak too softly, you will lose the attention of your listeners. Their thoughts wander to professional activities, family problems, or the next vacation. Closely related to pronunciation is the modulation and tonality of the voice. If you hit the right note, you make an impact. Everyone can train and improve their voice. There are a variety of exercises for this purpose, some of which I introduced to you in voice training. So, speak clearly and distinctly with a pleasant voice that people enjoy listening to for hours on end.

Step 4: Speak slowly, take pauses. Another cardinal mistake in speeches is that the speaker speaks too fast. Even speaking slowly on purpose, most will still speak too fast. If you want to have an effect, you have to speak slowly and take pauses. Thoughts can only settle with the listener and remain in memory if the listener has sufficient time to comprehend them. The greatest effect comes from the right length of a pause at the right time. However, this presupposes that the speaker is absolutely at rest within themselves and has full command of their subject. If you are mainly occupied with yourself and the content of your speech, you cannot use such effective stylistic devices as pauses. Many speeches are unfortunately delivered true to the motto "The faster I talk, the faster I finish my speech."

Step 5: Use body language. Effect always and everywhere: You make an impact. From the moment you first enter the room or stand on stage or in front of your audience, body language regularly takes place unconsciously.

In video trainings you can analyze positive and negative characteristics of yourself and others to increase your impact. A bad habit of many speakers is that they have one – or even worse both – hands in their pockets during a presentation. They think this makes them look especially casual, cool, and convincing. Others simply don't know where to put their hands and put them in their pants pockets. In my video trainings, I have been asking for many years how speakers with their hands in their pockets come across to the audience. I regularly get the following answers from most participants: "Arrogant, presumptuous, distancing, or seeing themselves as something better than the audience." So, those who want to come across as arrogant and overbearing should continue to keep their hands in their pockets. To everyone else, I recommend using the impact of positive body language. Former US President Barack Obama has excellent body language. Watch his gestures and facial expressions on YouTube during his speeches.

Step 6: Strong start, stronger finish. There is no second chance for a first impression. If you want to captivate your audience, you should think carefully about how you start. The first sentences of a presentation or speech are important. The conclusion is even more important. If you want to be remembered for a long time, you need a strong finish. Ideally, the audience is prompted to take action.

Step 7: Personal examples. The last and, in my opinion, the most important quality of an effective speech is that they include personal examples in their presentations. Share a specific example that you have experienced. Experience the situation again; but in front of your audience. If you talk about yourself, you come across as convincing and credible. You are authentic if you tell the experience as if you are telling it to a colleague or friend if you were not standing in front of a larger audience. In the meantime, this presentation method has long been established under the term "storytelling" and there are numerous books on this subject.

Follow these seven steps for effective presentations. PowerPoint is not the focus here. Should you now ban PowerPoint from presentations as a matter of principle? No! Of course, PowerPoint has its right to exist. Especially when it comes to creating "hand-outs" for example, to document project results, final presentations, or training documents. But if you want to present effectively, you should pay attention to completely different things than optimized PowerPoint slides. Anyone who makes PowerPoint slides the focus of their presentation is consciously or unconsciously distracting themselves. You often achieve a higher degree of effectiveness without PowerPoint. The targeted use of a

TABLE 15.1   Orientation guide for the use of PowerPoint

Occasion	yes	maybe	no
Order acquisitions		X	
Results presentations for consulting projects or final presentations		X	
Trainings	X		
Motivational speeches			X
Speeches			X
Staff meetings		X	
Advisory board and supervisory board meetings	X		

flipchart or a drawing on a tablet generates much more attention than a perfectly formatted PowerPoint slide.

Table 15.1 can serve as a guide for the use of PowerPoint. This table is certainly not to be understood dogmatically but should serve as a guide. In the future, check carefully on when and how you use PowerPoint slides. In this context, I would also like to point out how participants of presentations usually perceive information.

CHAPTER SIXTEEN

Effective Communication Tools

THE FOURTH TOOL OF successful professionals is the proper use of effective communication tools. Unlike rhetoric, which is about the "how," communication tools are about the means. The "how" in communication is much more important than the means. These are tools that support you in your professional and personal life. Nowadays, in critical situations with employees, customers, family members, and friends, text messages, chats, or emails are too often sent when a face-to-face conversation would be the more adequate means of communication. What's more, in written communication often neither the right "tone" or expression are used, nor is an appropriate form maintained. Essential information such as body language and voice cannot not be transmitted in an e-mail, chat, or text message (unless it is a video or voice message). On the other hand, phone calls or face-to-face meetings are usually more time-consuming than an email, chat, or text message, which the recipient can then read or listen to when they want.

A communication tool is effective if it helps you achieve your goals. Using the right communication tools can significantly increase a professional's effectiveness and efficiency. With this in mind, the following suggestions and tips are intended to help you consider when to use which means of communication to transmit information to colleagues, family members, and friends.

There are basically three types of communication tools: You can communicate orally, in writing, or in a video conference. All these can deliver the desired results when used correctly. However, the crucial question is: Which means should you communicate with and in what form? The means are essentially about the technical means of communication.

The following **verbal means of communication** are important for a professional:

1. Meetings with one or more counterparts
2. Telephone calls or video conferences with one or more counterparts
3. Presentations or speeches in front of a larger group of participants

AD 1: MEETINGS

Before the COVID-19 pandemic, many professionals spent a considerable amount of their time in meetings. This was especially true for executives. This is too rarely a productive time. Increasing complexity has contributed to the fact that there are many more meetings today than in the past. As a result, meeting effectiveness is more important today than ever before. Meetings can be a highly effective communication tool, however, there are important rules to follow. Malik claims that improving the effectiveness of meetings starts with eliminating meetings. In most of the professional services industry, too many meetings are held. The increasing number of meetings has also meant that each meeting often generates a series of other meetings. Therefore, it is important to question if a particular meeting is really necessary and whether there are no other ways to do the work or solve the problem?

Furthermore, good teamwork does not mean that all team members must always be in all meetings at the same time. Good teamwork is characterized by minimizing the number of meetings.

Preparation and follow-up are crucial to a meeting's success. Both the preparation of a meeting and the follow-up take time. The meeting leader needs to allocate time within their weekly planning for the preparation of the meeting. If not enough time is invested in preparation, the result is frequently a bad meeting. The central tool for preparing a meeting is the agenda. This is the task, duty, and right of every meeting leader. In principle, there should be no meetings without an agenda.

It is advisable to send the agenda to all meeting participants in advance of the meeting, if possible, in order to coordinate it with them. This gives each meeting participant the opportunity to influence the agenda.

A good agenda has few rather than many items. But it must contain important agenda items that justify the simultaneous and personal presence of the participants. The principle of focus is also important here. Effective meeting preparation also includes estimating the time needed to complete each agenda item. Even if you can't meet the times, they still serve as landmarks that should not be waived in a good meeting. This applies equally to the meeting leader as well as to the meeting participants.

TIP

Many professionals have participated in meetings where it was quickly foreseeable that the planned meeting time would not be sufficient. In such cases, it is advisable that either the chair or a meeting participant indicate that not all agenda items can be dealt with in this meeting or that items will have to be dealt with in a shorter time than allocated. In a situation like this, it becomes clear whether the meeting leader is able to distinguish between essential and non-essential items and react flexibly. Either a correction of the agenda items should be made and only the essential topics dealt with or, if possible, the discussions should be shorter or the meeting adjourned. Once again, the professional recognizes how important the principle of focus is and that they should always concentrate on the essentials.

In a meeting it becomes clear whether or not a professional is suitable as a leader. This becomes apparent to all participants because they often instinctively notice whether or not the meeting leader is on top of things. Leading meetings requires preparation, discipline, and experience. Like many things in life, leading a meeting must be learned and practiced through experience. There are a few points that should be kept in mind, which include:

■ Adherence to the schedule

■ Results-oriented and tight management of the meeting, and

■ Paying close attention to speakers

Depending on the length of the meeting, sufficient breaks, drinks, and food should also be included.

A critical success factor of any meeting is the lack of action orientation after the meeting. After each agenda item, the chair of a meeting must ensure that there is clarity about the required activities. Thus, it is a matter of defining responsibilities and deadlines for implementation. The responsibilities and the deadlines belong in the minutes of the meeting. Meeting minutes should be the rule rather the exception, even if they are only resolution minutes with keywords. The individual activities resulting from the meeting should be defined there, as well as the responsible persons and deadlines. After all, a meeting without subsequent activities raises the question of whether the meeting was necessary at all.

A central task of the session manager is to ensure that the necessary activities are also implemented. Their task is also to organize a follow-up. Only if the participants of a meeting know and feel that the leader of the meeting does not forget anything and consistently takes care of the completion, will the meeting be taken seriously. Furthermore, only in this way will the professional as a leader be taken seriously and management effectiveness emerge. This is where the task of controlling a manager comes into play again.

AD 2: PHONE OR VIDEO CONFERENCES

The pandemic has led to a fundamental change in working practices and processes for many professionals. Physical meetings where professionals met in conference rooms or offices have been replaced by video conferencing. Microsoft Teams or Zoom as well as other video conferencing providers have become a useful tool for every professional today.

It is possible to participate in a video conference not only via a desktop PC or laptop, but also with any smartphone. The integration of telephone and video calls, chat functions as well as screen sharing, and break-out rooms has significantly changed collaboration among professionals. The new normal is called hybrid working or remote working. While remote working often focuses on home office solutions, hybrid working means that a professional can work from anywhere in the world (with an internet connection) and that the processes in the company are geared toward hybrid working. This is probably not yet the case everywhere in the professional services industry, but the future workplace for many professionals will no longer be exclusively the office. In particular, when employees work in home offices or other places, it requires trust from management. If supervisors don't trust their employees, remote work and hybrid work are difficult to achieve. On the other hand, employees must have internalized the principle of personal responsibility, otherwise it will be difficult to achieve excellent work results.

Telephone calls are another way to communicate verbally. The importance of the landline phone has decreased dramatically in our group of companies.

Internally, we communicate almost exclusively on the basis of Microsoft Teams. Either without or with video function. Cell phones are then essentially used for phone calls with clients.

It is almost impossible to imagine life without cell phones. Today, constant accessibility is almost only interrupted by dead spots. In addition, a smartphone or tablet can also be used for video conferencing or video calls.

The first question that arises with every phone or video conference is whether the content of the conversation could also be communicated in writing or, if necessary, discussed at a later date during a face-to-face meeting. Telephone calls and video conferences can be a curse or a blessing. On the one hand, a professional is expected to be available at all times; on the other hand, they are expected to work effectively and efficiently. However, every phone or video call keeps a professional from being effective and efficient because they are interrupted. For this reason, I recommend the following five rules when talking business on the phone:

Do not be available at all times. This applies to your office hours as well as when you are on the road. You decide when you want to make or accept a phone or video call.

Be prepared when you call clients or employees:

- What is the goal of the call?
- Are there follow-up activities associated with the call?
- Is the timing of the call appropriate? Too early in the morning, during lunch break, or too late in the evening are often times that should only be used for urgent calls.
- Is a written record of the content necessary for documentation purposes, so that an e-mail might be more adequate?
- Is the phone video call really necessary?

Do not accept calls when performing a professional activity (for example, reviewing audit reports, expert opinions, etc.). The effort to "get back into it" is disproportionate to the benefit of the interruption.

Always honor your obligation to maintain confidentiality and do not make confidential calls in public places (for example, trains, restaurants, and so forth).

Get to the point quickly and engage in small talk only in exceptional circumstances.

> **NOTE**
>
> Phone calls and video conferences can be a big productivity killer. In self-management, we discuss in detail how to manage yourself effectively and efficiently. If you take every phone call, you will be less productive and achieve goals later or not at all. For this reason, it's especially important that you don't take every phone call when working in the office. Depending on the role you hold in your company, you will receive a large number of calls from telemarketers on a daily basis. Professionals are financially strong customers to whom one likes to sell products and services. In my companies, I have clearly regulated that I never take such calls personally. My employees always ask telemarketers to communicate their concerns to me by e-mail. As a rule, I receive only a few e-mails afterward, and I then tell my employees how to proceed the next time the telemarketer calls.

Maybe you have voicemail set up on your smartphone or landline phone? For me, the only time I end up with voicemail is when I am in a dead spot, or my cell phone is unreachable. One advantage of the mailbox is that your messages can be recorded. The big disadvantage is that you have to check the message and respond. While it may be that some issues have since been resolved, in many cases it will simply be a message for you to call back. This gives you one more unscheduled to-do, which in the worst-case scenario also has to be carried forward into the next day. For this reason, I have not set up a voicemail in my office. If the caller wants to speak to me urgently, he will try again. In addition, most callers don't suppress caller ID, so I can at least tell if the caller is a personal contact. To call back, I can use travel time in the car, or the blocks of time reserved for phone calls.

AD 3: PRESENTATIONS OR SPEECHES

Presentations and speeches are another form of oral communication. In contrast to meetings and telephone calls, a presentation is usually a monologue and takes place in front of a larger audience. The occasions for speeches and presentations are manifold, and they can take place with clients as well as with colleagues. In a speech, it is important to use the tools of rhetoric correctly. If it is not a specialized presentation, it is regularly about motivating clients and employees in a certain direction. For this reason, I would like to point out once again that motivational presentations in particular will regularly be more successful if PowerPoint is not used or is used only to a limited extent.

The following essential **written means of communication** can be used in practice:

- letters (including offers or engagement letters)
- e-mails
- text messages
- memos
- minutes
- reports

For a professional, it is irrelevant whether the medium of written communication is paper or electronic in digital form. What all written communications have in common is that they should be used effectively. However, most written communication is formulated with the sender in mind rather than the recipient. Effective written communication, on the other hand, should be written with the recipient in mind. Many professionals now too often have an aversion to the traditional written form, preferring verbal communication via smartphone; a professional thinks that communication by phone is faster than in writing. However, the written form often takes less time, not more. It saves time. Written communication, especially electronic by mail, chat, or text message, makes you independent of personal presence and is now possible from almost anywhere. The most important thing is that the written form gives you opportunity to think, and it often forces you to think.

The critical question in any written communication is, "What effect shall this message have on the recipient?" Most professionals are aware that regardless of any content of a written communication, the real work begins now. The message must be edited to give it the greatest possible chance of triggering the intended effect on the recipient. Often, one or more activities should follow.

NOTE

For many years, I have made sure that when activities are to be initiated, the written communication concludes with a call to action before the obligatory closing phrase at the end of a text. Since in many cases the last sentence is better remembered anyway, this should be the call to action. Completely independent of who the recipient of the information is, I always use the word "please" in a call to action. Unfortunately, the two important words "please" and "thank you" are used far too rarely. This is true in both written and verbal communications.

All messages should therefore be designed with the recipient in mind, so that they have a chance of triggering the intended effect for the recipient. Successful professionals are effective. Effective written communication means finding out as best as possible who the recipient(s) are and what they are most likely to respond to. A professional can only ever determine this on a case-by-case basis, but a few thoughts should help you become a little more sensitive in your written communications. For example, if the communication concerns a client, it is critical to know what your client's professional background is. If you know that the recipient is a lawyer, then it is better to avoid numbers, graphs, and tables and when possible work with text only. If, on the other hand, the recipient is an engineer, then you should minimize text but use graphics and, above all, mathematical curves in coordinate systems. The engineer's eye is trained for this, and it arouses their interest. For employees from the accounting department or among professional colleagues, text and sometimes graphics should often be minimized, but instead a lot of numbers should be presented in tables. The typical finance person and controller prefers numbers. Finance people (and accountants), by the way, often have a talent for finding at a glance exactly the number that is wrong in a table.

Unfortunately, far too often, simple rules of a factual and logical structure of texts are not mastered in written communication. Many professionals do not bring structure into a text. The question arises whether they have a structure in their thinking. Often the linguistic expression, grammar, choice of words as well as spelling and punctuation leave much to be desired. However, clarity, conciseness, and accuracy of language are essential for an effective professional. Actually, these are skills that may be assumed in academics. However, this is not always the case. Since a professional's services are usually provided in the form of written reporting, exactness, precision, and conscientiousness are also expected in written communications. Anyone who does not fulfill these qualities in communications with clients must expect that the client will draw conclusions with regard to their professional performance. By the way, anyone who has children knows that they often communicate with each other using only single words and abbreviations. Text messages from teens cannot be understood by every adult because of their coding. Sadly, in the age of PowerPoint, it has also become a bad habit for people often only writing in keywords or sentence fragments instead of complete sentences.

Written documents should facilitate communication and not make it more difficult. They should relieve the memory, facilitate the overview of essential things, and help keep track of the flood of information. Effective written communication must be oriented to this.

In concluding this chapter on effective means of communication I offer a few thoughts on technical means of communication. Professionals mainly use desktop computers, notebooks, smartphones, and tablets as their technical means of communication. The extent to which other technical means of communication will change our profession in virtual worlds in the future will not be discussed in depth here. What is much more exciting in a digitalized world, however, are the so-called "collaboration tools" professionals will be using in the future. Collaboration means the joint and networked cooperation of people in projects, groups, or even teams with the help of the internet and electronic media. There are a number of products that can be used in project communication to make processes more effective and efficient and to simplify control. These products include, for example, Microsoft Teams, Trello, Slack, and Asana. In a broader sense, video conferencing tools such as like Zoom, GotoMeeting, Webex, and Teamviewer are also included. In this book you will find mind maps that can be used via apps and cloud platforms for collaboration in project teams. Professionals are directly feeling the effects of the age of digitalization. Practically overnight, the pandemic has completely changed many processes irrevocably. Holding professional video conferences requires technical knowledge of light and sound. This also includes professional equipment (webcams or cameras, microphones and stands, monitors, a powerful PC, and stable internet connections). Professionals who skimp on the necessary equipment and act too conservatively will lose out. They will lose clients, but also young and qualified employees who are tech-savvy. Accountants know that the digitization of financial accounting has begun. Receipts are scanned and automatically posted, which is where jobs are eliminated. Collaboration tools should make processes transparent for all team members. Above all, they should contribute to effective communication across teams all the way to the client. Effective professionals use the technical communication tools for project success. It is advisable, regardless of age and length of time in the profession, to keep a close eye on technical developments here.

CHAPTER SEVENTEEN

Work-Life-Balanced-Scorecard

IF YOU WANT TO be exceptionally successful, you must focus all your time and energy on the ONE Thing that leads to success. A life that must be in balance to be successful is a misconception. Life purpose and life meaning are the ingredients for a successful life. Those who know their life purpose and life meaning will pursue the things that are in harmony with their mission and sense of life. Extraordinary results require focused attention and time. Having time for the ONE Thing means not having time for another thing. And that makes balance an impossibility. Those who want to be successful will always have periods in their lives that make balance with other areas of life impossible. Those who want to be exceptionally successful will have even more phases in their lives that make balance with other areas of life impossible. However, if you want to be happy in your life, you need equilibrium in the different areas of your life. Therefore, you should not permanently focus exclusively on your professional life. Use your private life for a balance. You lead a happy life when your life is in harmony with your life's mission and purpose. However, if you permanently neglect your personal life, don't be surprised if you lack the balance and energy needed to achieve your life's purpose. As you get older, there is a high probability that an inner emptiness will appear. You are particularly successful professionally, but not happy because you have failed to build positive relationships with others in your personal

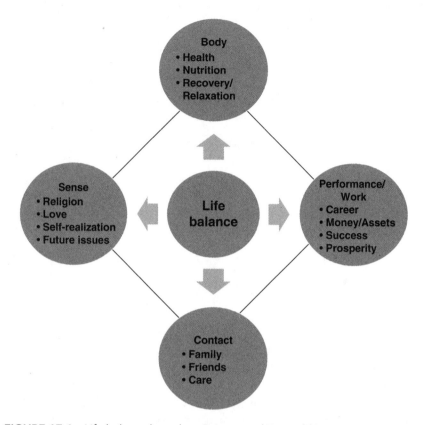

FIGURE 17.1 Life balance based on Seiwert and Peseschkian

life. Failed marriages or life partnerships, children who turn away from you, and no friends in your private life are the result of a professional's life being focused exclusively on their job.

In Chapter 3, we discussed the principle of focusing and concentrating on little or on ONE Thing. Different areas of life were presented. Lothar Seiwert and Nossrat Peseschkian focus on four areas of life and have developed the following life balance model. Analyze for yourself the four areas of life shown in Figure 17.1.

There is no generally binding guideline for how much time you should spend in any one of the four areas of life. Just as a person feels stress individually, they feel the time balance in different areas of their life. Everyone must determine their own individual time balance feeling here.

Body and health:
- What is my current state of health or how often have I been ill in the last 12 months?
- Were there any illnesses, if applicable, showing first signs of occupational overload?

Work and performance:
- What professional successes have I achieved in the last 12 months, and what is my current professional situation?
- What professional opportunities and risks do I see in the next 12 months or in the next few years?

Family and friends:
- What is my private situation?
- What is the state of my partnership?
- How are my family relationships and my relationships with friends? Have I cultivated these relationships sufficiently?

Meaning and culture:
- What motivates me and why?
- What are my life motivations and strengths?
- Why do I do what I do?

If you haven't yet analyzed how you spend those 8,760 hours a year, do it now. Determine the amount of time you spend in each area of your life during the year. In the next step, you can determine in which areas of your life you want to shift time.

 ## BALANCED SCORECARD AS A MODEL FOR THE WORK-LIFE-BALANCED-SCORECARD

In order to create and control the balance between work and private life, you can use the fifth tool of a successful professional. It is the Work-Life-Balanced-Scorecard, which I developed. The Balanced Scorecard (BSC) is a controlling instrument and goes back to Robert S. Kaplan and David P. Norton. Today, it is widely used in companies and is generally accepted. For many years, the BSC has also been an established instrument in the field of strategic controlling of companies. Its advantage over other methods of corporate management is that

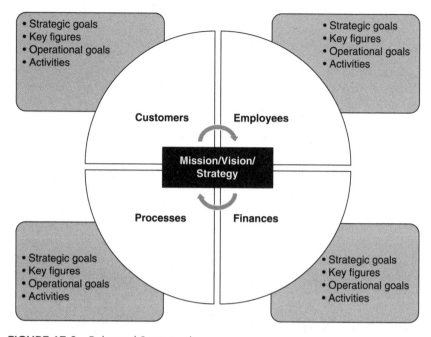

FIGURE 17.2 Balanced Scorecard

it takes a holistic view of several perspectives and is not limited exclusively to the financial side of the company as are traditional controlling instruments.

It uniquely links a company's long-term goals with concrete activities and thus, provides companies with an immediate guide to action. Figure 17.2 shows the basic structure of a Balanced Scorecard of companies.

Based on a clearly defined strategy and vision, the graphic makes it clear that the BSC includes in its considerations not only the financial but also the customer, process, and employee perspectives. The starting point for the considerations is the long-term corporate goals, which are reflected in a corporate vision. Concrete operational corporate goals are derived from the long-term corporate goals. The previously defined key performance indicators show the degree of target achievement and are used for control purposes. The BSC is a holistic approach. The link between long-term (corporate) goals and concrete (daily) activities makes the instrument suitable as a support for successful corporate management. Quite a few professionals, especially the large auditing firms and law firms, have recognized this and use the instrument in their companies for management and control.

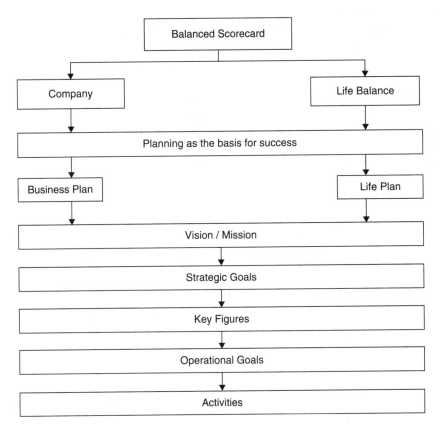

FIGURE 17.3 From business plan to life plan

The concept of the BSC in the company can also be applied to the life of a professional. Figure 17.3 shows the links and similarities between the BSC for a company and for the life of the professional.

Planning is an essential basis for success. This applies to both entrepreneurial and personal success. The best strategy will fizzle out if it is not accompanied by careful planning that weighs the various methods of achieving the goal that ultimately leads to action.

At the beginning, as already described, is the vision or long-term goal. Clarifying the following two questions serves as a starting point:

■ Where should the company and where does the professional want to be in the long term?
■ What should the professional's life look like in the distant future?

The answers to these questions are closely related to the professional's self-confidence and self-esteem. In addition, communication with oneself and with others is a crucial factor for success in both areas of life. If you constantly talk negatively to yourself and others, you will – "self-fulfilling prophecy" – often get the events in your life as you imagined them.

Based on the visions, strategic goals for the business as well as for the private life are formulated. Comparable to a compass, the metrics serve to verify that you are moving toward the goals. The goals should be SMART, as outlined earlier: They should be specific, measurable, action-oriented, realistic, and timed. Operational goals drive short-term actions and activities.

A common pattern in the thinking and actions of highly successful professionals is their focus on results. Successful professionals achieve positive results for their clients and ultimately for themselves. Whether a professional wants to apply this focus on results to their private life is a personal decision. Often people do something in their life not because of the results, but for completely different reasons.

TRANSFERRING THE CONCEPT OF THE BSC TO PRIVATE LIFE

My Work-Life-Balanced-Scorecard combines both thoughts and helps day by day to bring implementation-oriented balance into your own life and at the same time, not losing sight of the essential and important goals. Figure 17.4 shows how it works.

The creation of a Work-Life-Balanced-Scorecard requires clarification of the following questions in three areas:

Values:
- Which values are important to you?
- Which values have priority for you?
- Are your values compatible with your personal and professional life?

Life motives:
- What are your motives in life?
- What really drives you?
- Are there extrinsic motives in your life?

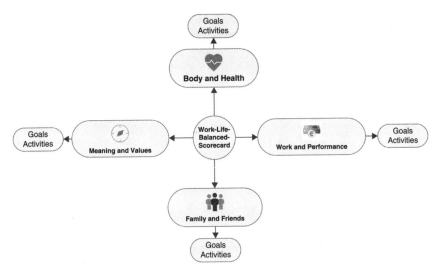

FIGURE 17.4 Work-Life-Balanced-Scorecard

Life Roles:

- What life roles do you currently have?
- How much time do you spend on which role?
- Is the time commitment of each role consistent with your values and life motives?

Clarifying these questions is the starting point for long-term professional and personal goal setting.

WORK AND PERFORMANCE

Accountants, lawyers, and their staff often work 60 hours or more per week. Professional life dominates private life. Relaxation and recovery phases are often shifted to vacations and are usually too short. Time for life partners, family, or friends becomes a bottleneck in these cases. The question of the meaning and motives for this one-sided time allocation can often not be answered clearly by professionals. Ultimately, a lifestyle that is lopsidedly focused on the job can lead to health damage, if it comes to physical and mental overload. There is often a lack of balance in a professional's life. The Work-Life-Balanced-Scorecard shows how professionals can create a balance between their professional and private life and thereby live in harmony with their private and professional goals.

It is up to each person to decide whether or not they want to develop a vision for their life. But isn't it interesting that the autobiographies of particularly successful personalities show that most of these people had visions?

 ## BODY AND HEALTH

A healthy body with a lot of energy is the source for carrying out professional and private activities. People who exercise regularly and eat a healthy diet do a lot for their bodies and generally have reserves of strength that others do not. There is also the question of whether you allow your body enough sleep to regenerate. We all know that both professional and private success is only enjoyable if you are healthy.

Professionally successful people especially spend most of their waking hours on work. Stephen R. Covey posed the question, "How Many People on Their Deathbed Wish They'd Spent More Time at the Office?" How much you work depends on your goals, values, and life motivations. That's why clarity in these areas is so important. Quite a few people, when asked, "What would you do if you knew you only had one day to live?" Would you seek closeness with family or friends rather than going to the office?

 ## FAMILY AND FRIENDS

An intact partnership, family, or friends can be a valuable and important source of energy for professional life. Too often, particularly successful people take refuge in their work, as the fights they have to get through with their partner at home are much more energy-sapping than the daily office work. However, if you don't work on your partnership, and if you don't schedule time to take care of it, you will most likely lose your partner one day. Professionals often like to work with checklists. Checking the relationship quality of a life partnership can easily be done with the following four points:

1. Values
2. Joint activities
3. Sex
4. Resonance

A long-term and harmonious partnership is based on the couple's shared **values**. Values are usually formed quite early, with imprinting often coming from parents or people who had a considerable influence during childhood and adolescence. A person's values change less and less as they age. Around the age of 20, most people have a set of values that is quite solid in itself. The values form the daily framework for action and also influence decisions in everyday life. Not all values are equally important. It is therefore important to determine:

▪ What are important values for me?
▪ What are important values for my partner?

Work out the similarities and differences. Values that are important to you should also be important to your life partner.

EXAMPLE

A conscientious, tidy, and punctual person is likely to exhibit these characteristics at a later age. This applies equally to career orientation and sense of family. A person for whom career comes first will also maintain this value firmly for several years. A deeply faithful person will probably not become an atheist.

Clarity about the values that are important to you and those that are important to your partner is the foundation of a functioning partnership. If these sets of values do not match, problems in a partnership are inevitable.

Furthermore, a couple should have **joint activities**. Those who do nothing together except on vacations often live side by side. For specialists who have turned their "hobby" into a profession, everyday working life is often omnipresent. This is even more true if "career" is a particularly important value for the professional. These professionals usually subordinate everything to their job. This inevitably leaves little time for joint activities with their life partner. Those who spend little time with their partner (and possibly their children) should not be surprised if their life partner suddenly has another partner. The following questions help to determine the status quo:

▪ What were the joint activities with your partner (without children) in the last 12 months?
▪ Do you have regular dates with your partner?

Joint activities often begin with common interests and hobbies. Shared positive and happy experiences in a partnership are the link even in challenging times. Positive memories of time spent together help overcome crises in a partnership.

The next point of a happy and functioning partnership has an evolutionary biological background. Without **sex** we would not reproduce, and we would become extinct. Sex is therefore the starting point for the survival of the species. For many people, intimacy and sex are part of a happy relationship. This point may become less important as we grow older. However, this does not apply to the topic of tenderness and intimacy in a relationship. If neither sex nor intimacy take place in a relationship, then a couple lives together like brother and sister. And there are clear differences between a life partnership and siblings.

The last item in the checklist is a couple's **resonance**. It is about communication between couples. This does not mean that a couple must always be of the same opinion, nor that a couple never argues. Rather, what is meant by resonance is that a couple talks to each other frequently and gives the other an insight into their soul. Above all, this includes empathy. If one partner no longer feels understood by the other, there is a lack of resonance. In my talks, I often address people directly and say, "If you feel like you're talking to a parking meter when you talk to your partner, then you no longer have resonance." Some people laugh and some remain thoughtfully silent. People who don't feel understood often lose interest in having sex with their partner, too. Talking is not only important for happy and functioning partnerships. Talking is just as important in functioning and successful client relationships and in good relationships with employees. This is where the circle from private to professional success closes.

The previously mentioned points are the four secrets of functioning partnerships that lead to a happy relationship. The foundation for extraordinary success is an intact private relationship with the life partner. This is the starting point to professional and financial success. Your relationship with your partner in life can positively or negatively impact your professional and financial successes. Everyone who has been through a divorce knows the financial impact of a separation, which, by the way, can often be substantial even with a prenuptial agreement. The "right" partner at your side can either inspire you or clip your wings. Use these four points to check whether or not you have the right partner by your side. These are the same four points that should be present at the beginning of a partnership, by the way.

MEANING AND VALUES

In the end, most people have no time left for the question of the meaning and values of their lives. However, values are the guideline for all our actions. Meaning is the basis for fulfillment and satisfaction in life. For this reason, I regularly ask myself the following three questions:

1. What do I want to do in the future?
2. Why do I want to do it?
3. What are my key tasks in the future?

These questions help me become aware of my motives and values again and again and to check whether they are in line with my current and future key tasks.

 ## HOW DOES BALANCE COME ABOUT?

How much time each individual spends in these four areas of life is something that everyone must know for themselves. There is no patent remedy here. Conscious discussion and weekly, monthly, and annual planning that ensures that activities take place in all four areas of life is the basis for balance in the life of a successful and happy professional. The Work-Life-Balanced-Scorecard is not only a tool to help you bring balance into your life, but it is also a tool to ensure that you will only achieve your goals in each area of life if there are concrete activities behind them that actually get done. Accordingly, it supports the principle of action orientation.

The four perspectives of the time balance model make it clear that a balanced life does not only include the areas of performance and work. For a happy life, the areas of body and health, family, and friends, and meaning and values are also important. In particular, the questions of Why? and about the future take up too little time for many people.

But how can goals, key figures, and activities be developed according to the levels of a balanced scorecard for the areas of health and body, family, and friends, or even values and meaning? Simple examples also show that without planning – in the sense of mentally anticipating future action – success is not possible. For example, if you want to do something for your body and health (weight loss) you need a realistic goal that should be measurably achieved in a certain time. This is always connected with certain activities like running, cycling, etc., as well as healthy nutrition. Here it is necessary to find suitable key figures as well as dates by which the goal should be achieved. For example, a strategic goal for an overweight person could be the reduction of body weight, by a certain weight (key figure), for example X lbs. by a certain date. As an operational (intermediate) goal, a specific weight reduction (key figure: for example, four lbs. in four weeks), can be set as an intermediate target in the next step. Essential activities on the way to realizing the strategic goal are, for example, regular running, cycling, swimming (key figure: number of days and duration of running), healthy nutrition (number of calories consumed with meals, cholesterol levels, etc.).

This example shows that the Balanced Scorecard technique can be easily applied to other areas of life. Even for the area of family and friends, clear strategic goals can be defined (for example, a happy, and harmonious family life), which are underpinned by clear key figures (happy time spent together with life partner, children, friends) and activities suitable for achieving the goals.

Transferring the concept of the Balanced Scorecard to private life and developing it further into a Work-Life-Balanced-Scorecard can be used to create a balance between the professional and private lives of professionals. However, a prerequisite for successful application is goal clarity. Those who know exactly what they want in their professional and private life will be more successful. The creation of a Work-Life-Balanced-Scorecard alone requires an intensive analysis of professional and private goals. For this, knowledge of one's own values, life motives, and life roles are a "conditio sine qua non." Nothing changes in a person's life unless they change. Since we are often prisoners of our own habits, concrete motives are needed to implement certain changes and new activities. A serious illness as a sign of professional overload or the separation from one's life partner due to a lifestyle that is one-sidedly focused on professional life can be avoided by using the Work-Life-Balanced-Scorecard.

Conclusion: Outlook into the Future

I N A VUCA WORLD, the question was raised whether new principles, tasks, and tools are necessary for professionals to cope with the increasing complexity in their daily professional and private lives. The book is entitled "Soft Skills for the Professional Services Industry." From the wide variety of soft skills, a selection was chosen. Various principles, tasks, and tools of successful professionals were presented. Soft skills are soft competencies that can be learned. The initial requirements are not the same for all professionals. However, this is true for all things that are to be learned. Learning a language or a sport requires talent and training. Not everyone has the talent to become a language genius or top athlete. Due to hereditary factors and social conditioning, not all professionals have the same starting conditions when it comes to learning soft skills.

However, with regular training, everyone can improve. Perseverance and the willingness to acquire these soft skills are the prerequisites for a positive personality change and a successful life. The book is intended to give you an impulse to integrate the presented soft skills into your life and to apply them on a daily basis. Since professionals have always been intensely concerned with technical knowledge and the hurdle to pass the professional exams is high, there was usually no opportunity to deal with soft skills during the training. In professional exams, soft skills are not relevant to the exam, and in the studies the topic is usually only dealt with in passing. In the first years of a professional's life after training and studies, specialist literature dominates their life until the professional exams have been passed. Only a few professionals deal with soft skills in this phase of life. Once they have passed their professional examinations, at the latest, a professional's field of activity expands to include management tasks. In addition to the specialist tasks, there are now management tasks and tasks in connection with the acquisition and support of clients. By this time, every professional realizes that it is not only professional competence that counts, but that soft skills are decisive for professional (and private) success.

For the most part, the soft skills presented here apply to both professional and private life. Separating them would be neither meaningful nor useful. The soft skills have been divided into principles, tasks, and tools. The principles of successful professionals are soft skills which, in my opinion, are also fully relevant in private life. Some professionals will object that they do a number of things in their private lives that are not result-oriented, for example. This is to be agreed with. Nevertheless, a failed partnership or a poor relationship with parents, children, and friends is also an outcome.

The soft skills related to the tasks of a professional are presented from the perspective of the professional. A separation into factual and management tasks is not useful. For this reason, a professional's key tasks are presented in the tasks. Marketing is of particular importance in this context. Without engagements, even the best expertise of a professional is of no use. The acquisition of new clients and their subsequent support are the basis for the activities of professionals and their employees. In doing so, professionals first sell themselves and then their company. Our professions are "people's business." For a good Rainmaker, the corporate brand is interchangeable. Clients will follow them if they change companies. This is not to say that investments in the corporate brand should not be made. Large law firms invest large sums in the visibility of their brand. The sums that these firms invest in developing the soft skills of their employees are comparatively small. The professional services industry and large international firms would be well advised to consider whether investments in the soft skills of their employees might not be more profitable in the future than investments in the corporate brand. Particularly in the age of digitalization, in which artificial intelligence, machine learning, and other technical developments are replacing humans, people who still work for other people are becoming even more important than before. As long as companies are still managed by people and not by machines, soft skills will make a difference.

In Part Three, Tools were presented that professionals should deal with extensively. This chapter is probably unfamiliar territory for many colleagues, which for the most part they have not yet entered. This is especially true for the tool of mental training. Those who do practice mental training will notice the biggest changes in their lives. Many professionals are not known for being particularly excited about change and tend to be very conservative. The changes a professional can achieve through the regular practice of mental training are considerable. And this means positive changes in both their professional and personal life.

The principles, tasks, and tools of successful professionals presented here help to master the still increasing complexity in professional and private, everyday life. It is common knowledge that learning is a lifelong process. In a changing environment, those who stand still and do not continue to develop will lead neither a successful nor a happy life. The principles, tasks, and tools of successful professionals are timeless. Those who observe them and integrate them into their daily lives will be more successful and also happier. Happiness comes from success. If you succeed in aligning your life with these principles, tasks, and tools, you will be on your way to a successful and happy life.

Many people believe that they must be successful in order to be happy. They have developed the belief that happiness comes only when they are successful professionally and financially. In his best-selling book, "The Happiness Advantage," Harvard professor Shawn Achor has found the opposite based on his extensive research findings:

- We become more successful when we are happier and more positive, not the other way around.
- Happiness is the joy we feel when we realize our potential.
- The happiness benefit is not the belief that we don't have to change, but it is the realization that we can change.

We can use our brains to change how we process and respond to events. If a professional, despite their critical attitude while working as a lawyer or an auditor, searches the world for positives, they will find happiness, gratitude, and optimism. Part of success is failure. There is no shame in not achieving goals and failing. However, if you fall down and stay down, you have utterly failed. This can haunt a professional for a lifetime. A child who learns to walk and falls down has the urge to get back up. This is natural behavior. We should all preserve this childlike behavior. When we see failure as an opportunity for growth, we become successful, especially if we know why we failed and that we will do better the next time. The greatest crises often offer the greatest opportunities. It's a question of how you respond to crises. The most successful professionals believe that their actions have a direct impact on their results. As you practice the soft skills presented in this book, my wish for you is success and a happy life!

About the Author

Andreas Creutzmann is a valuation expert, entrepreneur, and speaker. He is a German Certified Public Accountant (Wirtschaftspruefer), Tax Consultant (Steuerberater), and Certified Valuation Analyst (CVA). Business valuations have been Creutzmann's specialty. He has over 30 years of cross-industry experience in the valuation of international corporations as well as small and medium-sized companies in all relevant industries (e.g., banking, insurance). As an expert witness, Andreas supports the presiding judges of the major regional and higher regional courts in a multitude of court procedures under the German Stock Corporation Act by ascertaining appropriate cash compensations. He graduated with a degree in business administration from the prestigious University of Mannheim.

Since 2000, Andreas Creutzmann (CEO) has been the founder and majority shareholder of the IVA VALUATION & ADVISORY AG, Frankfurt (www.iva-valuation.de), as well as the Executive Director of Creutzmann & Co. GmbH Accounting and Tax Advisory Firm, Landau (www.creutzmann.de). He has been active in the business world for nearly 30 years and successfully built several accounting firms and established a continuing education company for professionals.

As the founder and chairman of EACVA, Andreas Creutzmann has initiated and established the Certified Valuation Analyst accreditation (CVA) in Europe. Since then, more than 1,200 valuation professionals have been trained and certified as CVAs in Germany, Austria, Switzerland, and across Europe. With the creation of the title "Certified Valuation Analyst," he has established a new profession for valuation professionals in Europe. The National Association of Certified Valuators and Analysts (NACVA, www.nacva.com) calls Andreas an "Industry Titan" of the Valuation Profession (www.nacva.com/titans).

Andreas has been an active speaker and author for 20 years. He is a speaker and lecturer in the field of finance, investment, and business valuations as well as in the area of marketing and management of professionals. He is an instructor in EACVA's CVA-training program and has been a lecturer for many years in the master's degree programs at select universities. In addition to lecturing and teaching in the field of business valuation, he is involved extensively in the marketing and management of professionals. Successful professionals do certain things differently than less successful ones. In his articles on marketing and management, Andreas shares his practical experience as an entrepreneur on the subject of success with professional colleagues. Find out more on his website at www.creutzmann.eu.

Bibliography

Achor, Shawn: The Happiness Advantage: The Seven Principles that Fuel Success and Performance at Work, 2010

Amon, Ingrid: Die Macht der Stimme: Mehr Persönlichkeit durch Klang, Volumen und Dynamik, 8th edition, 2016

Bly, Robert W.: Become a Recognized Authority in Your Field, 2002

Boy et al: Projektmanagement: Grundlagen, Methoden und Techniken, 1999

Brand, Heiner/Löhr, Jörg: Projekt Gold. Wege zur Höchstleistung – Spitzensport als Erfolgsmodell, 2008

Bailey, Chris: Hyperfocus: How to Be More Productive in a World of Distraction, 2018

Bloch, Robert L.: Erfolgreich denken lernen – Meine Warren-Buffett-Bibel: Die Grundsätze des Starinvestors, 2016

Christiani/Scheelen: Stärken stärken: Talente entdecken, entwickeln und einsetzen, 3rd edition, 2013

Covey, Stephen: The 7 Habits of Highly Effective People, 2020.

Creutzmann, Andreas: The ONE Thing: Die überraschend einfache Wahrheit über außergewöhnlichen Erfolg in: Create your Life, Tempus-Verlag, 2017

Creutzmann, Andreas: Lebensprinzipien der Shaolin in: BewertungsPraktiker, October–December 2009, p. 50–51

Creutzmann, Andreas: Irrtum Power Point: Wirkungsvolle Präsentationen in: BewertungsPraktiker, April-June 2009, p. 37–39

Creutzmann, Andreas: Wirksame Kommunikation in: BewertungsPraktiker, January–March 2009, p. 32–35

Creutzmann, Andreas: Rhetorical Skills Help Win New Business – What Valuation Professionals Can Learn from Obama in: The Value Examiner, November/December 2008, p. 21–23, (Editor: NACVA)

Creutzmann, Andreas: Selbstmanagement: Mit klaren Zielen ins neue Jahr in: BewertungsPraktiker, October–December 2008, p. 41–42

Creutzmann, Andreas: Spitzensport als Erfolgsmodell für Berater? in: BewertungsPraktiker, July–September 2008, p. 30–35

Creutzmann, Andreas: Was Bewertungsprofessionals von Obama lernen können in: BewertungsPraktiker, April–June 2008, p. 24

Creutzmann, Andreas: Bewertungsprojekte effektiv und effizient managen in: BewertungsPraktiker, January–March 2008, p. 24–27

Creutzmann, Andreas: Die Work-Life-Balanced Scorecard in: BewertungsPraktiker, July–September 2007, p. 19–23

Creutzmann, Andreas: Wie Berater zu "Rainmakern" werden – Teil I: Marketing-strategien und Marketingaktivitäten in: BewertungsPraktiker, January–March 2007, p. 20–21

Creutzmann, Andreas: Wie Berater zu "Rainmakern" werden – Teil II: Soft Skills von Rainmakern in: BewertungsPraktiker, April–June 2007, p. 20–22

Creutzmann, Andreas: Grundsätze, Aufgaben und Werkzeuge erfolgreicher Profession-als, Teil I: Grundsätze als Basis für den Erfolg in: BewertungsPraktiker, April–June 2006, p. 21–23

Creutzmann, Andreas: Grundsätze, Aufgaben und Werkzeuge erfolgreicher Profession-als, Teil II: Aufgaben in: BewertungsPraktiker, July–September 2006, p. 20–23

Creutzmann, Andreas: Grundsätze, Aufgaben und Werkzeuge erfolgreicher Pro-fessionals, Teil III: Werkzeuge in: BewertungsPraktiker, October–December 2006, p. 19–23

Dauth, Georg: Führen mit dem DISG®-Persönlichkeitsprofil: DISG®-Wissen Mitarbeit-erführung, 3. Aufl., 2012, (Kindle-Version)

Davis, Katie/Seider, Scott: The Theory of Multiple Intelligences, in: Cambridge Hand-book of Intelligence, Chapter: 24, Publisher: Cambridge University Press, Editors: R.J. Sternberg, S.B. Kaufman, pp. 485–503

Drucker, Peter F.: The Practice of Management, 2006

Enkelmann, Nikolaus B.: Mentaltraining – Der Weg zur Freiheit, 2001

Enkelmann, Nikolaus B.: Rhetorik Klassik: Die Kunst zu überzeugen, 7th edition, 2004

Enkelmann, Nikolaus B.: Das Power-Buch für mehr Erfolg. In fünf Jahren die Num-mer 1, 2005

Fox, Jeffrey J.: How to Become a Rainmaker: The Rules for Getting and Keeping Customers and Clients, 2000

Friedrich, Kerstin: Erfolgreich durch Spezialisierung, 2014

Fuchs, Helmut/Huber, Andreas: Die 16 Lebensmotive: Was uns wirklich antreibt, 2002

Gardner, Howard: Frames of Mind: The Theory of Multiple Intelligences, 3rd edition 2011

Gigerenzer, Gerd: Risk Savvy: How to Make Good Decisions, 2014.

Gigerenzer, Gerd: Gut Feelings: The Intelligence of the Unconscious, 2007

Gladwell, Malcolm: Outliers: The Story of Success, 2008

Häusel, Hans-Georg: Think Limbic! Die Macht des Unterbewussten verstehen, 5th edition, 2014

Harding, Ford: Rain Making: The Professional's Guide to Attracting New Clients, 1997

Heimsoeth, Antje: Mentale Stärke: Was wir von Spitzensportlern lernen können, 2017, (Kindle-Version)

Heßler, Armin/Mosebach, Petra: Strategie und Marketing im Web 2.0: Handbuch für Wirtschaftsprüfer und Steuerberater, 2013

Hill, Napoleon: Think and Grow Rich, 2015

Kahn, Oliver: Ich. Erfolg kommt von innen, 2008, München

Karsten, Jürgen: Das Mentalprinzip: Wie Sie denken, was Sie wollen und bekommen, was Sie denken, 2009

Kartmann, Siegfried W.: Wie wir fragen und zuhören . . . könnten!, 1998

Kast, Bas: Wie der Bauch dem Kopf beim Denken hilft: Die Kraft der Intuition, 2007

Keller, Gary/Papasan, Jay: The ONE Thing: The Surprisingly Simple Truth Behind Extraordinary Results, 2013

Koch, Richard: Das 80/20 Prinzip: Mehr Erfolg mit weniger Aufwand, 4th edition, 2015

Konrad, Boris Nikolai: Alles nur in meinem Kopf: Die Geheimnisse unseres Gehirns, 2nd edition, 2016

Kriffer, Paul: Atemtechnik: Positive Energie, weniger Stress, Entspannung und besser schlafen durch Atemübungen, 2018, Kindle-Version

Küstenmacher/Seiwert: Simplify your life: Einfacher und glücklicher Leben, 17th edition, 2016

Lauster, Peter: Wege zur Gelassenheit, 2018

Lo, Min-Tzu et al: Genome-wide analyses for personality traits identify six genomic loci and show correlations with psychiatric disorders, in: Nature Genetics 2017 January; 49(1): 152–156. doi:10.1038/ng.3736

Malik, Fredmund: Managing Performing Living: Effective Management for a New World, 2016

Matthews, Gail: Goals Research Summary, 2015: https://www.dominican.edu /academics/lae/undergraduate-programs/psych/faculty/assets-gail-matthews /researchsummary2.pdf

Mayer, Jan/Hermann, Hans-Dieter: Mentales Training: Grundlagen und Anwendung in Sport, Rehabilitation, Arbeit und Wirtschaft, 3rd edition, 2015

McCormack, Mark H.: What They Don't Teach You at Harvard Business School, 1984

Murphy, Dr. Joseph: The Miracles of Your Mind, 2010

Öttl, Christine/Härter, Gitte: Networking: Kontakte gekonnt knüpfen, pflegen und nutzen, 2004

Pöhm, Matthias: Der Irrtum PowerPoint: Präsentieren Sie noch oder faszinieren Sie schon?, 2006

Pöhm, Matthias: Das NonPlusUltra der Schlagfertigkeit: Die besten Techniken aller Zeiten, 7th edition, 2019 (Kindle-Version)

Reiss, Steven: The Reiss Motivation Profile: What Motivates You?, 2015 (Kindle-Version)

Robbins, Anthony: Unlimited Power, 1986

Robbins, Anthony: Awaken the Giant Within: How to Take Immediate Control of Your Mental, Emotional, Physical & Financial Destiny!, 1991

Schieblon, Claudia (Hrsg.): Marketing für Kanzleien und Wirtschaftsprüfer, 4th expanded and completely revised edition, 2019

Schuller, Robert H.: If It's Going to Be, It's Up to Me, 1998

Seiwert, Lothar: Wenn du es eilig hast, gehe langsam: Wenn du es noch eiliger hast, mache einen Umweg Der Klassiker des Zeitmanagements mit neuen Tools, 2018 (Kindle-Version)

Seiwert, Lothar: Das 1x1 des Zeitmanagement: Zeiteinteilung, Selbstbestimmung, Lebensbalance, 2014

Seiwert, Lothar/Gay, Friedbert: Das 1x1 der Persönlichkeit: Mehr Menschenkenntnis & Erfolg mit dem persolog®-Modell, 4th edition, 2019 (Kindle-Version)

Sprenger, Reinhard K.: Das Prinzip Selbstverantwortung, 13th edition, 2015

Sprenger, Reinhard K.: Die Entscheidung liegt bei Dir! Wege aus der alltäglichen Unzufriedenheit, 15th edition, 2016

Staller, Thomas/Kirschke, Cornelia: Die ID37 Persönlichkeitsanalyse: Bedeutung und Wirkung von Lebensmotiven für effiziente Selbststeuerung, 2019

Stäuble, Matthias: Dein Weg zur mentalen Stärke: Mentaltraining und Lebensschule für Sportler, Trainer und Betreuer, 2015 (Kindle-Version)

Tepperwein, Kurt/Aeschbacher, Felix: So geben Sie Ihr Bestes: Ein ganzheitliches Mentaltraining in 7 Stufen, 2004, Frankfurt am Main

Tracy, Brian: Focal Point: A Proven System to Simplify Your Life, Double Your Productivity, and Achieve All Your Goals, 2001

Tracy, Brian: The 100 Absolutely Unbreakable Laws of Business Success, 2002

Tracy, Brian: High Performance Leadership: Der Schlüssel zu erfolgreicher Führung und Motivation, 1999

Tracy, Brian: Luck factor. Die Gesetze des Erfolgs, 3rd edition, 2000

Tracy, Brian: Eat That Frog!: 21 Great Ways to Stop Procrastinating and Get More Done in Less Time, 2017

Tracy, Brian: Goals!: How to Get Everything You Want – Faster Than You Ever Thought Possible, 2nd edition, 2010

Walther, George: Power Talking, 1991

Waugh, Tory: 101 Marketing Strategies for Accounting, Law, Consulting, and Professional Services Firms 2004

Wise, Anna: The High-Performance Mind: Mastering Brainwaves for Insight, Healing, and Creativity, 1997

Wolf, Jurgen: Focus. The Power of Targeted Thinking, 2008

Zittelmann, Rainer: Psychologie der Superreichen, 2nd edition, 2017

Index